THE ESSE
BOAT
MAINTENANCE
MANUAL

THE ESSENTIAL BOAT MAINTENANCE MANUAL

Jeff Toghill

THE LYONS PRESS

First Lyons Press edition, 2001

Copyright © 2001 New Holland Publishers (Australia) Pty Ltd
Copyright © 2001 in text: Jeff Toghill
Copyright © 2001 in illustrations: Jeff Toghill
Copyright © 2001 in photographs: Jeff Toghill

First published by New Holland Publishers (Australia) Pty Ltd, 2001

ISBN 1-58574-327-5

The Library of Congress Cataloging-in-Publication Data is available on file.

While all care has been taken to ensure the information in this book is correct at
time of publication, the author and publisher accept no liability for accident, injury,
or any other misadventure incurred in relying on this book.

ACKNOWLEDGEMENTS

So many people helped with the collation of this book that it would be impossible to acknowledge all of them, and I hope that those who are missed will bear with me. Of particular assistance were Azko Nobel Pty Ltd, International Paints Ltd, North Sails, Intergrain Timber Finishes, International Marine and Outboard Marine Corporation.

On a more personal basis, my thanks to the innumerable waterfront people to whom I owe a beer for their input, in particular the Skoljarev family of tuna fishermen, Ben Selby of Beneteau Yachts for his British input, my old seafaring mate John Milne, who kept his professional eye on the whole thing, and La and John Lovell who loaned me their house so I could live and work in the environment of a busy boat harbour while putting this book together.

Last, but quite definitely not least, my grateful thanks to my wife, Diana, who scrambled around the mucky waterfront environment with me as assistant, model, photographer and general dogsbody. As usual with my books, her assistance and forbearance made the whole project feasible and enjoyable.

Jeff Toghill

CONTENTS

1
Introduction

Before starting maintenance work on any boat, it is important to have a basic knowledge of how it is built, the structure of the hull and deck, and how the stresses and strains experienced when the boat is moving, especially in a seaway, are handled. If any part of the hull is damaged, the repair work must be carried out in such a way that it does not leave a weak spot, otherwise the next time the boat is under stress the repair job could fail, with disastrous results. It does not take a university education in naval architecture to understand the structure of the boat and how an effective repair job should be carried out. Basic knowledge is all that is required to understand how to go about repairing or maintaining a boat.

For example, when hauling a boat on a slipway or storing on land for maintenance of underwater areas or for winter layup, it is important that the hull is correctly supported. A boat is designed to float in the water with an even pressure distributed around the hull to support her weight. When out of the water, the hull is only supported at specific points and unless these points are strategically located to distribute the weight evenly, the hull will suffer 'hot spots' where excess pressure may dent or even crack the hull. Even worse, if the hull is not properly supported it may become distorted. One problem that can arise in this situation is distortion of the hull structure as a result of the weight at each end bending the hull structure in the middle—a situation known as 'hogging'.

So it makes sense, in a book on maintenance, to begin by explaining the basic make-up and structure of a boat so that the boat owner is not only aware of what needs to be done but also why it must be done in a certain way. Anyone can patch a hole, but to make a patch that will not fall out or allow water in when the boat next puts to sea is the difference between having complete confidence in the safety and security of the vessel, or crossing your fingers and hoping that she will make it to the next port.

THE HULL STRUCTURE

Every boat is a box. There are many different shapes of boxes, of course, but every hull is basically designed the same way, be it a motor boat, yacht or row boat. The sea can be an unkind mistress and will severely punish a hull that is not prepared for the unique

Unless the boat is properly supported out of the water, parts of the hull will be stressed and perhaps distorted.

stresses and strains of a seaway. So, every boat is designed to withstand the effect of waves passing under or around the hull, picking it up and slamming it down, and wracking or twisting it. The structural members used to counter these forces and keep the hull in one piece fall into two major categories—longitudinal and transverse.

Longitudinal members are the keel, deck stringers and hull stringers (if any), which run from bow to stern and prevent the boat from bending in the middle. They may be in the form of heavy lengths of wood, steel or aluminum angle or fiberglass reinforcing, depending on the material from which the hull is built.

Transverse members prevent the box shape of the hull from being twisted out of shape, wracked from side to side, or collapsed inward when in a seaway. They consist mostly of deck beams and bulkheads which are common to all types of hulls although perhaps not all made from the same material.

When a boat rides over a big sea, she is momentarily suspended on the crest of the wave under the middle of the hull with the bow and stern hanging in the air, a condition mentioned earlier in relation to hauling and storing, and known as 'hogging'. When the boat is in the trough between two waves, the reverse applies; the ends are supported and the weight is concentrated on pushing down the middle of the hull—a condition known as 'sagging'. At other times, especially when the boat is running at angle to the seas, she will

Even in small boats, the wear and tear of a sailing season can create plenty of maintenance work.

be corkscrewing all over the place and putting enormous twisting strains on the hull—rather like taking a shoe box and twisting each end in opposite directions. This is known as 'wracking'.

It is these three principle stresses that can severely damage a hull, and the longitudinal and transverse structural members are designed to counter them and hold the hull together. Obviously, it would be very unwise, in the course of a repair job, to cut or remove any or part of these structural members. It might, for example, seem convenient to remove a bulkhead to fit new interior fittings and make more cabin space, but this could be tantamount to suicide—for when the boat is next in a seaway and the transverse stresses require the resistance of every available bulkhead, there will be nothing there and the hull structure will collapse. Similarly, cutting into deck beams, stringers or any other structural member, for whatever reason, will weaken the hull and make her vulnerable to wave action stresses when next at sea.

Sailing in a seaway puts severe stresses on the hull and equipment.

It follows, therefore, that when a boat is damaged and has to be repaired, it is vitally important that the repair, especially to a structural member, is properly carried out to withstand any stress it may encounter at a later date. Apart from this, it is important for regular maintenance work to be carried out on all parts of the vessel to ensure that there is no deterioration of the structural members or of the hull skin which will weaken them and make them ineffective when the vessel is at sea. Rot in wooden members, rust in metal frames and osmosis in fiberglass skin are typical of the sort of problems that can arise in the course of using a boat, and that only regular maintenance can prevent.

MOTORS, MASTS, AND SAILS

The reason for frequent and competent maintenance of the power unit that drives the boat—be it mast and sails or motor—is fairly obvious: if it is not kept in good shape, sooner or later it will fail. That can mean big problems when a motor stops and the boat is far from shore, or the rigging gives way and the mast and sails collapse over the side. While not necessarily disastrous, such happenings can be inconvenient at best, dangerous and costly at worst. Careful maintenance of the motor, as with a car, will ensure that when called upon it will respond quickly and efficiently. Careful maintenance of mast and sails can also avoid inconvenience and difficulty as well as considerable cost.

Fiberglass—the wonder material

Boat shows are great places to discover the latest maintenance materials and techniques.

Most modern pleasure craft are constructed of glass reinforced plastic (GRP), commonly known as 'fiberglass'. The basic structure of this material consists of a core of fine glass strands enclosed in a chemical resin, in much the same way that steel mesh is enclosed in concrete to create a strong structural building material. The glass fibers may be woven into a cloth, providing much the same 'mesh' as the steel reinforcing in concrete, or randomly scattered as loose fibers throughout the body of the resin, which is applied as a liquid and then chemically hardened to a very tough surface.

The resin is usually an epoxy resin with good workability and low viscosity. A popular brand is International HT9000, which is widely used for a variety of boat repair and maintenance purposes. The resin has a limited shelf life and it is better to buy quantities to suit as required rather than buy a large amount and store it for a long period. The catalyst used to activate the resin and convert it from a liquid to a solid is called the hardener, and this must be mixed at the manufacturer's recommended rate. As a guide, around 1% is usually sufficient in warm, dry conditions while up to 3% may be needed if the temperature is low and the humidity high. Laying up fiberglass in cold, wet conditions is not recommended.

The curing time will vary but on average, with reasonable climate conditions, the resin should cure in around 30 minutes; the higher the temperature the faster the curing time. Ideally 77°F (25°C) is the temperature to aim for, although the mix will not be degraded by a slightly lower temperature, it will just take longer to cure. Similarly, larger quantities of resin will tend to cure faster than smaller quantities so the best procedure is to pour

Glass reinforced plastic (GRP) is the 'wonder' material of modern boat building.

small mixes of resin into a flat tray so they don't bulk up and shorten the curing time. Frequent mixes of small quantities is always better than mixing one large pot.

TIP: THE THREE GOLDEN RULES FOR MIXING RESIN AND HARDENER—MEASURE QUANTITIES ACCURATELY, STIR SLOWLY, MIX THOROUGHLY.

For most maintenance and repair work the resin and glass laminate can be laid up by hand, using a bristle brush to stipple the resin through the cloth, or a roller if the area to be covered is extensive. The important factor in applying the resin is to ensure that it saturates the cloth totally and penetrates through to the surface underneath. Excess resin can be sanded off when the job is finished, and it is always better to apply too much resin and sand back later, than to apply too little. Where large areas are concerned, especially when a hull is being laid up, the resin/glass mixture is forced through specially-built 'guns,' which mix the resin and fibers as they are sprayed into a mold to give the required shape of the hull. As a rule, a resin gel coat is sprayed into the mold before lay-up of the laminate in order to provide a high gloss finish to the outside of the hull when it is popped from the mold. A release agent, often a waxy substance, may be used to prevent the resin sticking to the mold.

Because it is impervious to water, GRP is used to build boats of all shapes and sizes.

Taking the boat out of the water always makes maintenance much easier.

Fiberglass is an ideal material for boats of all types since it is strong and durable and its surface is resistant to most of the chemicals that damage painted hulls. It is also impervious to rust and rot (two factors that create headaches for boat owners of metal and wooden craft), and repair work is quickly and easily carried out. Indeed, there is very little that affects GRP other than the general wear and tear of normal use. But despite these qualities, fiberglass is not maintenance free, and the surface of the synthetic material can become just as marked or damaged by physical contact as any other surface. Routine maintenance is necessary to keep the boat looking in showroom condition, and winter lay-up time is the ideal time to attend to all the dings, scratches and other repair jobs that have accumulated throughout the summer season.

CLEANING FIBERGLASS

The dirty marks that result from everyday mishaps such as bumping into a pier or another boat, loading onto a trailer, and oil and rubbish in the water, will spoil the appearance of a fiberglass boat just as they would spoil the paint work of a boat made from any other material. However, where a painted hull will need some considerable touching up and probably even repainting after the marks have been removed, a GRP hull will probably need nothing more than a wipe off with a cloth and detergent, or at worst the use of a fiberglass cleaner.

Washing down the boat after each use will remove grime and dirt that has accumulated during use (and that may otherwise cause deterioration of the surface), and keeping the boat covered when not in use will provide long-term protection from dust and chemicals in the air. Together with sunlight these create the main problems of deterioration in a fiberglass surface, so hosing down and keeping the boat under cover are two basic steps that will help keep the boat in good condition and reduce the need for more extensive maintenance. These things can be done whether the boat is taken home on a trailer or left on a mooring or at a marina. For small boats, an overall cover such as a plastic or tarpaulin sheet can be used, although the boat will look neater if she has tailored covers that enhance her appearance. But appearance is not as important as keeping out dust and dirt as well as rainwater, especially if the boat is located in or near a big city, where pollutant gases can create havoc with all synthetic materials.

If the boat is left in the water, the upper parts can be similarly protected with covers, although it may be difficult to cover the topsides above the waterline. The underwater areas are not affected by the same problems but may be attacked by marine growth. These are dealt with separately in Chapter 11. Sun reflecting off the water and chemical pollutants in the water will tend to stain the lower sections of the hull near the waterline, but as it is not practical to cover these the only precaution is to ensure they are cleaned and polished when any signs of damage starts to appear. A strong fiberglass polish rubbed hard into the surface may help remove some of the staining, even at the risk of losing some of the sheen of the gel coat.

Launching and retrieving from a trailer can result in scratches to the gel coat.

As mentioned, even a slight bump against a pier will leave a mark on a pristine GRP hull, and a boat that is well used will soon show signs of wear and tear unless a routine maintenance program is adopted. And of course, marks and blemishes that are not treated will lead to further deterioration in the appearance of the hull, in some cases even deterioration of the hull material. Water getting into a scratch or gouge that is not filled can creep through the fibers and affect the laminate, which in turn could lead to a weakness in the hull structure. So apart from washing down and covering the hull, any significant damage should be removed or repaired as soon as possible.

The first step in cleaning a fiberglass hull is to wipe down the affected surface with a cloth or sponge soaked in detergent solution. If that does not remove all the marks, a light fiberglass polish should be used, but make sure it is not a cutting or scouring polish or it will remove the high polish of the gel coat. If these do not work, acetone or thinners, used sparingly, may do the trick. It is important not to use acetone or thinners too frequently and to wash off the treated area immediately after use, to prevent possible damage to the high gloss surface of the gel coat.

TIP: WHEN CLEANING THE HULL WITH ANY LIQUID, BUT ESPECIALLY ACETONE OR THINNERS, WEAR GLOVES AND EYE PROTECTION.

Stubborn marks may need harsher treatment with a special cutting polish, and there are a number of polishes specifically made for fiberglass that are available from boat stores. This polish must also be washed off after use or it may mark or stain the fiberglass. Indeed, the harsher polishes, even though specifically designed for use with GRP, can damage the surface if care is not taken. At worst the gel coat can become scratched, at best the highly polished surface will be dulled. On a hull with a high gel sheen, a dull patch stands out like a sore thumb. Unfortunately, if the marks cannot be removed with normal mild polishes, there is no alternative and scouring polishes will need to be used, even a very fine wet and dry sandpaper as a last resort. It will be up to the owner of the boat to decide which is the lesser evil—a badly marked hull or the loss of the highly polished surface.

REMOVING SCRATCHES

If the damage is more severe and has resulted in scratches or gouges in the hull, then the work becomes more a question of repair rather than just cleaning. The degree of repair required will depend on how badly the hull has been scratched; whether the surface of the gel coat has been only slightly damaged, or whether it has been penetrated and the laminate beneath gouged. Unfortunately, because it is such a highly finished material, the fiberglass of a boat's hull is very susceptible to the scratching that is hard to avoid in normal everyday use. The slightest bump against a sharp corner or ragged edge on a pier, or even the touch of a dinghy coming alongside, can scratch the gel coat. Trailered boats, of course, are more vulnerable than most as launching and retrieving at the ramp can lead to numerous contacts with objects that will damage the surface. If the scratch is light, it is not a great problem and can be fixed fairly easily, but if the scratch is deep or the surface is gouged, then the laminate may be exposed and this can lead to serious problems unless properly fixed.

Sometimes very light scratches can be polished out using a fiberglass polish, but scratches of any depth must be filled to prevent the possibility of water entering the laminate. Filling a moderate scratch or gouge is not a problem, but almost certainly the job will result in damage to the surrounding surfaces and require further treatment to restore the original appearance of the boat. Severe scratching and gouging may need rebuilding of the laminate—a major repair job that will require restoration of the gel surface when the repair is completed, or possibly a paint job.

Resin fillers are available from marinas, chandleries and most boat shops and these can be used to fill light to moderate surface scratches or gouges. They come in a number of forms, and the manufacturer's instructions must be followed to ensure the right mix of hardener to resin is achieved. The damaged area must be well cleaned with a detergent solution (acetone or thinners if necessary) and thoroughly dried before the filler is applied, usually with a putty knife or spatula or some other tool that will enable the resin

Boats lying to a mooring are less likely to suffer damage than those tied up alongside a pier or marina.

to be worked well into the scratch. To a certain extent these fillers can be used to repair quite deep gouges and even holes, depending on the size, the depth and the location of the damage. Where the hole is of any size, or where the structure of the hull skin or the hull itself is concerned, filler will not be strong enough. Then it will be necessary to cut back around the damage and re-lay the laminate with fiberglass and resin, as described later in this chapter. If the cavity is too large, the filler may fall out when the boat is in use, and apart from negating the repair work, this could lead to a dangerous situation.

REPAIRING DAMAGE

Where there is severe damage and the hull skin has been pierced or seriously damaged, the structural strength of the fiberglass must be restored, and this involves rebuilding the laminate. Once again, there are limitations as to how much can be rebuilt, but for the purposes of this section we will assume that the damage is to the skin only and the structural features of the boat have not been affected. It may be possible to just use filler, if the hole is not too large or the gouge too deep. But where the job is beyond a filler, the damage will need to be cut away, reshaped and rebuilt, which will involve the use of fiberglass cloth and resin. More serious damage, particularly where the structure of the boat is affected, may need to be turned over to the marina boat builder, so the repair job does not create any weakness that may later affect the safety of the boat.

The procedure for repairing a hole in the fiberglass skin is not difficult, but first the damaged area must be shaped and prepared so that the new skin will not only fill the hole, but also match the surrounding surface. Often damage of this type—probably from a bump or collision—leaves depressed sections or cracked and ragged edges, and these will need to be cut away as they will interfere with the satisfactory bonding of the new patch. Loose, torn or shattered sections of skin must be removed and the whole damaged area cleaned up until the skin surrounding the hole is firm and undamaged, and any depressions pushed out to the final appearance will match that of the rest of the hull. Once the damaged area is prepared, the procedure for the repair work is as follows:

1. Clean up the 'wound' with acetone or thinners to remove any dirt, grease or chemicals that will interfere with the bonding of the new patch.
2. With a chisel, sander or angle grinder (depending on the size of the damaged area), chamfer the edges of the hole from both sides so that they form an inverted 'v' around the edges to give the new GRP a good hold on the old surface.
3. It is best to work from the inside if at all possible, as this will be the area less visible when the repair is finished. Secure a backing piece over the outside of the hole, using masking tape to hold it tight against the old skin. A piece of marine plywood or stiff cardboard (depending on the size of the hole) covered with a plastic sheet is ideal. If correctly secured, this will prevent the resin from oozing through from the inside work, while the plastic sheet (or cellophane) will give a smooth finish to the outside of the repair.
4. With the backing piece in place over the hole, check again to ensure that any damaged material has been removed so that the new laminate will bond with the old without creating any unevenness in the finished surface. Sand away the surrounds of the hole to remove any paint and give the new material a good key.
5. From the inside, fill the hole with pieces of fiberglass cloth shaped as near to the hole as possible to meet the bevelled edges and thus make a uniform bond. Chopped strand or "mat" fiberglass can be used instead of woven cloth, but this usually is not as strong as the woven material for this type of repair work and is more difficult to handle. The number of layers of cloth will be determined by the thickness of the skin surrounding the hole; the aim is to build the damaged skin to its former thickness and then add a little more to provide reinforcing.
6. Measure out a small quantity of resin and mix it with the correct amount of hardener. Use a pipette or some similar equipment to ensure the exact amount of hardener is used.
7. From the inside of the hull, work the resin mix into the first layer of cloth, ensuring that it soaks well through the fiberglasss and into the bevelled edges of the hole to

When first laid up the GRP patch will appear rough, but it can be finished to look like new with filler, sanding, and a coat of paint.

bond firmly to the old surface. With a moderately stiff brush 'stipple' the resin hard into the cloth to remove air bubbles and ensure that any cavities are filled. Add further layers of cloth and apply resin in the same way. If the surface is vertical there may be problems with the resin running from the cavity or 'creeping' on itself. If this happens it will be necessary to apply smaller quantities and try to hold the next layer until the previous one has started to cure. Build up the inside surface a few millimetres above and onto the surrounding skin to ensure the patch has a good bond with its surrounds.

8. When the resin has cured, the inside of the patch will need to be sanded back to flush with the surrounding surfaces. This can initially be done with a sander but to get the best finish, hand sanding with fine wet and dry sandpaper is recommended to achieve the best result. The wet and dry paper (fine grade) is used with soapy water, the paper being thoroughly immersed in the water then applied to the damaged area with a light circular rubbing action. It is important to build up a slurry to soften the harsh scouring effect of the grit on the paper which needs to be dipped in the water frequently in order to keep the whole surface area wet and the slurry thick and viscous.

9. The backing piece can be taken off the outside and if the surface needs further treatment, which it probably will, the same wet and dry sanding will remove any unevenness, especially around the edges of the patch. Buffing the surface with a

The fiberglass cloth is thoroughly saturated with the resin and all air bubbles stippled out.

lambswool pad will help restore some of the original surface, but is unlikely to return it to its former pristine appearance.

From this point on, it will be personal preference and the location of the repair as to what sort of finish is applied. If a showroom finish is required, or if colors have to be matched, then a fiberglass primer followed by a coat of polyurethane paint will be necessary. Spray painting always provides a superior finish, but is rarely successful with small areas and it may be necessary to repaint the entire hull to provide a satisfactory finish.

TIP: IN HOT WEATHER KEEP RESIN COOL AND OUT OF DIRECT SUNLIGHT. IN COLD WEATHER KEEP THE RESIN AT ROOM TEMPERATURE BEFORE MIXING THE HARDENER.

MAJOR REPAIR WORK

When large areas of the boat are damaged, or when structural members are affected, the repair work takes on a different aspect. Damage of this type can require complex repairing and can affect the structure of the boat if it is not done correctly. For this reason it would be a wise move to call in a professional rather than attempt a repair job which, although perhaps suitable for harbor sailing, could endanger the boat when she puts out to sea and encounters adverse wave conditions. A number of individual fiberglass repair jobs other than the patching described here, are covered in Chapter 15 of this book, and these are mostly within the scope of an amateur boat owner. But for major repair jobs, safety demands that a professional be called in.

FINISHING

Where a hull or cabin section of a fiberglass boat has been repaired, the finished surface will almost certainly not match the surrounding area. Most modern fiberglass hulls have a gel coat finish with a high gloss and this will be affected by any form of repair work, whether it be patching or rubbing back with polish or wet and dry sandpaper. The gel coat will lose its gloss and stand out as a distinctly dull patch in the high gloss of the undamaged surfaces. Colors, too, create problems in returning the boat to her original condition; the color of the patched area will almost certainly not match the original surface color and this will spoil the attractive appearance of the boat.

Whatever the cause, the outcome of any significant repair work will most likely be a paint job to restore the boat to its original appearance. It might be possible to just paint the damaged area, particularly if the repair job is located somewhere that is not particularly visible, but in most cases, particularly with large surface areas such as the hull skin, a complete paint job will almost certainly be called for. Since normal wear and tear in use will eventually reduce the appearance of the fiberglass to the point where no

The new repair job shows the make-up of the fiberglass cloth and resin composite. Sanding back will restore the surface and clean up the edges.

amount of polishing or cleaning will restore it to its showroom condition, the chances are the hull will be enhanced by a paint job anyway. It is nearly impossible to restore the original appearance of the gel coat once it has suffered the ravages of wind and weather, the effect of chemically polluted air and water, and the repairs that result from bumping and scraping in use.

So, if the boat has been in use for some time the choice will be an easy one; the whole hull will come in for a coat of paint. Modern paints can achieve quite remarkable results, and indeed some boat builders prefer to give their craft the protection of a coat of paint when first built, so durable and attractive are the modern paints. Some even prefer a polyurethane paint finish to the traditional gel coat, laying up the boat with the laminate directly onto the mold and then using polyurethane paint to provide the finishing coats.

The secret in painting a GRP surface is the same as with any other type of material—careful preparation before the painting begins. If the surface to be painted is not well prepared, no amount of painting or re-painting will achieve a satisfactory result and in most cases the money spent on high-quality paint will be wasted. All surfaces to be painted must be clean and free from grease, oil or any other material that may prevent good adhesion of the initial coat. A solution of detergent in water may be sufficient while paint thinners and acetone can be used where the grease or grime is stubborn. Then a light rub with fine wet and dry sandpaper will provide a key to which the paint can grip. This is particularly important when the fiberglass surface is shiny and smooth, as is the

To restore the hull to its original condition a full paint job may be necessary.

Spray painting offers the best result when large areas are to be covered. Note careful masking of windows and waterline.

case with gel coat, and a little elbow grease used at this stage can pay dividends in the final result. Full details on painting GRP is given in Chapter 7 of this book.

When fiberglass is laid up in a mold, a release agent is used to prevent adhesion of the laminate to the mold, and this chemical may remain on the surface for some time. It is often a type of wax that makes it very hard for paint to adhere to the surface, so it must be removed before painting begins. Wiping off with white spirit, or some cleaner recommended by the paint manufacturer—sometimes thinners will work—will prepare most surfaces, and scuffing with wet and dry sandpaper should ensure that the last traces are removed. A final wash with detergent and water will remove any traces of the cleaning agent and sandpaper slurry, and ensure that the surface is clean and ready for the first coat of paint.

Polyurethane paint is the most popular with experienced fiberglass boat owners and when applied carefully, particularly when sprayed, can produce a finish closely resembling the original gel coat that gives a boat such an attractive finish when it is first popped out of the mold. But modern manufacturing techniques are producing newer and better paints all the time, so it would be wise to check with the manufacturer, the chandler, or the local marina manager to see the latest paints available and suitable for the job in hand.

Spray painting is rather more involved than brush or roller application, but the end result is so superior it is well worth the extra effort. It is not easy, and a degree of skill is required to use a spray gun effectively. Brief instructions in the art of spray painting are given in Chapter 7, but much practice and trial and error are required. Otherwise a great deal of time and effort will be wasted and the finished job will spoil rather than enhance the appearance of the boat. If time and expertise are not readily available, it would be best to turn the job over to a professional spray painter. Even a small boat can be costly to paint and if the end result does not achieve the desired result, then the money and effort has been wasted.

Painting fiberglass, whether with a spray gun, roller or brush, is similar to that for any other material. While different types of paints may be used the techniques are basically the same. The first coat on a previously unpainted fiberglass surface must be an etch primer in order to prepare the surface for subsequent top coats and give them a firm grip on the smooth fiberglass surface. Then the subsequent coats and rubbing back between them uses much the same techniques as for painting wood, aluminum or any other surface. Full details are provided in Chapter 7 of this book.

3

Wood—the old faithful

There is a tendency to think that since the advent of fiberglass, wood is no longer a material used for boat building. In terms of hull construction that is true to a certain extent, and the modern synthetic resin materials have certainly made inroads into the use of wood for hull construction. The ease of construction, low maintenance and high strength of GRP has resulted in it almost totally superseding wood as the favored material for hull structure.

The days when ships were wood and men were steel! Wood is still a popular boat building material for many boat owners.

However, there is still a strong following for wood boats among a small fraternity of boat owners, particularly youngsters with their sailing

dinghies and small outboard fishing boats, and those who find the aesthetic quality of wood far superior to the new 'plastic'! Then again, wood is unsurpassed as a fitting out material and even the most modern synthetic boats have extensive wood fittings to enhance their interiors and deck furniture. There is nothing quite as aesthetically appealing as wood trim and wood decks, and used in conjunction with a fiberglass hull, they add beauty to the boat while at the same time retaining the low-maintenance qualities of the synthetic material. As a result, most boats, particularly large yachts and motor cruisers, employ a combination of synthetic fiberglass and traditional wood to provide the ultimate in attraction and practicability.

Wood is very user-friendly, particularly for persons useful with their hands, and adding bits and pieces to a boat is more readily achieved using handyman tools and easily obtainable wood than attempting to construct a mold and lay up a GRP fitting. Apart from the 'double handling' involved in first making the mold then making the fitting, anyone who has worked with fiberglass materials will know how exacting (and messy) the process is when only small pieces are being made. And maintenance is not entirely avoided, because if a fine finish is required, then a coat of polyurethane paint is almost certain to be needed in both cases.

WOODS

Of first importance when working with wood is to know the material. There is a huge range of woods available with many having a specific purpose in boat work. For example, many types of wood are very vulnerable to rot, which is a constant worry on board a boat where water is always present. One of the most traditional of all ship building woods—oak—is very susceptible to dry rot, while other popular woods are susceptible to wet rot. Both types of rot, and other problems which attack wood, are prevalent on boats, yet there are woods which are less susceptible—some not susceptible at all—to these problems, and which can offer the warm aesthetic appeal that wood provides without the worry of excessive maintenance.

Basically, there are two types of wood employed in boat work; hard wood and soft wood. Hard woods are mostly from slower growing trees and thus have tight grain structures, while the soft woods mostly have more open, straighter grains. For these reasons soft wood is much easier to work, but hard wood has greater resistance to wear and is usually less susceptible to water problems. Weight is also a consideration, depending on which part of the boat is being worked on. Hard woods such as gum and teak are heavy while the faster growing pines are lighter, and this accounts for the extensive use of Oregon. In the course of building or fitting out a boat, a shipwright may use a number of different woods, each matched to suit a specific requirement. The following are the most suitable woods for boat building or fitting out and are generally available in most parts of the world:

The additional maintenance required for wood is its major drawback.

Spruce

Spruce is renowned for its strength and light weight and is extremely popular in boat yards across the world. It is very easy to work and ideal for interior fittings but it is not particularly resistant to rot and requires regular maintenance when the boat is in use.

Cedar

Cedar is also very popular for interior furniture and fittings because of its magnificent appearance, but it is also popular for planking and decking as it is a soft wood and easily worked. Although it has a natural oil which tends to resist rot, it absorbs water very readily and becomes heavy if left immersed for any time.

Oregon pine

This is probably the most widely used of all woods for general boat work, particularly for planking and decking. Oregon does not shrink or swell as much as most woods, it is very easy to work and fairly resistant to rot, although it needs careful maintenance. There are many different versions of pine, most of which are closely related to Oregon. But the true Oregon has a characteristic light and dark grain and should not be confused with other similar woods.

Ash

Another wood much sought after for interior fittings and furniture, mainly because of its beautiful blonde coloring. Used with darker colored woods such as teak, jarrah or mahogany, it makes attractive contrasts with interior furnishings and fittings. It can be used for structural work and is quite well suited for this task.

Elm

Used principally for structural members, such as beams and knees, elm is a fairly hard wood, but works quite readily and has much the appearance of ash although it is not as strong.

Mahogany

Becoming hard to obtain these days, mahogany has been used extensively in boat building over centuries, particularly for planking and decking. It is a very hard wood and provides an attractive dark appearance when finished with a gloss coat. Honduras and African mahogany are the two best known of these woods.

Oak

This has been the traditional boat building wood for centuries, particularly for frames and other structural members as it is very strong and hard to work. Despite its strength, it is vulnerable to rot although this can mostly be prevented by treating the wood with chemicals before it is fitted into place.

Teak

Arguably the best of all wood for boat work because of its resistance to rot and worm, teak unfortunately has some major disadvantages. It is very hard to work and dulls the blades of tools very quickly, probably due to the minute specs of silicone ingrained in the wood. However, it does not shrink or swell and stands up to weather well even when not painted or varnished. It is hard and heavy and makes an attractive wood for fittings and furniture where its appearance can be enhanced by a coat of clear finish.

Spotted gum

This is a very hard wood, close grained and not easy to work, but is ideal for many uses on boats because of its resistance to rot and great strength. It is mostly used for structural members although it can be brought up to a fine appearance, given a good finish. It is generally considered to be the best of the gums for shipwright work.

Maple

This is mostly a soft working wood, very porous and short grained and does not bend too well as it tends to split easily. However, maple cuts well and can produce attractive color

Choice of the right wood can make a big difference to the structural strength of the boat as well as her appearance.

finishes so it is a popular wood for interior furnishings and fittings. There are a number of different type of maples, mostly from the Pacific area, and these vary in appearance and structure. Advice from a wood yard might be advisable before purchasing maple for any specific purpose.

TIP: LARCH IS A GOOD BOAT BUILDING WOOD BUT IT IS ONLY AVAILABLE IN SOME PARTS OF THE WORLD.

Plywood

Marine grade plywood is made by laminating thin sheets of wood in an uneven number of layers. The sheets are so placed that their grains run at right angles to each other thus offering great strength at relatively low thicknesses. The adhesive used to bond the sheets together is a high quality marine waterproof glue, usually a synthetic resin type, and when correctly made, plywood is one of the strongest and most useful of all types of wood for boat use. The laminated material is waterproof, very strong, and will stand immersion in water for a period of time. It is very popular with boat builders, both amateur and professional, as it can be cut to any shape, easily bent when in long pieces and can be joined by scarfing without loss of strength.

The warm beauty of wood can be readily seen here. The right woods must be used to achieve such a result.

The most important factor in selecting plywood for use in a boat, whether for interior or exterior use, is to ensure that it is full marine grade. Modern techniques have improved the quality and waterproof characteristics of marine plywood, and it can also be impregnated with anti-rot chemicals for areas which may be hard to reach for routine maintenance. Some of the more recent processes for impregnating the wood are barely discernible in the finished product and it can be varnished or oiled without inhibiting the final appearance of the job.

Plywood can be purchased in a number of different-sized sheets with different thicknesses. Providing it is of quality marine grade, the type of wood used in making the laminate is not usually of importance, and providing it has been impregnated, it can be used in any part of the boat's construction or as interior or deck fittings. The ends can be somewhat vulnerable to damage because of the cross grained effect of the laminations, and care must be taken when working with plywood or the ends grain may splinter or be otherwise damaged. The ends should be carefully planed and sanded before being placed into position and, preferably, sealed with a cover strip.

BUYING WOOD

When selecting wood to be used for the building, repairing or fitting out of boats, only the highest quality material should be used. Wood for major work should be selected for straightness of grain, low shrinkage and freedom from defects. The structural strength of the wood can be affected by knots, shakes, sapwood, incipient decay, compression failure and brittleness, and under the stresses and strains of a boat in a seaway they may collapse; using lower quality wood will only result in more repair work at a later stage. While the strength of the wood may be less important in fitting out and other decorative work, if the best results are required, then the best wood should be used.

There are two forms commonly available at most lumber yards; wood that is rough sawn, has not been planed and still has the rough edges of the original milling, and dressed wood that has been planed to a smooth finish and an exact measurement. Obviously it is best to purchase dressed wood as this eliminates the need for further planing. However, this is more expensive than rough sawn wood and where cost is a factor, or where dressed wood is not available in sizes suitable for a particular job, rough sawn wood may have to be purchased and planed back to the dimensions required. Wood may be dressed on two sides or all sides and when the dressing or planing has been completed the finished wood will be a standard size. These standard sizes vary in different countries around the world and some are given in English measurements, some in metric.

A magnificent example of wood boat building, but what about the maintenance!

When buying wood at the yard, examine each piece carefully, noting the direction of the grain, the way in which the planks are cut, and particularly what grade it is given. Different countries have different methods of grading, but a common grading is the 'Select' or 'Clear select' with a number. Thus 'Clear select No 1' is the highest grade, indicating the best quality wood. The grades are determined by the number of knots in a given length, as well as other factors which might affect its quality.

In order to use wood to advantage in boat building, repair or fitting out, it is important to understand the characteristics of the wood. For example, some woods split easily when worked one way but not when worked the opposite way. A piece of wood cut one way will have greater strength to withstand stresses than when cut another way. Also, wood shrinks or swells much more across the grain than along the grain. All these are useful factors to know when deciding on what wood to buy for fitting out or repairing a boat, and since there are so many variations it would be impossible to cover them all in a book of this type. The best procedure is to consult an expert at a wood yard on which would be the most suitable wood for the job at hand.

New wood is usually sawn into planks with the grain running either across the plank or vertically through it. Where the grain run is across the plank it is said to be slash sawn and when the grain runs up and down, the wood is said to be rift sawn. The direction of the grain is also important for strength. A square plank will better support weight and stresses when the grain runs in the direction of the load; when the grain runs across the direction of the load it is liable to bend more easily. Here again, the full details of how different cuts of wood will perform is too complex for this book and an expert at the wood yard should be consulted in order to obtain the best results.

All wood must be weathered or seasoned before use because the different rates of shrinkage in different parts of the plank will cause the wood to become curved and distorted. When wood is milled, it is soft and moist from the sap in its fibers, so it has to be dried. This can be done in the open air of the wood yard or in kilns where the drying process is speeded by heating. It is vitally important when selecting wood for any purpose to ensure that it has been correctly dried or it will continue the drying process when in position and warp or become disfigured, not only spoiling the appearance of the boat but also weakening the structure. This applies particularly to large dimension wood used for structural fittings, but it also applies to all cut woods (as opposed to laminated or built woods) used for fittings or furnishings.

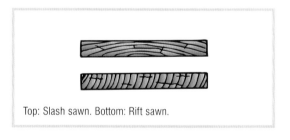

Top: Slash sawn. Bottom: Rift sawn.

As already described, selecting the way in which the grain runs in a plank can affect its strength, and strength is always a major factor in wood used for boats. A classic example is in the beam knees used to secure the corners of the boat between the beams and the woods (ribs). These knees are a major factor in holding the hull together and come under great stress when the boat is wracking in a seaway, so they must be strong. They can be

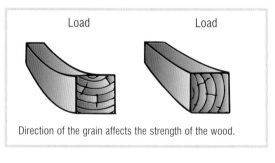

Direction of the grain affects the strength of the wood.

Shrinkage during seasoning tends to distort the shape of the plank.

Grown wood knees were an important part of ship building in the days of wood ships.

fabricated from plywood, and this would certainly be strong enough, but its appearance would do nothing to enhance the interior appearance of a nicely furnished boat. So, wood knees are selected with the grain running around the curve of the knees to provide maximum strength and superb appearance. Indeed, when wood was a major boat building material, it was specifically grown to achieve this shape and appearance, giving the fittings the not surprising name of 'grown knees'!

Even in fabricated wood structures, it is important to see that the grain runs the right way to provide maximum strength as well as—in many cases—optimum appearance. Interior fittings are often made from wood, and here the use of the right wood in terms of color and texture, as well as a pleasant visual effect from the curving patterns of the grain, will add enormously to the appeal of the furnishings and help give the interior of the boat a sophisticated, elegant appearance.

WOOD FITTINGS

In few, if any, other industries is wood required to be cut into such complex shapes as in boat building and fitting out. The curves of a vessel require special shaping for almost every piece of wood in its construction and the aesthetic look of both interior and exterior fittings call for considerable shaping skills for both utilitarian and aesthetic purposes. The superbly fitted and finished beam knees mentioned earlier are an example of this and there are many other instances—particularly in interior furniture—where curved wood is selected or cut as much for the way in which it provides an appealing appearance, as for the strength it offers. Since it is easily shaped and can be finished with a wide variety of paints and varnishes, wood provides a very versatile material for building, fitting out and repairing boats and, with few exceptions, can be easily handled by the amateur handyman.

A wide choice of woods enables the appearance of the boat to be enhanced.

Interior furniture, cockpit fittings, deck, handrails, doors, hatches, and instrument panels are just a few of the uses of wood on board, even where the main hull construction and some of the interior furniture, are of fiberglass, aluminum, steel or concrete. Of course this type of use is mostly restricted to large vessels, but even small fishing, sailing or ski boats use wood for floors, seats, benches, bait boxes, and the like. So no matter what the boat, there is usually a need for some wood work to be undertaken to enhance its appearance or usefulness.

This work involves cutting and shaping as well as fastening and painting, and all these in turn require tools. Any woodworking expert will emphasize that the skill in producing good woodwork lies in the correct use of the correct tools. A book on maintenance is perhaps not the place for a detailed exposé on woodworking tools and how to use them to best effect, but it is important to mention some of the tools used for shaping wood in boat work. Many are standard tools to be found in any handy person's tool shed, but some have special uses. Details of tools and techniques are given in Chapter 5 of this book.

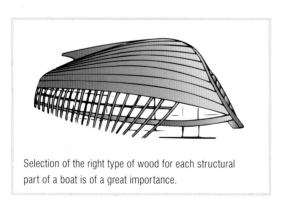

Selection of the right type of wood for each structural part of a boat is of a great importance.

TIP: USE A TEMPLATE TO CUT WOOD WHERE POSSIBLE: IT SAVES EXPENSIVE WASTE AND ENSURES GOOD FITTING.

CLEANING WOOD

Wood hulls are invariably painted or varnished so the cleaning procedure is that used for any painted surface, no matter what the material beneath it. Few boats use anything other than glossy paint for exterior finishes, although cleaning would probably be easier if the finishes were less highly polished. This is because all but the lightest form of cleaning tends to damage the high-gloss paint surface, albeit only to a slight degree. But if a part of a pristine hull has been firmly cleaned to remove some mark or abrasion, the chances are the gloss will be dulled, and that will stand out against the remaining gloss surface, giving the appearance of deterioration. If coarse cleaners or abrasive materials such as wet and dry sandpaper are used, damage to the paint surface will become very obvious. Few, if any, cleaning materials can be used for any length of time without dulling a gloss finish.

An old wood hull has great aesthetic appeal, but the paint and varnish topsides will need constant attention.

For this reason, warm soapy water is the best cleaner to use initially, although this will only remove superficial dust and dirt. Stronger detergent solutions can be tried if this does not

Rust from steel fittings and fastenings is the most common cause of deterioration in the paintwork of wood boats.

Cracks and small damage can be repaired with a putty or epoxy filler.

work with obstinate or ingrained marks. At this point, the chances of damaging the high gloss of the paintwork will be minimal, but the next step, when scouring or abrasive materials are used, can cause damage. Sugar soap or a solution of washing soda and detergent are both powerful cleaners and will remove even the most stubborn stains. Unfortunately they will almost certainly take some of the gloss from the paint surface. Sandstone, scourers and other harsh commercial cleaners will have much the same result and this must be born in mind before the cleaning job is undertaken with heavy duty cleaners like these. Such cleaners should only be used when the surface is to be repainted or the loss of the gloss finish is acceptable.

A degreasing liquid will be necessary where oil or grease stains are in evidence but these cleaners also tend to have a detrimental effect on the high gloss paint surfaces. They can also be fairly tough on the skin, so gloves should be worn for all cleaning work and a bucket of fresh water should be kept nearby for when the cleaning is done. Stubborn stains such as rust can be removed with Brasso or car polish, but if all else fails it may be necessary to use a very fine wet and dry sandpaper as the last resort. This, of course, will totally wreck the appearance of the paint job, and once again should only be used when the surface is to be repainted.

Minor repair jobs, and small areas where the high gloss of the paintwork has been affected by hard cleaning, can sometimes be restored by using a lambswool buffer and a wax polish. If this is not effective, such spots can sometimes be touched up with a spray can of gloss paint or lacquer, to cover the damaged area and renew the appearance of the paint work. But rarely are such touch-up jobs totally invisible, especially where colors are involved and the new paint has to be matched to the color of the old surface. If the boat is to be restored to her original pristine condition then only a full repaint job will achieve the desired results and return the hull to its showroom finish.

After filling, the repair is sanded back and given a coat of primer.

REPAIRING DAMAGE

As with any other material, wood hulls suffer from the day-to-day bumps and grinds of normal use, and since a painted surface is every bit as vulnerable as the gel coat on a fiberglass boat—perhaps more so—treatment for minor damage can be much the same for both. Scratches and minor gouges, for example, can be filled with an epoxy filler, then sanded back and repainted. As with fiberglass, the scratched area must be clean and dry before the filler is applied, and from that point the procedure is the same for both materials. Once it has set, the filler can be sanded back to flush with the surrounding surfaces using a fine grade wet and dry paper prior to spot priming and painting.

If the gouge is deep, and bare wood is revealed, it will need to be given a coat of primer before applying the filler. Spot priming will again be necessary when the filler has hardened and been sanded back, before the top coats are applied. Polyurethane paint is the most popular and the most effective, although it is, of course, more expensive than oil paint or acrylic. Spraying offers far and away the best results in terms of appearance although spraying small repair jobs can be rather finicky. Full details of painting are given in Chapter 7 of this book.

When the damage is more extensive than just scratches or gouges, the repair work starts to take on a different dimension. Obviously much will depend on how extensive the damage is, where it is and how much expertise is required to repair it. Because they are built from many different pieces—as opposed to fiberglass boats which are mostly cast as a whole—repairing different parts of a wood boat can call for different techniques and different woods. Repairing stove in hull planks, for example, will probably require a new section of plank to be scarfed in and is likely to also involve repairing ribs, maybe even stringers and other structural parts as well as recaulking the planks. The same repair on a fiberglass boat will probably be fixed by the basic patching technique described in the previous chapter.

4
Metal—aluminum and steel hulls

Metal is a popular boat building material, and the popularity of individual metals is strangely divided between small and large craft. Few small boats are made of steel, while larger craft, especially commercial craft, favor this material for its hard-wearing characteristics. In contrast, aluminum is not widely used for the construction of larger craft—although it is becoming more popular as time goes on—yet is extremely popular for small craft, especially fishing boats and runabouts. Neither metal is favored much for yachts, where fiberglass is undoubtedly the king. Since this book is aimed mainly at leisure craft, it will deal only superficially with the maintenance and repair of steel boats, the reference to metal concerning mainly small aluminum craft.

Steel hulls need special treatment when first built in order to keep rust at bay.

CLEANING

All steel vessels have to be painted, so cleaning the painted surface of a steel hull will differ little from cleaning any other painted hull, although rust stains are unique to steel surfaces and need special attention. Most aluminum hulls are also painted, although some small craft—especially commercial craft such as oyster barges—prefer the bare aluminum, as it is easier to maintain than a painted surface and commercial operators are not so concerned with the appearance of the bare metal.

Initially, as for any other painted surface, a wash down with a detergent solution will remove light marks, dust and dirt. More ingrained stains will need stronger treatment and here, as with fiberglass or wood, it becomes a question of what strength of cleaner to use as harsher cleaners are likely to damage the paint, particularly if it has a high gloss finish. However, unsightly stains such as rust 'bleeds' must be removed as they will impair the appearance of the boat, and in this case there is no choice but to use harsher scouring cleaners. There are products which claim to remove rust stains from paintwork without damaging the surface, and because improving technology may one day come with a satisfactory rust remover, it may well be worth trying one of these. But most either fail to remove the bleed, or else remove the paint as well as the bleed, and in the long run it may be that a kitchen scourer or sand

Aluminum can be painted like any other material, but a special etch primer must be applied first.

soap will be necessary. The final solution is fine wet and dry sandpaper, but that will almost certainly make it necessary to repaint the surface.

REMOVING DENTS

Of all the different materials, removing dents from aluminum is probably the easiest. Aluminum dents relatively easily, so by the same token the dents are equally easy to remove although much depends on the gauge of the metal and the degree of denting. The thicker gauge of steel used for boat hulls does not dent so easily but where light gauge steel is used, dents can again be removed without too much effort. The procedure for taking out dents depends a great deal on where they are located. A dent in an aluminum mast, for example, will be very difficult to remove. On the other hand a dent in the panel of an aluminum hull, providing it is not too severe, or in a place where there is not too much curvature, can usually be removed quite easily. Where there is doubt, particularly with masts and spars, they should be sent to the manufacturer, as a poorly carried out repair job will not only look bad, but could also weaken the metal.

A rubber mallet has many uses in the workshop, particularly where aluminum is concerned.

Moderate dents in the lightweight aluminum of a small boat hull can mostly be removed with a rubber hammer. A wooden block, considerably larger than the size of the dent, is placed across the concave side of the dented area so it totally overlaps the dent. The rubber hammer is then used on the opposite side, hammering gently with a circular motion and increasing the impact as it becomes necessary. Denting usually causes the metal to stretch, so the hammering should start at the outside edge of the dent and circle slowly in towards the middle, pushing any stretch back the way it came. If carried out successfully, this method will gradually remove the dent and return the aluminum plate to its original condition.

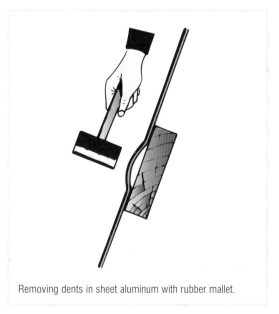

Removing dents in sheet aluminum with rubber mallet.

Stubborn or deep dents may need to be heated to enhance the hammering. A gas torch or blow torch played gently onto the metal will assist in removing the dent and also reduce any stretch that may have been induced in the metal from the impact that caused the dent. It is important not to overheat or the metal may become distorted, and the hammering must be done between applications of heat, with the mallet used swiftly and evenly across the damage in the same circular motion, while the metal is still warm. Both with or without heat, the dented area will need repainting when the job is finished.

RUST AND CORROSION

Metal and salt water are not good bedfellows, and since most boats are used in salt water, metal on board boats and ships is always susceptible to rust or corrosion. The problem is greater with steel than with aluminum, since rust will attack the normal steel alloy without hesitation whereas aluminum, providing it is of a good marine grade, will withstand the attack more readily. Both forms of corrosion come about in much the same way—the galvanic action of two dissimilar metals. This is discussed in detail on pages 118 and 120 of this book. Steel, being basically an alloy of iron and carbon, is subject to electrolytic action the moment it is immersed in an electrolyte (salt water). Small localized electric currents are set up between anodic and cathodic elements in the alloy, the effect being a gradual disintegration of the metal. This results in pitting of the metal where the anodic

Rust is the scourge of any seagoing
boat where steel fittings are used.

parts are eaten away, and fine deposits of rust settling on the cathodes. Since both are part of the steel structure, rusting does not appear as separate actions, but one single galvanic action producing surface rust and pitting of the steel in the same place.

Aluminum is also an alloy and is also subject to the galvanic action when placed in an electrolyte. Here the pitting is the same as with steel, but the powder deposited on the cathodic element is aluminum oxide, a white powder familiar to anyone who has worked with aluminum on boats. Pure metals resist corrosion better than metals containing impurities, therefore different grades of both aluminum and steel can be used to reduce the corrosion problem. For example, small additions of copper improve the resistance of steel to corrosion, while the addition of nickel and chromium produces stainless steel, which in certain grades is almost totally corrosion resistant. Similarly grades of aluminum alloy can be obtained which reduce corrosion problems considerably—these are broadly referred to as 'marine grade' aluminum. However, highly resistant grades of both metals are a great deal more expensive and can add considerably to the cost of the boat or its fittings, so they cannot be used universally, and mostly a compromise is reached, as a result of which the use of some lesser grades together with the accompanying risk of corrosion, must be expected.

When rust occurs, the steel has been partly demolished and cannot be recovered. The important factor in maintenance work with steel is not so much to repair any damaged areas, but to prevent the rust progressing further. Once rust has gained a foothold on mild steel that is subject to constant sea water contact, it will rapidly eat away the steel and reduce it to a dangerous state if not treated. Brushing with a wire brush will remove the rust powder on the surface of the plate, although if the rust has gained a severe foothold there will be flakes of rusted metal beneath the powder on the surface. These must be removed by chipping away with a small hammer until the steel beneath shows through clean and shiny. Any flakes left behind will continue the corrosion process and gradually undermine any repair work, so it is essential in the first instance to remove all flaking areas. With the steel clean and shiny an anti-corrosive liquid should be applied. There are a variety of commercial brands available and the local chandler should be consulted as to which is the best for the job at hand. Some require the surface to be cleaned back to shiny metal, others prefer a light rust powder to be left on the plate as this combines with the chemicals in the anti-corrosive to seal the repair.

TIP: WHEN CHIPPING RUST ALWAYS USE PROTECTIVE EYEWEAR.

Much the same process can be used to remove aluminum oxide from corroded aluminum, although this rarely deteriorates to the point where the metal begins to flake. But because aluminum alloy, especially in mast walls and the like, is relatively thin, the corrosion can quickly break down the metal and create a hole. Usually, a good stiff wire brush will remove the white powder and an aluminum anti-corrosive can then be applied. Both steel

The correct marine grade of stainless steel must be selected if rust and corrosion problems are to be avoided. The bolts in the closer samson post are obviously not the correct grade.

and aluminum repairs should be painted once they have been treated and sealed, using a primer followed by a polyurethane topcoat that suits the particular area of the boat. Underwater areas, of course, will need a finishing coat of antifouling composite.

TIP: TO AVOID CORROSION, ALWAYS USE MARINE GRADE STAINLESS STEEL FOR FITTINGS ON AN ALUMINUM BOAT.

REPAIRING DAMAGE

Where the damage to a metal hull is greater than just a dent—for example a hole or a crack—it will be necessary to either use a filler or else repair the damage by patching or welding. Neither is very satisfactory from an aesthetic point of view, but the safety of the boat may be at stake and it will be essential to effect some sort of repair before putting to sea again. The easiest and obviously the best solution is to run the boat into the marina and have their workmen do the job professionally. This is expensive and may not be convenient, but repairing metal involves a considerable amount of expertise which most boat owners do not have, and in any case the visual result of inexpert patching or welding can be worse than the original damage. However, a brief description of the technique for patching is provided. Details of the basic welding procedures are contained in Chapter 6.

If the crack or hole is small, an epoxy filler may be all that is required to fix it. Special fillers for metal can be obtained from auto shops, but small holes and cracks can usually be filled with a standard epoxy filler providing the damaged area is clean and dry. The filler is driven hard into the crack or hole and when cured can be sanded off flush with the surrounding surface. Where the damage is more extensive it will be necessary to fit a patch or fill it with weld metal. Using the metal from the welding rods as a filler will work with holes that are not too extensive although the final result will need to be ground down heavily to restore the original appearance of the surface.

Fast aluminum hulls may be susceptible to damage if used at speed constantly in a seaway.

A patch is usually the simplest solution and it requires only a small piece of similar metal, shaped to cover the damaged area well, which is then secured in place. The patch should be fitted on the inside to be less visible and placed on a bed of mastic or some other synthetic material to make it waterproof. Pop rivets are mostly used to secure an aluminum patch, although a professional would probably prefer to weld it. Riveting is not usually practical with a steel patch and the welder is the choice for this job. After the patch has been secured in place the outside area can be filled and faired off to hide the appearance of the repair work as much as possible. It goes without saying that if the damage is part of a dent, the dent will need to be removed first. The whole area can then be primed with a suitable primer and the job finished with top coats of two-part polyurethane paint.

5
Tools and techniques

Nothing makes a job easier and better than using the right tools. And nowhere is that truism more applicable than when doing maintenance work on boats. Unfortunately, the full range of tools required to do the best job with every type of repair or maintenance work would be beyond the means of the average boat owner, so a compromise is necessary in many cases. Even professional boat yards find it too expensive to carry all the right machines to suit every repair job.

For this reason, the tools covered in this section are those which are essential for some work yet adaptable for a number of jobs, and at the same time are those which fall within the budget of most boat owners. Many of the tools described here are mainly for use with wood but by the same token, many can be adapted for use with fiberglass. Some—hacksaws and drills for example—can even be used for working with metal, although metals such as steel and aluminum may require some special tools, such as welding equipment. But as most of the repair and maintenance work described in this book is within the capabilities of the average handyman, the tools described are not specialized and for the most part are similar to those found in any home workshop or garage.

SAWS

The saw is probably the most used of all tools, especially with wood work. There are also saws for cutting fiberglass and others for metal, although often one saw can be adapted for use in a number of different areas. Since, generally speaking, most fitting-out work and a great deal of repair work involves the use of cutting, it is worth spending a little time examining what saws are available and which is the right one for each specific job.

There is a wide variety of saws available and although each has a special purpose and is the best saw for that purpose, it would be expensive and unnecessary to buy them all, since some can be used for a number of different purposes. Power saws are great labor saving devices but of course are not cheap, so one, or at most two, power saws should be included in the workshop equipment. Hand saws are relatively inexpensive and very useful for all kinds of boat work. They involve the input of a little more elbow grease but can be used for much finer work than power saws and are particularly well suited to interior work with wood fittings and furnishings.

POWER SAWS

Power saws can make repair and maintenance work much easier and simpler, especially when working with large sections of wood. There is a wide variety available and each has its special use. While most can be hand-held, some are permanently mounted on a workbench. The following are the most commonly used power saws for boat work, and the type of job for which they are best suited:

Circular saw

Ideal for cutting wood of all sizes, but most useful for large sections such as planks or structural members. These saws may be hand-held or bench mounted, but will only cut in a straight line. As a rule, the teeth are fairly large and therefore the cut is rough and will need sanding for any fine finishing.

Band saw

Probably the most useful saw for intricate fitting-out work on a boat since it is designed to cut curves, and most boat work requires curved sawing. It is usually permanently mounted on a bench and has a belt-like blade which runs over two wheels set vertically one above the other. The blade comes in different widths for cutting sharper or less acute corners which makes it ideal for cutting furniture or fittings to specific shapes.

Jig saw

This is a portable version of the band saw in that both have narrow blades and are used for cutting curves. However, the resemblance ends there for the jig saw is a small hand-held power tool with a single fixed blade that operates with a fast up and down sawing action rather than the continuous one-way action of the band saw. The blade in the jig saw can be easily changed with a screwdriver or wrench to cut different materials.

TIP: FOR A USEFUL GENERAL PURPOSE HAND SAW, SELECT ONE BETWEEN 24" AND 25" LONG WITH TEN TEETH PER INCH OF LENGTH.

HAND SAWS

Hand saws require a little more effort in use than power saws, but they are far more versatile, and invaluable for use with the complex shapes experienced in boat repair work. They do require a degree of skill if they are to give the maximum return with the least effort, unlike the power saws which just need guidance and an electricity supply. The secret of using a hand saw is to ensure that it is correctly sharpened. This is best

Holding the hand saw correctly makes sawing easier. Point the index finger along the blade.

done by a professional, because nothing makes harder work of sawing than incorrectly set teeth. It is possible for amateurs to set the saw, and there are instruments to help with this, but since ease of use is related directly to correct setting, the cost of a professional sharpener is well justified in labor saving terms. Similarly, setting up the wood correctly can reduce the effort required to cut it. A vice or sturdy bench is essential to hold the wood firmly and it is important to get into a comfortable sawing position with the wood at the right height to avoid too much bending or reaching. A firmly held piece of wood will cut much more easily than one that gives with each pressure stroke or moves as the blade bites in.

The saw should be held firmly with the forefinger of the sawing hand running along the handle and pointing down the blade, which should be angled at about 45 degrees to the wood, and the operator's head should be looking straight down the blade. Firm, even strokes ensure a steady cut and relieve the pressure on the arm muscles. A good maxim is to 'let the saw do the work' and not push or force the blade. Jerky, uneven strokes will create pressure that will bend the blade and dig the teeth into the wood fibers, making the work so much harder than need be. Smooth, flowing strokes with little weight on the saw and little pressure on the blade, will see the saw cut through even the hardest wood with surprising ease.

Selection of the right hand saw for the type and weight of the wood being cut is important to make the job as easy as possible. The basic hand saws required for maintenance work are as follows:

Panel saw
This is the main hand saw used for straight cutting. It comes in a variety of sizes and types of which the two most important are the cross cut, which is used, as its name denotes, to cut across the grain, and the rip saw, used when cutting with the grain.

Tenon saw
The tenon is a smaller, rectangular hand saw with fairly fine teeth used mainly for fine sawing, especially for making joints or cutting light wood where a bigger saw would be too rough.

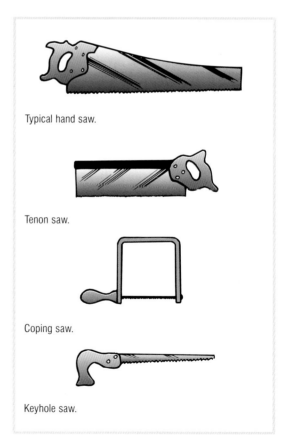

Typical hand saw.

Tenon saw.

Coping saw.

Keyhole saw.

The power saw and power plane reduce the effort required for the toughest jobs in maintenance work.

Coping saw

This is a light saw in the shape of a bow, for cutting curves or holes as it has a thin blade and fine teeth. A fret saw is used for similar work, particularly where the curves are very tight.

Keyhole saw

Also known in different forms as a pruning saw or compass saw this is similarly used for cutting curves and holes, but has a wider, more robust blade that will not cut such fine curves as a coping saw or fret saw.

Hacksaw

This saw has fine teeth and is used mainly for cutting metal. The blade is thicker than a coping or fret saw so it is not used for cutting curves, but it is not as wide as a tenon saw.

It is important to keep saws in good condition and the teeth sharp if they are to do the job cleanly and with minimum effort. Rust will appear on blades that are kept in salt-laden or moist atmospheres, and this will inhibit the use of the saw when it is next put to work. A light spray or film of oil will help to prevent rust, but the blade should be wiped clean before use to avoid staining the wood.

TIP: TO MAKE CUTTING EASIER, RUB A CANDLE ALONG THE SAW BLADE BEFORE STARTING TO SAW.

PLANES

The choice of planes is like that of saws; power planes for fast basic work, hand planes for finer work. Planes are used for reducing rough wood to a smooth, dressed finish and also for preparing a surface for sanding and painting. When rough sawn wood needs to be dressed or the dimensions of a piece of wood need to be reduced fairly drastically, the electric power plane is easy to use and gives excellent results. The depth of the blade can be adjusted to cut deeper or shallower, and when used with a smooth, steady action the plane will shave off even layers, leaving the wood surface smooth and level. This action is import-ant because a plane used by an inexperienced handler with rough, uneven strokes will gouge chunks and grooves out of the surface, leaving it looking unkempt and unattractive and making for a lot of unwanted extra work.

Hand planes are smaller and lighter than power planes and therefore better for fine work. They come in a wide variety of shapes and sizes of which the most common is the Jack plane; a metal plane about 15" long which has an adjustable blade for shaving deep or shallow cuts as it is pushed across the surface of the wood. A smaller version, about 9" long, is called a smoothing plane. As with power planes, a smooth, even planing action will achieve the best results; rough action will damage the wood surface. These useful little planes can be employed for all kinds of smoothing work, especially where moderate curves or corners are concerned. If a plane does not run smoothly the blade can be adjusted, and when it becomes blunt, the blade can be sharpened on an oil stone in much the same way as a chisel.

The surform plane is the only other type of plane that might come in for work in boat repair and maintenance jobs. It is a finishing plane with a coarser cut than a sander, but less

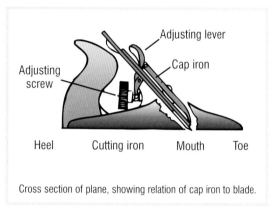

A Jack plane.

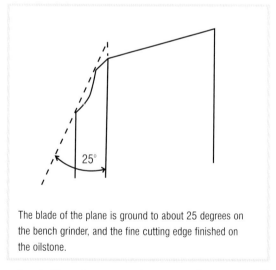

Cross section of plane, showing relation of cap iron to blade.

The blade of the plane is ground to about 25 degrees on the bench grinder, and the fine cutting edge finished on the oilstone.

dramatic than a plane. It is useful for cutting back fiberglass or polystyrene foam as well as wood, having a serrated surface that bites well into synthetics. The surform plane is widely used for shaping surfboards and flotation material.

TIP: WHEN PLANING ACROSS END GRAIN, PLANE INWARDS FROM EACH END TO PREVENT END BREAKAWAY.

SANDERS

Probably one of the most important tools for maintenance and repair work on a boat is the sander. Sanding is necessary for virtually every kind of surface at some time or another, and steel, aluminum and fiberglass as well as wood may need sanding in the course of repair or maintenance work. The most common use is for smoothing wood surfaces and preparing for painting on any other surface, but there is a wide application for sanding and as a result a wide range of sanding tools.

Professional users always have a number of power sanders to choose from, some costing hundreds, even thousands of dollars, because it is important to use the right sander for the job if a good result is to be achieved. Multi-speed sanders are particularly popular where fiberglass or paint surfaces are being sanded because they produce highly professional finishes and avoid the risk of scratching, but these are expensive and limited in their use for everyday boat work. The average handy-person power sanders, which most people have in their home workshop, are usually sufficient, although as with all tools, there is no question that the better the sander, the better and easier the job. The following are the sanders most used for maintenance work:

Disc sanders

These are the most basic type of sander, consisting of a power unit that rotates a disc at speed. The disc is usually rubber or plastic to which is secured a circular sheet of sandpaper. The speed may be variable and the sandpaper specially made to withstand the speed as well as match the type of sanding being done. There are many grades and types of disc sandpaper available, some with holes to allow the dust to be collected as the machine operates. Disc sanders must be carefully used, especially on fine or finished work as it is very easy to scratch or score the surface with the fast rotating disk.

Orbital sanders

Orbital sanders are basically similar to disc sanders but instead of a circular rotating disc the power unit drives an oblong pad that moves in an orbital pattern giving a smooth, even action that is far less likely to scratch or score the surface. Once again special sandpaper sheets are used to fit the pad, and these are mostly of finer grades since the orbital sander is mainly used for finishing work prior to painting rather than hard abrasive cutting, as is the case with the disc sander.

Random orbital sanders

These sanders are a further development of the basic orbital sander, using a random action to reduce the risk of scratching and scoring, at the same time providing a good cutting action, thus offering the best of the disc and the orbital types in one unit. These

Angle grinders can be used on work
that is too heavy for disc or belt
sanders. But care must be taken not
to score the surface. The operator
should be wearing a protective mask.

When hand sanding, a sanding block helps create a smoother finish.

are the most popular for fine finishing work and have fitted disks that can be changed to ensure the right grade of sandpaper is used.

Belt sanders

The most aggressive sander available, the belt sander is used to cut back the surface almost like a plane. Instead of a pad, the power unit drives a rotary belt with a contact surface usually 8" or more long, fitted with a coarse sand-paper that provides continuous cutting along its length. Such sanders have a limited use in repair or maintenance work but are often used in wood boat building where they are useful for reducing rough surfaces or sanding back large pieces of wood that may not quite justify the use of a plane.

Corner sanders

These have a triangular or pointed blade that enables them to sand into tight corners where circular or rectangular discs cannot go. They are basically similar to other power sanders although the pad is relatively small and thus limited for use where extensive sanding is required.

HAND SANDING

Despite the wide range of power sanders available, there will always be a need for hand sanding, especially in maintenance and repair work where most jobs are relatively small or need special attention. Where large surfaces or heavy work is concerned, the power sanders are ideal, but where intricate or detailed work is involved or when a fine finish is required, hand sanding will usually be necessary. Since most maintenance on boats relates to applying new coats of paint or repairing minor damage, hand sanding is usually involved somewhere along the line.

A very useful gadget for hand sanding is the sanding block—a rectangular block of cork, wood or plastic around which a sheet of sandpaper is wrapped. This prevents the sandpaper from folding or breaking up while in use and offers a firm base onto which pressure can be applied, thus creating firmer abrasion than when the sheet is used by itself. There are various sanding blocks that can be purchased at any handyman store, but any block of solid cork will do the job as effectively and more cheaply.

TIP: AS A SUBSTITUTE FOR A SANDING BLOCK MAKE A 'MITTEN' BY ROLLING THE SANDPAPER SHEET AND STAPLING THE ENDS. FITTING YOUR HAND INSIDE MAKES FOR A SMOOTH SANDING DEVICE.

SANDPAPERS

Because sandpapers are used for a wide range of purposes, from burnishing metal to preparing fine paint surfaces, there is a wide range of sandpapers to choose from. Different grades of grit offer fine, moderate and coarse abrasion, and these are usually given a code by which they can be recognized and ordered from the hardware store. Because different countries use different codes it is not proposed to list the codes in this book, but a glance at the sandpaper shelf in the local chandlery, or if necessary a chat with the marina manager, will soon indicate which grades are the best for marine work.

As important as the grades, is the material used in the structure of the paper. The term 'sandpaper' covers almost all types yet many different materials are used to create the abrasive medium.

With a range of grades and types of paper to suit anything that may crop up in the job, the next step is to select the right tool and paper to make the work easy and efficient. In most cases the ultimate aim is a fine, smooth surface without scratches or blemishes. The following tip will provide a basis on which paper should be used for each specific job.

TIP: USE GARNET OR GLASS PAPER ABOUT 40–80 GRIT FOR THE FIRST CUT ON WOOD OR FIBERGLASS, DRY 140–180 GRIT FOR FINISHING WOOD, WET AND DRY 150–400 GRIT FOR FINISHING FIBERGLASS AND WET AND DRY 400 GRIT FOR SANDING BACK PAINT BETWEEN COATS.

DRILLS

Since hand drills are virtually obsolete these days the choice of drills for woodwork comes down to the standard power drill and the battery operated drill. These drills come in a variety of shapes, sizes and power output and, with a wide range of accessories, can be adapted to many different jobs. A very useful innovation for work on boats is the battery operated drill, since the regular power drill mostly requires shore voltage, and this is not always easily available, especially if the boat is at sea or lying at a mooring. Large yachts and motor boats may have a 120 or 240 volt generator, in which case normal power tools can be used on board, but smaller craft mostly rely on battery power, 12 volts or 24 volts and these will not operate a drill designed for shore power. So the battery operated drill, although not as powerful as the plug in version, is more than useful for running repairs afloat.

A drill stand should be used for drilling metal.

The one limitation with using battery operated drills, especially cheaper units, is their lack of power when compared to a standard drill. It is worth buying one of the more powerful battery operated drills since it may save the hassle of hooking up to a power supply when a tough drilling job is encountered. A 12-volt drill will give plenty of 'grunt' for most jobs and will only require periodic recharging of the battery to keep it in good shape. These drills can, of course, perform a number of useful tasks, not least of which is as power screwdrivers. Yet another advantage with the battery operated drill is that the risk of electrocution is non-existent, which is not the case with AC powered electric drills.

Using the correct drill bit is important for successful drilling. As with any tools, economizing on price can often affect the quality of the bit and create problems when in the middle of a job. A good quality bit will pay dividends, as will choosing the correct type of bit for the job, in terms of ease of drilling and reliability. Wood, metal and masonry bits are available and should be used for their designated task. Although some can be interchanged (metal bits will drill into wood, for example), the result is never worth the effort, and the extra cost of getting the right drill for each job always pays off. A wood bit used for metal will end its effective life almost immediately. Bits can be sharpened by using a special machine available from most hardware stores, or they can be handed to a professional for sharpening. By sharpening good quality bits time and time again, a lot of money can be saved because bits are usually expensive

Drilling should be done with a steady hand and a gentle but firm pressure, in order to make the hole uniform and accurate. A drill that wanders will enlarge the hole and prevent the fastening from getting a good grip—this is especially the case with pop riveting, when the hole must exactly fit the rivet. Metal drilling requires the use of a press to achieve accuracy and to avoid many broken drill bits. A punch is necessary to give the bit a start and to prevent it wandering across the surface, leaving unsightly scratches. Wood drill bits can be used to drill into fiberglass.

SCREWDRIVERS

As with drill bits and drilling, the secret of successful fastening with screws is to use a screwdriver that matches the screw head. A screwdriver blade that does not exactly fit the slot in the screw head will result in difficult and irregular screwing or the burring of the slot edges, rendering the screw useless. Most screwdrivers can be purchased in kits, with a range of tools that will fit most screw heads, whether they be Phillips heads (crossed slots) or standard, single slot heads. Similarly, a range of inserts for battery operated drills can be obtained to match the screw heads when using the drill as a screwdriver. Since there is often a need to use a screwdriver on board, a set of screwdrivers or a battery operated screwdriver with a set of interchangeable heads should be carried on every boat.

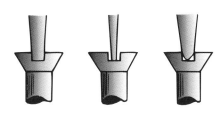

The use of the correct screwdriver for every job ensures easy and accurate fastening.

The blade of the screwdriver must fit the slot in the screw head (left). Difficult and irregular screwing will result from too fine a screwdriver (centre) or too thick a blade (right).

CHISELS

Used mostly for trimming wood, although they can be used for shaping compressed foam and fiberglass, chisels are a useful tool for boat work. There are several different sizes and varieties, of which the 'firmer' or flat blade is the most common for repair work. As with any tools, keeping chisels in good shape will pay dividends when they are required for use, and the sharpness of the blade is the prime factor in making the work easy and accurate. If the edge of the blade becomes pitted or damaged (often the result of striking hidden nails or similar objects) it may need to be sharpened on a grinder. If it is just blunt, an oilstone will restore the edge.

Sharpening a chisel blade on an oilstone is done by placing the cutting edge at an angle about five degrees greater than that used for grinding. The blade is stroked easily across the oilstone, using neatsfoot oil as a lubricant, until the required sharpness is achieved. The burring or 'wire edge' formed can be removed by

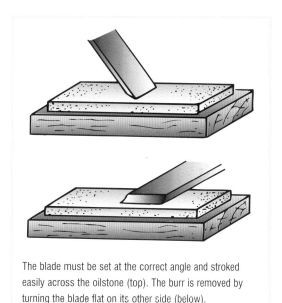

The blade must be set at the correct angle and stroked easily across the oilstone (top). The burr is removed by turning the blade flat on its other side (below).

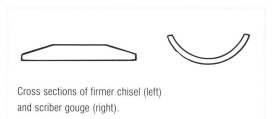

Cross sections of firmer chisel (left) and scriber gouge (right).

A wooden mallet would be better used
with the chisel than this hammer!

The essential boat maintenance manual

turning the blade over and rubbing it flat on the oilstone surface. The cutting blades of planes can be sharpened in the same way.

FILES

Always a handy tool to have in the workshop, files are mostly used for metal work although the coarser 'rasps' can be useful in smoothing rough wood. Files come in a wide range of sizes and with a wide range of surfaces. 'Single cut' files have the teeth running parallel in the same direction, and are mostly used for sharpening and finishing. 'Double cut' files have teeth crossed in a diamond pattern and are used for faster cutting and heavy duty work. Most files used for repair work are flat, although some round or half-curved files can be handy for cleaning round surfaces and holes. Triangular files are mostly used for corners.

OTHER USEFUL TOOLS

Hammers are very useful general purpose tools that can be used for a wide range of jobs, from knocking in and pulling out nails to knocking out dents. A ball hammer and a claw hammer will cover most requirements for repair work on boats, while a rubber mallet is the best tool for knocking dents from aluminum.

Pliers, **multigrips** and **pincers** are likewise useful for all sorts of purposes and one pair of standard pliers plus one long-nose type should be kept handy.

C-clamps are essential in marine work where gluing, screwing or bending is required. As with most other useful tools, they come in a variety of shapes and sizes and choosing the right clamp for the job is important. They are relatively inexpensive and it may be worth having a small selection available when commencing repair or maintenance work on board.

Angle grinders are perhaps somewhat limited in their use on wood or fiberglass boats, but the angle grinder is essential for steel vessels and indeed for any steel work. A multi-speed grinder can be used for a variety of tasks from cutting metal to buffing a polished surface, depending on the quality of the tool and the attachment on the spindle.

TIP: ALWAYS WEAR GOGGLES WHEN GRINDING, WITH BOTH BENCH GRINDERS AND ANGLE GRINDERS.

Pop riveters are useful tools that have replaced the days of cold hand riveting. They are ideal for all types of work, but particularly for masts and other aluminum fittings and

of course for aluminum hulls. There are a number of different types of pop riveters, and it is important to obtain one that has plenty of leverage to ensure a good draw of the rivet. The 'scissor' action type used by professionals is by far the best.

Bolt cutters are particularly useful for maintenance work when old rusted or seized rigging or fittings have to be cut away. They can save a lot of agony and arm work with a hacksaw.

Swaging tools are used almost exclusively for yachts and small sailing boats for renewing rigging.

Wrenches are the universal tool beloved by mechanics and engineers, but they can also be very useful for other boat maintenance work. For general purpose work and to avoid the purchase of an expensive set, the adjustable wrench is usually sufficient around the boat. But if work on the motor is done, a full set of box and open end wrenchs will be necessary.

Wire cutters can be very handy when rigging work is undertaken. It is well worth the extra expense of purchasing a really good set of wire cutters as they reduce the effort required to cut stainless steel wire rope. Bolt cutters are also carried on some larger craft where heavy rigging or chain is used.

Wire brushes are important if there are any steel fittings aboard that are liable to rust. Cleaning off powder rust can be done quite easily with this hand tool, and if a lot of such cleaning is involved, a wire brush fitting can be obtained that will fit onto a power drill.

Fastenings

Almost all repair work, and a lot of maintenance work, involves fastening. A broken hatch, a fitting that has worked loose, rigging that has come adrift—most things will need some form of fastening whether it be screwing, gluing, riveting or some other means of putting things back together again. A good repair job can be as strong as, or even stronger, than the original, provided the fastening is done correctly and the correct fastening is used—and that is the secret: the fastening must be done properly or instead of being stronger, a weakness will be created and any area of weakness in a boat at sea can lead to a dangerous situation.

Screwing and gluing is the most common form of fastening with wood, while pop riveting is probably the most popular with aluminum. Fiberglass may require just a 'potch' filler job or reconstruction of the laminate in way of the damage, and steel needs to be welded. Whatever the material, fastening is an important part of any repair job and must be done with the right fastener and in the correct manner or it will only lead to a bigger and more expensive repair job.

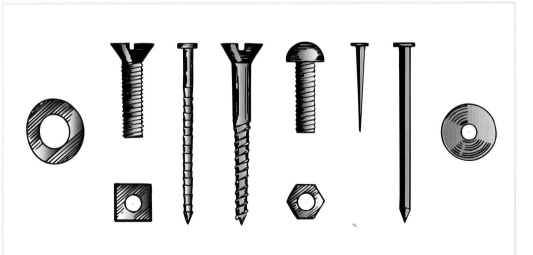

A typical range of fastenings used in boat work: (from left) washer, flathead bolt, anchor nail, brass screw, roundhead bolt, copper tack, copper nail, copper rove.

WOOD FASTENINGS

Gluing, screwing and nailing are the main forms of fastening wood, and there is a wide choice of fasteners to do the job. Not all are suitable for each situation, however, and it is important to use the right fastening or the repair work may fall apart at some later date. The following provides some information on what fastenings are available and when they should be used:

BRONZE AND BRASS

The greatest problem with metal fastenings in a marine environment is the likelihood of rust or corrosion. In wood boats, bronze and brass are widely used for fastenings and fittings as both metals are resistant to rust. They are both alloys of copper, tin and zinc, although the quantities of each may vary. For example, bronze is mostly a fusion of copper and tin. Brass, on the other hand, has little or no tin, but has copper and zinc in roughly the ratio 7:3. Phosphor bronze, which has a small percentage of phosphor, is the most popular alloy for any marine work, particularly fastenings. Brass is also popular but has a tendency to deteriorate as a result of galvanic action when in contact with sea water.

For interior work such as furnishings, where there is less likelihood of salt water affecting the fastenings, either brass or bronze can be used. Galvanized or stainless steel screws can also be used in these areas, but they do not have the aesthetic appeal of brass or bronze. For exterior and underwater work, where the fastenings may be exposed to the weather or water, phosphor bronze should be used. If this is too expensive, stainless steel or galvanized iron fastenings can be used but they must be protected from the elements either by dowels or plugs, or at very least, several coats of paint. It will not take long for the sea air to break down the galvanizing and then rust bleeds will appear, and these are very hard to remove.

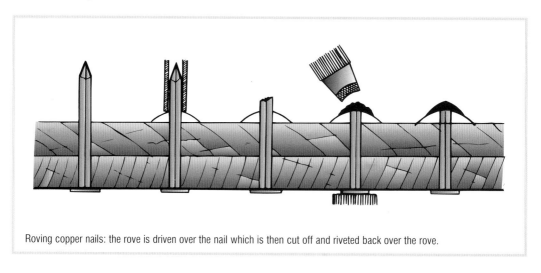

Roving copper nails: the rove is driven over the nail which is then cut off and riveted back over the rove.

COPPER

Once widely used for fastening planks in wood boats, copper is not widely seen these days other than for ornamental use. It is a soft metal with poor tensile strength and is subject to metal fatigue. It is mostly used as a component in harder metals such as bronze and brass.

Copper patches, while still useful for wood repair, have been mostly superseded by GRP patches.

STAINLESS STEEL

Probably the most widely used metal in any form of boat work, stainless steel is highly resistant to rust and corrosion. This makes it useful for a wide range of uses from fastenings and fittings to rigging and handrails. It needs no painting or treatment and generally keeps its shiny appearance regardless of wind, weather and other deteriorating forces. The only factor of importance when selecting stainless steel for marine use, is to ensure that it is of the correct grade. It is basically an alloy of steel with chromium and

nickel, but comes in different qualities, of which the loosely termed 'marine grade' is the one to select of use on board a boat. Stainless steel screws, rivets and bolts should be used wherever possible, but particularly where they are exposed to the sea air.

MONEL

Like stainless steel, monel is very resistant to all forms of corrosion and is thus ideal for marine use. However, it is generally more expensive than stainless steel—which is itself quite expensive—and is therefore not used as widely as the stainless metal. Nevertheless, where a tough repair job (particularly below the waterline) requires sound fastenings that will not be affected by any form of corrosion, monel can sometimes justify the expense.

GALVANIZED IRON (STEEL)

At one time a widely used metal on all types of wood vessels, galvanized iron (which is actually steel these days) has fallen out of favor because of its vulnerability to rust. While

the galvanizing is intended to prevent rust, the harsh maritime conditions tend to attack it after a while, leaving the metal beneath exposed and open to corrosion, particularly rust. Its tensile strength is generally less than that of stainless steel, although some cruising yachtsmen favor galvanized rigging over stainless because when it reaches the end of its useful life it gives good warning by 'whiskering' over a period of time. Stainless steel rigging, on the other hand, tends to become brittle and snap with little or no warning signs. Where galvanized fastenings are used they must be completely covered and sealed from contact with the atmosphere.

NAILS

Nails are not used widely in marine work these days, other than perhaps in interior work such as furniture and fittings. Older wood boats often had their hull planking secured by 'roves,' which consists of copper nails driven through the planks and then hammered back over copper roves to give a rivet effect. With the demise of planking, this type of fastening is rarely seen.

A small block of waste wood gives better leverage for drawing the nail and prevents damage to the wood surface.

SCREWS AND SCREWING

For repair or maintenance work on wood craft, particularly where it is exposed to salt air, bronze or stainless steel screws should be used, especially below the waterline, but brass can be used where there is no risk of corrosion such as in the interior furniture. There are many different types of tapered screws, ranging from flathead screws that can

Choice of the correct screw and matching screwdriver are important at any time, but particularly when screwing into tough wood.

be countersunk into the wood, to roundheads, while panel screws are of uniform thickness throughout their length. Self tapping screws are usually favored for screwing into metal although these can be used for any material.

TIP: NEVER USE BRASS SCREWS FOR UNDERWATER FASTENINGS.

Drilling the correct size hole can make screwing simple and effective. With battery operated drills used as screwdrivers, it may not be necessary to drill a hole for self tapping or panel screws, much depending on the hardness of the wood into which the screws are to be driven. Mostly a light hole is drilled, as much for a guide as to make screwing easy. With tapered screws drilling is essential and the technique is as follows: the bit matching the dimensions of the screw is used first to drill a hole part way into the wood. In the case of fastening two pieces of wood, this hole should be in the top piece of wood. A smaller gauge bit is then used to drill a 'guide' hole of smaller diameter in the second lower wood which enables the threaded end of the screw to get a solid 'bite'. As the tapered thread of the screw is drawn into the guide hole, resistance from the wider shank of the screw is eased by the first hole. In this way the most secure fastening possible is obtained without placing too much strain on the screwdriver yet ensuring the wood is drawn up tight.

Countersinking is the neatest and most proficient way of hiding the screw as well as protecting it from the elements. Having drilled the initial wide and narrow holes for the screw,

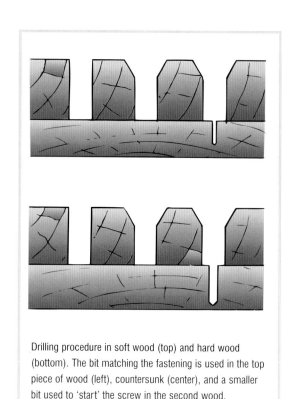

Drilling procedure in soft wood (top) and hard wood (bottom). The bit matching the fastening is used in the top piece of wood (left), countersunk (center), and a smaller bit used to 'start' the screw in the second wood.

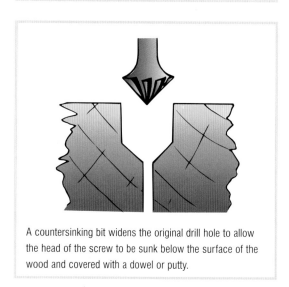

A countersinking bit widens the original drill hole to allow the head of the screw to be sunk below the surface of the wood and covered with a dowel or putty.

the top of the hole is enlarged with a countersinking bit to a depth which will allow the screw to be recessed below the surface of the wood. A filler or, for more aesthetic appearance, a dowel, is then used to plug the hole and conceal the screw.

GLUES AND GLUING

There are probably as many different types of glues as there are metal fastenings, but the choice for marine work is limited since whatever the type of glue used, it must be waterproof. While ordinary household glues may be used for interior work, on a boat there is always the risk that at some stage water may get into the cabin. When wood gets wet, many of the non-marine glues will disintegrate, so any extra cost involved in using correct marine glue will be rewarded by ensuring the job is secure no matter what conditions may be experienced. Likewise, paying extra for a top quality glue also pays dividends, for when a boat is experiencing the stresses and strains of working in a seaway or when the wind and weather take their toll, only the best glues will ensure that the repair job will not fail.

For wood repair the adhesives used for boat repair and maintenance mostly fall into two main categories. First are the synthetic compounds such as urea formaldehyde, resorcinol formaldehyde and phenol formaldehyde, and secondly the epoxy group of compounds. These are all good for marine work, especially for use with plywood construction or repair. It is obviously not possible to list all the commercial brands available, there are so many and often procedures for their use differ from one to another. However, all manufacturers issue detailed instructions with their product and it is important to follow these instructions when using the glue.

Generally speaking, a good quality glue will create a bond as strong as, if not stronger than, the wood it joins. This accounts for some of the strength of plywood; the cross-grained laminates are strong in themselves, and when fastened with a good quality marine glue make an extremely strong composite. Many glues have the added advantage of gap-filling, which is obviously a bonus in repair work where gluing sections with awkward corners or uneven faces can be difficult. As a rule, epoxy glues are thicker than

Avoid glue spills and use dowels to cover screw heads if an impeccable clear wood finish is required.

PVA glue and will fill minor cracks and gaps. Indeed, glues such as International HT9000 have a special additive called HT110 Extender which acts as a thickening agent to avoid drainage from the joint, and the degree of gap filling fulfilled by this produce can be increased by varying the amount of the additive. Where large gaps are concerned, wood shavings or micro balloons can be mixed with the glue to resolve the problem and avoid leaks or an unsightly finish.

Epoxy glues are mostly supplied in one- or two-part packs and mixed just prior to use. As with any resin/ hardener mix, measurement of the two components is critical and great care must be taken to ensure the right amount of each is used. The effectiveness of the glue depends on the correct balance of the two components and an incorrect mix may lead to a weak bond in the repair job. Screwing and gluing is a practice followed by many of the older

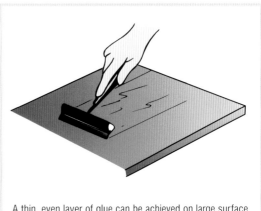

A thin, even layer of glue can be achieved on large surface areas by use of a squeegee.

Gluing is an important part of any wood joinery, including scarfing.

shipwrights, but with the improved strength of modern glues, this is not really necessary, although the screws are sometimes useful in holding the joint together while the glue sets.

Once mixed, the glue must be used quickly, and on a small or difficult job it may be necessary to divide the quantities rather than mix the whole pack. The maximum pot life will be indicated in the instructions and this must be carefully watched, for if the glue starts to cure, not only will the job become difficult, but the effectiveness of the glue will also be reduced. Curing can be speeded by using heat, and this is something that must also be watched, especially when working in very hot or very cold temperatures. A temperature of, say, 95°F (35°C), can considerably reduce the pot life of a mix, so gluing a repair job in mid-summer heat can, in some climates, need fast work. Conversely, the curing can be slowed by lower temperatures.

TIP: USE A REFRIGERATOR OR HEATER TO KEEP THE TEMPERATURE OF THE GLUE AT A REASONABLE LEVEL—AROUND 77°F (25°C).

Basically, most glues need to be applied to a clean surface if they are to achieve maximum bond. The moisture content of the wood should be between 10% and 12%, certainly not above 18%, and oil or grease on the surface, or oily woods such as teak, should be wiped off with trichloroethylene or thinners before the glue is applied.

Resinous or gummy woods such as Douglas Fir or Oregon should be wiped with a 2% caustic soda solution to etch the gluing face, followed by a wash down with fresh water to raise the grain. It must then be completely dried out.

It goes without saying that dirt, dust, paint and other inhibiting factors must be removed, and for preference the surface should be slightly roughened to give a good key to the glue. Both faces of the wood to be joined should be coated with the glue unless the manufacturer states otherwise. Allow a few moments before placing the two faces together under pressure, as this enables the glue to penetrate into the wood and create a stronger bond, before any surplus glue is squeezed out.

Screwing or clamping are the most common methods used to hold the repair in place while the glue cures. It is important not to clamp too tightly or much of the glue will be squeezed out of the joint. As mentioned earlier, curing can be speeded or slowed by varying temperatures; a moderate temperature of 77° to 86°F (25° to 30°C) is ideal for curing most marine glues, although a higher temperature is always preferable to a lower temperature. If the wood is later to be clear varnished, it is important to ensure that no glue spills or runs out of the join or it will mark the surface and show through the clear finish. Cleaning up carefully is not so important if the repair work is to be painted, for any spills or runs can be sanded back and covered with the paint coat.

TIP: WIPE OFF BOTH FACES OF WOOD BEFORE GLUING , USING THINNERS OR SPIRIT. WASH OFF WITH FRESH WATER TO RAISE THE NAP, THEN ALLOW TO DRY.

METAL

There are three main methods available to the amateur boat owner for fastening metal to metal. Pop riveting is the easiest and welding requires the most expertise. The third, soldering, is limited to joining relatively small pieces of metal such as electrical wiring and small metal fittings and therefore has only a limited use. Before fastening metal to metal, it is important to keep in mind the problem of corrosion. Two dissimilar metals, when in contact with one another in a salt spray or water environment will be subject to galvanic action. Small currents of electricity will set up between the two metals and one will be eaten away by the galvanic action more commonly known as corrosion. Metals such as aluminum, brass and bronze are particularly susceptible to this action and steps must be taken to prevent it or the result will be a poor repair job, and possibly, costly damage to the boat.

The electric currents that create the galvanic action cannot exist unless there is an electrolyte to carry them from one metal to the other. Salt water is a notoriously effective electrolyte, which explains why one of the most likely areas for corrosion to occur is on the outside of the hull beneath the waterline, but even above the waterline, masts, booms and other aluminum or brass fittings can be affected. As a result,

Pop riveting is a method for fastening fittings on boats. A powerful riveter makes light work of any riveting job.

checking for galvanic action between metals is an important part of any boat maintenance. The under-water areas are dealt with in detail in Chapter 11 of this book, but as far as the joining of two metal fittings on deck is concerned, it is important to match the two metals and the metal fastenings joining them if corrosion problems are to be avoided. A 'shield' or insulator made of non-conducting material placed between the two different metals is one way of minimizing this problem, another is to ensure that the metals are as closely compatible as possible.

POP RIVETING

Cleats, sheaves, repair plates and similar fittings can be fastened very easily and securely to masts or other parts of the boat with pop rivets. These are metal rivets, usually aluminum or stainless steel, housed around a metal shaft that fits into a special tool. A hole is drilled where the rivet is to be used and a matching rivet inserted through the two pieces to be fastened together. Under pressure, the riveting tool pulls the head of the shaft back through the rivet, expanding it outwards and locking it into place, thus securing the two items together. The pressure is applied via the handle, which may be a simple grip-type handle or a scissors mechanism which applies enormous pressure. The lighter tool may be quite adequate in carrying out much of the riveting on board, but the heavier equipment will make the work easier and more secure and enable much heavier rivets to be used.

The two pieces to be joined need not necessarily both be metal, as pop riveting can be used with materials such as heavy duty plastic and nylon providing it will withstand the pressure of the rivet being drawn up tight. Synthetic mast and deck fittings can usually be pop riveted in place, but soft materials and wood are not suitable for this fastening procedure. Close fitting of the rivet and the hole through both pieces to be fastened is important, and to ensure this, the pieces must be clamped securely together during the drilling and while the rivet is inserted. The riveting tool is then lowered onto the

Cold riveting is still widely used in metal boat construction.

protruding rivet shaft and pressure is applied to the handles until the slack is taken up. It is often worth dipping the rivet in a sealing compound if it is likely to be exposed to the elements. This ensures that it will not leak and also helps prevent the possibility of galvanic action starting up if the metals are not exactly compatible.

A hard pressure applied to the handles will pull the rivet into place and snap off the shaft so that a solid riveted join is made and the only way to remove the rivet once firmly secured in place is to drill it out. Bear in mind that while the top outer end of the rivet (nearest the riveting tool) will be more or less flush with the surrounding surface, and quite neat in appearance, the underside will be rather unattractive since the expanded head of the rivet will be sticking out of the drilled hole. This will be of no consequence in mast fittings or

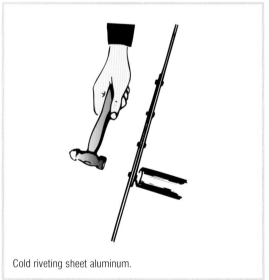

Cold riveting sheet aluminum.

the like where the inner end of the rivet is concealed, but it can be a nuisance if it protrudes through a the deck or any base where it is visible to the eye.

COLD RIVETING

Cold riveting is not used greatly in amateur repair work since it is more complex and requires more skills than pop riveting. Briefly, it involves the use of a solid aluminum rivet which is inserted into the drilled hole and hammered home. A second hammer or 'dolly' is held against the head of the rivet and the other end hammered vigorously until the metal 'burrs' and spreads, tightening the rivet into the hole and fixing it firmly in place. This is the traditional method of riveting for any metal, but in small boat repair work has been mostly superseded by the much easier pop riveting.

WELDING

This is the popular and probably most secure method of joining metal, but there are a few factors that inhibit its use in amateur repair and maintenance work. Firstly, it requires a considerable degree of skill, and secondly, good welding equipment is fairly expensive. For the occasional use required by most boat maintenance work, purchasing such equipment and undertaking the training required to use it efficiently seems rather an excessive enterprise unless, of course, the boat in question is of steel construction, when welding will be required quite frequently. However, modern home welding sets are somewhat less expensive and can handle most small jobs that might be required for maintenance or repair of the average boat, so an enthusiastic boat owner might well find a small welder a useful acquisition for the annual maintenance.

Using an electric arc welder

Extensive or difficult welding jobs should not be tackled by an amateur, but the everyday tasks that crop up when the boat is on the slipway for annual maintenance, or when she is being refitted or repaired, can mostly be handled by a person of modest skills using home handyman welding equipment. The following is a guide to the basic requirements and techniques for small welding jobs:

- An electric arc welding set
- Electrode holder with insulated cables
- Hand shield or helmet with tinted glass
- Grounding clamp
- Quantity of covered electrode rods (3.25 mm or 4.0 mm diameter)
- Chipping hammer
- Wire brush
- Clear goggles (for chipping slag)
- Gloves
- A suitable workbench and vice or clamps to hold the pieces being welded

Electric arc welding is within the reach of the average handyman, but aluminum welding requires special equipment and techniques.

When an electric current jumps across a gap between two electrically charged pieces of metal it creates a spark. The spark used in welding, called the arc, creates temperatures of around 4000°C which is sufficient to melt some metals. If the edge or ends of the pieces of metal are close together, they will melt and fuse creating a permanent join on cooling. This is the principle of electric arc welding and it is put into practice by connecting one side of the electric supply to the metal pieces to be welded together, and the other to the electrode of the welding equipment. The tip of the electrode is brought close to the join between the metal pieces and the arc jumps across, melting both pieces of metal and the electrode, and creating a crater. The molten metal from the electrode is worked into the crater and mixes with the molten metal of the pieces to be joined. When left to cool the fused metals create a bond that secures both pieces together.

While it sounds easy, there are of course certain requirements that must be met if the work is to be successful. Firstly, the metal pieces to be joined must be completely clean so that no oil, dust, grease or other pollutant interferes with the quality of the weld. The intense heat will create gases from such impurities, which will leave blowholes in the weld metal. Pollutants may also make the work harder by preventing the spark from firing when striking the arc. With the plates cleaned and ready, and before starting to weld, it is a good idea to undertake a few practice runs on spare metal plates in order to get the feel for using the welding rods. It is important to use the correct electrode rods for the work and the correct amperage setting; in both cases the manufacturer's recommendations should be followed. The metal to be welded must be secured firmly into position with clamps or vice and the area cleared of any hindrance so that the work can be done quickly and comfortably.

TIP: KEEP ALL WELDING TOOLS DRY—WATER AND ELECTRICITY DO NOT MIX!

Striking the arc

There are two main methods of striking the arc, both equally effective. The first method involves tapping or touching the metal with the end of the electrode at an angle of 90° to the work, and then withdrawing it until the arc is fired. The electrode should be held at an angle of about 70° towards the direction of travel and should be held as close to the plate as possible without the rod sticking (freezing) to the weld. If the arc is hard to strike, the process can be helped by striking the electrode on a spare piece of metal to get it started and then applying it to the work. The rod will strike more easily when the tip is warm.

The second method involves scratching the metal with the rod rather than tapping it. This action is not unlike that of striking a match, with the rod sweeping down and along the surface of the plate then immediately rising; the arc should fire at the point where the tip is at working level above the plate. If the electrode sticks to the plate with either of these methods, it must be jerked quickly sideways with a twisting action to pull it free. If this fails, the current must be turned off quickly or the rod immediately released from the holder.

The welding technique

The most basic method of welding involves making what is known as a 'straight bead,' or a clean straight deposit of weld across a join. The electrode is held at an angle of around 70° to the plate in the direction of travel and moved forwards at a speed that deposits the required amount of metal onto the join. An arc length of around 1/8" (3 mm) with a 1/8" (3.25 mm) rod should enable this task to be carried out without sticking or unevenness. There must be no sideways movement in the electrode and the rod must be

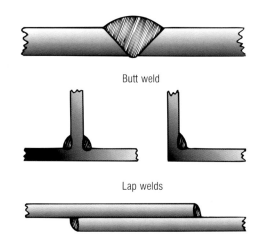

Butt weld

Lap welds

Common weld joints.

moved so that the weld metal fills the crater with the slag solidifying on the top. At the end of the weld, the arc is broken by pausing then withdrawing the arc slowly, moving it back over the weld about 3/8" (10 mm) and increasing the angle of the rod to the metal to vertical and beyond, then lifting it clear. This will ensure that the weld metal fills the crater completely.

As with any skills, the technique for making an efficient weld requires a lot of practice, and real work should not be attempted until a degree of proficiency has been reached. As with using a spray gun, practice runs on spare material can avoid the angst of ruining the job, or ending up with an unsightly result, or even worse, an unsafe weld. There are always spare bits of metal to be found around boat sheds and marinas that can be used for practice. Only when the practice pieces are near perfect should the

A neatly finished butt weld.

welder be turned towards the proper job. When the welding is done, the job is finished by chipping and wire brushing to remove the slag before priming and painting.

Other welding systems

There are many different types of welds used for different types of joins or used for joining different materials. Joining metal can also be done with oxy-acetylene gas, and indeed this is preferred by some steel fabricators for small work. This work is somewhat similar to soldering, where the high temperature (3000°C) of the oxy-acetylene gas mix is used to melt metal rods at the surface to be joined so that the melted metal joins the two heated surfaces together as it cools. Welding aluminum requires the use of Argon gas in yet another technique for joining metals. However, this is no manual on the art of welding, so it is no place to go into the finer points. Suffice it to say that once having mastered the basic technique of using welding equipment, whatever the method used, it is only a matter of practice, plus perhaps some more advanced instruction, before the average boat owner should be able to handle most of the welding requirements for his boat.

SOLDERING

Although soldering is similar to welding in that it involves the joining of two pieces of metal by using molten metal, there are also many differences. To begin with, a soldered join is not nearly as strong as a welded join, so soldering is mostly confined to the smaller jobs around the boat such as connecting wiring and metal piping, plugging holes or cracks in metal tanks or containers, or making up small metal fittings that are mainly ornamental and will not be subject to heavy loads. Soldering requires far less skill than welding and much cheaper equipment. Indeed, the requirements are so few that many boats carry a soldering iron in the tool drawer as a matter of course.

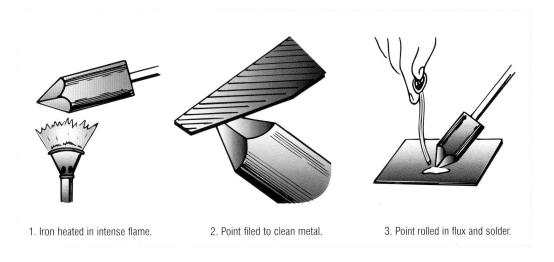

1. Iron heated in intense flame.   2. Point filed to clean metal.   3. Point rolled in flux and solder.

TIP: SOLDERING ALUMINUM REQUIRES A SPECIAL SOLDER.

The basic needs for soldering consist of an iron—which may be heated by electricity, gas torch or any other type of flame-solder, flux, abrasive paper and a file. A flat piece of metal for 'tinning' will be needed and a cloth to wipe off excess flux or dirt. Before use the iron must be tinned, which is a process whereby the point of the iron is cleaned and given a thin coat of solder so as to ensure maximum transfer of heat onto the job. The iron is heated to a moderate heat then the copper tip filed back or rubbed back on abrasive paper until it is shiny. The tip is then coated with flux and solder, both of which are applied together if the solder has a flux core, or separately, with the flux first. While still hot and the solder molten, the tip of the iron is rubbed up and down on the spare piece of metal to ensure a good, even coverage of the solder. A wipe with the rag and the iron should be bright and shiny and ready to start the job.

Flux assists the solder to take to different metals, cleaning the surface at the same time. Despite this, a great deal of work must go into cleaning the metal to be joined, for lacking the intense heat of arc welding, the soldering procedure will not burn off any impurities. Sandpaper or emery paper is the best to clean up the surfaces to be joined, and when cleaned, flux should be applied immediately. The iron is then brought up to its recommended heat and placed against the metal to be joined, heating both pieces at the same time. Solder, usually in the form of a rod or coil, is placed against the hot tip of the iron until it melts and runs into the join. With everything at the desired temperature, the iron can be moved across the surface slowly and smoothly in order to work the molten solder right into the join. The two pieces being joined must be held firmly in position until sufficient solder has been run between them and smoothed out to make a solid finish. When this has been done, the iron can be removed and the whole unit allowed to cool, when the solder will solidify and create a firm join.

FIBERGLASS

Since most modern leisure craft are made of fiberglass, securing fittings and other items to fiberglass is a common practice when fitting out the boat. For maintenance and repair work there are also many occasions when fastening is needed, so it is fortunate that GRP is such an easy material to work with. There are a number of techniques that can be used; fiberglass can be glued, screwed or bolted, and since it is a laminated material, it provides good strength for anything secured to it. However, that strength is tensile strength, which is spread through the laminate, and if excess stresses come to bear on one small area, the seemingly indestructible GRP can collapse.

THROUGH BOLTING

A hypothetic example will best illustrate this; if an eye bolt is to be fastened to the fiberglass deck of a boat for towing and it is just through-bolted with a nut on the inside of the laminate, the chances are that when a tow is under way the huge strain on the

Safety rails must be firmly bolted
through the deck to withstand the
impact of a heavy body being thrown
against them.

small area under the nut will not spread the load sufficiently and the bolt will pull out of the deck. If the deck is reinforced underneath the bolt with a large steel or plywood pad (or thicker fiberglass) that spreads the load over a large area, there will be little or no risk of the bolt pulling out. There are numerous fittings on a boat that need this sort of treatment, mostly deck fittings that are likely to come under the most severe strain. Using a pad is the only way to spread the load; the size and shape of the pad depending on the type of fitting and the load it is likely to bear.

TIP: USE A PIECE OF WOOD OR LOOSEN THE NUT TO PROTECT THE THREAD IF IT IS NECESSARY TO HAMMER THE OPEN END OF A BOLT.

The problem becomes even more acute when the deck is of sandwich construction because the foam, honeycomb or balsa core is liable to be crushed by the stress on each end when tightening the nuts to secure the fitting. In addition to spreading the load across the surface, steps must also be taken to prevent the layers on either side of the sandwich material from becoming compressed under load. One way of achieving this is to use a 'collar' around the bolt where it pierces the deck. A piece of steel tubing cut to the exact depth of the hole is placed over the bolt and the nuts tightened onto washers on either side. The collar will prevent any pressure being exerted on the core material between the outer and inner laminates while allowing the fitting to be securely bolted into position.

SCREWING
Although screwing into fiberglass is possible, the laminate is usually fairly thin and there is not much for the screw to bite into. It is a particularly risky procedure attempting to screw into the side of the hull. Yet many interior fastenings, as well as some repair jobs, make it necessary to screw fittings to the laminate, although such fittings should be only light and not likely to come under any great strain. Tap screws are the best to use, and it should not be necessary to drill a hole, especially if using an electric screwdriver. But if the laminate proves too tough, a pilot hole can be drilled, taking care to measure the width of the laminate against the length of the bit.

Light furnishings can be secured to the hull in this way, although a safer and probably more satisfactory way would be to glue them into position and secure them with glass tape heavily impregnated with resin.

GLUING
Epoxy glue can be used quite successfully for fastening things to fiberglass providing the surfaces are very clean. When gluing to a gel coat, it will be necessary to first clean the surface and follow this with a light sanding to remove the high gloss and provide a key for the adhesive. With interior surfaces it may be necessary to remove any wax or resin

Fittings that come under stress must
be through-bolted with pads or
plates above and beneath the deck to
spread the load.

and grind down any uneven surfaces before wiping down with a solvent or thinners and removing dirt and dust. In all cases, the surface of the laminate or gel coat must be sanded if adhesion is to be satisfactory.

A two-part resin glue must be mixed in the quantities recommended by the manufacturer and applied in moderate temperatures. It is applied to both surfaces which are then clamped together or secured in place until the resin has cured. Providing instructions are followed carefully, it is possible to glue almost any material to fiberglass with a good epoxy resin glue—fiberglass itself, wood and even metal.

POP RIVETING

There is no reason why light fittings cannot be pop riveted to a fiberglass base, providing a pad is placed on the underside. The narrow end of the rivet will pull out of the laminate if it is not secured by something more substantial. Ideally, a metal plate will provide a good pad, not only allowing the rivet to obtain a good grip to prevent it being pulled through the fiberglass, but also spreading the load of the fitting across a substantial area of the GRP, as recommended for any fittings in fiberglass.

7

Paints and painting

Because of the unique environment in which boats are used, the demands on paint are far greater than those used in most shore situations. Virtually every element of sun, sea and weather works against the showroom finish, color attraction and corrosion resistance that paint is intended to provide. For this reason, painting a boat is far more demanding than painting a house and careful choice of the right paint for each individual job is essential if the craft is to be shielded from anything the elements can throw at it, yet retain its looks and it protective capability. Moisture, salt, corrosive elements as well as the impact of the waves all do their best to destroy the protective coat of paint, and for this reason paint

No matter what material the hull is made of, there will always be something that needs painting.

manufacturers spend a lot of money and time researching the best coatings to withstand these attacks and keep the boat looking good and free from damage.

Although the older oil-based paints still have a wide use in marine work, modern acrylic and polyurethane paints are the most popular in general use for above water coatings of a hull. Underwater paints and composites are dealt with separately in Chapter 11 of this book, as these have special properties not usually associated with normal paints. Clear varnishes, which for many decades were oil-based or synthetic, are now also available in water-based acrylic gloss which may sometimes contain UV resistant factors. One of the advantages of the water-based products is their lower levels of toxicity and the ease with which equipment and spills can be cleaned up.

PREPARING THE SURFACE

Painting a boat is no different to painting a house or any other structure. Different paints are used for exterior and interior as well as for the underwater areas, and different finishes can be obtained, although for exterior work, a gloss finish is usually the most popular. As described earlier, oil-based, water-based or polyurethane paints can be used, and the paint can be applied by spray, roller, or brush, depending on personal preference and the surface to be painted. Likewise, there are plenty of colors available in marine paints, and although perhaps the choice of colors is not as wide as with house paints, nevertheless, there are usually colors to meet most preferences.

As with all paint jobs, the secret of success lies in the preparation work, particularly if the surface has been previously painted. In that case, all chipped or flaking paint must be removed and the surface sanded hard back to remove uneven edges. Hard sanding may be necessary, using a random orbital sander or even a disk sander if the old paint proves stubborn, after which hand sanding takes over to provide a good finish. With steel or aluminum a wire brush may be necessary to remove rust or corrosion but fiberglass usually needs only light hand sanding to remove any loose paint or to provide a key for the new coats on the high sheen of the gel coat.

Where the old paint is badly deteriorated it is wise to remove it altogether or it will provide an unstable base for the new paint and probably flake off a few months after the job is finished. If heavy sanding does not remove all the paint, it may be necessary to use scrapers with a paint remover such as Intergrain Liquid 8, and follow up with sanding to remove all traces of the old paint. Any sign of deterioration in the hull material must be treated either chemically or surgically, since covering it with a new coat of paint will only exacerbate the problem. Any areas of rot will need to be cut out and rebuilt, whereas rust and corrosive patches on metal hulls will need to be treated with chemical anti-corrosive and patched if need be.

On new surfaces it will be necessary to use a primer to match the material being painted. There are many primers available; both fiberglass and aluminum must be

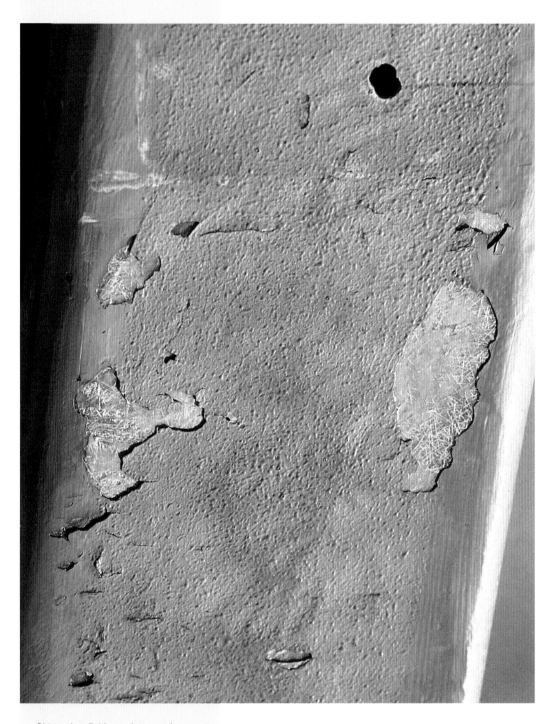

Chipped or flaking paint must be removed or the new paint will not take to the surface.

primed with an etch primer, and there are separate etch primers for each material. This gives the surface a 'key' on which to paint the finishing coats and give them a firm grip. Wood paints now come in primer/finishing form so a separate primer may not be necessary. However, where there are patches of bare wood on a surface that is otherwise painted, a touch up with a reliable wood primer prior to starting the full paint job would not go astray. Steel will also need a primer, usually one of the tar-epoxy compositions to reduce the risk of rust getting a hold.

When the preparation of the surface has been completed, and prior to the first coat of paint being applied (by any method) it is important to ensure that the atmosphere is right for a paint job. Humid, steamy weather is not really suitable, nor are very cold conditions. Ideally, the atmosphere in which the painting is to be carried out should be temperate to warm, dry and dust free. This latter is extremely important as any dust will inhibit a fine finish to the paint job. A wipe over the surface with a damp rag (soaked in water in the case of acrylic paints, turpentine in the case of oil paints and thinners where synthetic paints are used), is the first step, and a thorough vacuuming of the surrounding areas will ensure that dust is removed. Where the job is outside, wind will obviously be a factor and painting in any sort of a breeze must be avoided. This is particularly important with spray painting

Sanding is the best and easiest way to prepare for painting where the surface has to be taken well back.

where not only will the dust be blown onto the newly painted surface, but a fine mist of paint will be blown around as it is being sprayed onto the surface, leading to uneven application and a less than satisfactory job.

TIP: MASKING WITH PAPER MASKING TAPE OFTEN ALLOWS PAINT TO SEEP UNDER THE EDGE. USE LOW TACK PLASTIC/VINYL MASKING TAPE.

SPRAY PAINTING

Without question, spray painting provides the most attractive finish of all, but it is the most difficult of the painting techniques to use, especially for amateurs. A top finish requires not only the best equipment but also considerable skills and experience. It is very easy to completely ruin a paint job very quickly when applying paint by spray gun, and novices are likely to waste many litres of expensive paint, to say nothing of time, before they get any kind of result. If a top class job is required, such as a total hull repaint, it might be wise to call in a professional, although this can also be an expensive exercise. However, despite the problems, the boat owner with the patience and time to acquire spray painting skills will find it is not as difficult as it at first appears, and the end result is well worth the effort.

Good equipment and good quality paint are the first important factors in achieving a satisfactory spray paint job. There are many cheap spray units available, some of which are electrically operated, some use an air compressor and some even work off a vacuum cleaner. These may be suitable for small jobs, but for a paint job that encompasses the entire hull and which will enhance the appearance of the boat, it is best to get hold of good equipment and in this regard, compressed air operated spray guns are often the best. Good quality paint is also important, as is the solvent used as a thinner, and if a top result is required the best results will always be achieved by using the best paint products.

Once again, preparation of the surface is vital if the spray job is going to be successful. First the hull must be cleaned and all dirt, grease, oil and contaminants removed, as well as any dust and dirt from sanding operations. Any repair jobs such as filled scratches or patching of previous paintwork must be examined to see that the job has been done adequately, primed correctly, and the surface rubbed back ready for the final coat. Anything that is not to be painted (such as fittings) should be removed if possible, if not they will need to be carefully masked with paper and masking tape before the job commences. Any demarcation areas, such as the boot topping line or varnished rail capping, need to be completely covered with paper and secured in place by masking tape. Much the same applies to windows and portholes if they are in the area to be sprayed. It is always surprising how far the mist from a spray job can carry, even when there is little or no wind, so care must be taken to see that there is nothing that can be affected within a safe distance (150') of the work when it is in progress.

No form of painting gives quite the same smooth quality as spray painting, particularly when done by a professional.

The secret of good spray painting is to build up a number of thin coats rather than complete the job with one heavy coat. For this reason the paint for spraying usually has to be thinned before use, and the consistency of the mix must be carefully controlled. Just before starting the job, the thinners and paint are mixed precisely to the manufacturer's instructions and then the gun loaded. A practice run with a spare piece of wood is also a good idea as this not only indicates if the consistency of the mix is correct, but also gives the operator a chance to practice his painting action before starting on the boat hull itself.

TIP: ALWAYS USE AN AIR-FED BREATHING MASK TO COUNTERACT HARMFUL FUMES WHEN SPRAY PAINTING.

The spray painting technique involves swinging the gun evenly across the surface, leaving a light spray of paint as it passes. The distance off the surface will vary according to the gun, and manufacturers' instructions will usually offer a guide. Keeping the gun nozzle at the required distance and selecting an area of good working width—say around three feet—the gun is moved smoothly from one side of this area to another, covering it with a fine layer of paint. Then sweep back on the next level down, and back again on the

Smooth, even strokes are the secret of good spray painting. Protective clothing and mask are also essential.

next level, and so on until the entire working strip is covered. Some spray painters like to then follow this pattern with a similar pattern running vertically up and down instead of across. The important factor at all times is to keep the gun moving steadily, especially at the end of each sweep, for any hesitation will cause excess paint to collect and start to run. Practice is the only way to become perfect at spray painting, and a lot of practice is required to get the swing of the nozzle just right. When the first working section is finished, the next section can be started using exactly the same technique and slightly overlapping the first section and so on until the whole hull has been covered.

When the first coat has dried thoroughly, a light sanding with fine wet and dry paper followed by a wipe down is all that is required before the next coat. Once again the sweeping movement of the gun is repeated, although many spray painting experts think the pattern should be varied with each coat in order to avoid hot spots. This is quite a good idea and it should be tried in practice first and if successful applied to the job. Everyone has a different action when spray painting and this is where the importance of practising on a spare piece of wood pays off. As the practice swings become more and more even, and the sweeping pattern becomes more efficient, the paint job will start to look really professional after each coat. There was probably never a more appropriate truism than 'practice makes perfect' when applied to spray painting.

The paint must be thinned to the correct viscosity before using in the spray gun.

ROLLER PAINTING

Using a roller for applying a coat of paint has many advantages, principle of which is the speed of the operation and the satisfactory finish to the paint job. The main disadvantage is that rollers can only be used on large surface areas such as the hull exterior, and even then the edges and corners need to be cut in with a brush. Lambswool rollers are considered by most experts to be preferable to foam or any other material, and the width of the roller depends on the size of the area to be covered. An average sized roller of 7" to 10" (200 mm to 250 mm) is convenient for most jobs, although on large underwater areas wider rollers may be required to apply the anti-fouling.

TIP: NEVER WEAR WOOL CLOTHING WHEN PAINTING; THE FIBERS WILL INEVITABLY GET STUCK TO THE PAINTWORK.

Preparation for roller painting is the same as for any other type of painting, and any type of paint can be used. The roller is saturated with the paint in a roller tray and squeezed out by rolling up and down the ramp of the tray until an even coating is achieved. If the roller is overloaded the paint will spray everywhere and if there is insufficient paint, it will not coat the surface evenly and patches will show. With the roller correctly loaded it is run back and forth across the surface, leaving an even swathe of paint. Finishing strokes with the roller running in straight lines gives the final job a smooth appearance. As mentioned, corners and obstructions will need to be cut in using a brush, as will any edges where the roller cannot go. Masking tape can help by allowing the roller to go close up to an edge without overrunning a demarcation.

Smooth, even strokes with the roller working steadily across the hull will provide a steady flow of paint onto the surface and ensure an even finish with no hot spots or runs to mar the appearance. One of the advantages of roller painting is that it puts a fairly heavy layer of paint on with each sweep across the surface without the risk of runs, thus reducing the number of coats required. It is particularly useful when anti-fouling

The roller is a favorite tool for painting large surfaces.

Anti-fouling is often applied by roller so a heavy coat can be applied quickly over a large area.

beneath the waterline as this is a wide, mostly unbroken surface area that enables the roller to work effectively, and also provides an even coat of the anti-fouling composite across the bottom of the hull. Masking tape along the waterline is usually all that is needed to keep the job tidy. When the boat is careened between tides, brushes are often too slow to get the job done before the oncoming tide moves in and this is where the roller can be handy. Light wet and dry sanding between coats, as with any type of painting, ensures a top quality finish with the final coat.

BRUSH PAINTING

Paint roller and tray.

Most boat owners are proficient at painting with a brush, particularly those who have older wood boats where painting is a constant chore. Except for primer and undercoat, discussed later in this section, similar types of paints can be used for wood, metal or fiberglass boats when applied by brush. No thinning is required in most cases, and the one- or two-part polyurethane paints are usually the most popular since they are easy to apply, long lasting and result in a fine appearance.

To ensure a good finish across the entire surface without patches of light and shade, the initial action of putting the paint onto the surface should involve working the brush backwards and forwards, literally in almost any direction, spreading the paint as smoothly as possible. Then hold the brush lightly at an angle of 45° to the job, and when a limited area has been done and before the paint starts to dry, stroke it gently but evenly across the surface in one direction, gradually working down the newly painted surface until it has all been 'stroked out'. This removes any

1. A good firm grip for large surface areas.

2. For finishing strokes this grip offers a smooth easy action.

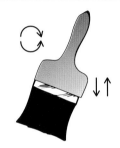

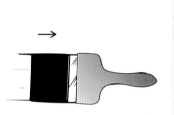

1. Heavy strokes backwards and forwards to lay even coat of paint.

2. Irregular hard strokes to work paint into surface.

3. Gentle, smooth strokes in one direction to give fine finish.

Brushes are necessary for painting in tight corners and around fittings.

unevenness and scraggy brush marks, and leaves the paint surface clean and smooth. The procedure is repeated each time a section is painted, preferably before the previous section has dried. Where more than one coat is required, the surface must be rubbed down with a light wet and dry sandpaper between coats.

TIP: CLEAN THE BRUSH EVERY 20–30 MINS TO PREVENT DRIED UP PAINT CLOGGING THE BRISTLES.

CLEAR FINISHES

Clear finished wood can give a very attractive touch to any boat, be it of fiberglass, aluminum, steel or wood construction. It is particularly attractive with synthetic and metal boats since the beautiful warm colors of wood add a pleasant, soft touch that is impossible to obtain with paint or any other material. Cabin structures, seats, cockpits and in particular interior fittings, provide an attractive touch to the boat if they are finished in wood. To obtain the full benefit of the wood it must be given a clear finish. Oil, varnish or synthetic finishes can be used, the latter providing the toughest resistance to the weather, but oil and varnish offering the richest color to the wood. Sikkens deck oil is a favorite with experienced boat owners, as it enhances the natural appearance of the wood yet provides excellent protection, but there are other varnishes and oils available, and there are many polyurethane clear finishes which offer excellent weather protection, as well as an attractive appearance.

Clear finishes need constant attention if they are to maintain their appearance. Once water gets in, the wood stains easily.

Even more than the preparation for painting, preparing the wood for a clear varnish is the key to success. Where a coat of paint will hide marks on the wood surface, they will show through a

Clear varnishes enhance the beauty of wood hulls.

clear finish, and unless the prepared wood is totally free from all blemishes or stains the final result will be impaired. This is particularly important when the wood has been previously painted or varnished, as even the smallest blemish is likely to show through. Glue runs, water stains or rusty fastenings will also ruin a pleasant appearance while screw holes should be filled with a dowel rather than putty or filler. Hard sanding is necessary to restore the original appearance of the wood, and a random orbital sander will be best for the job followed by hand sanding to minimize scratching. If necessary the wood can be stained before applying the clear finish, but often the finishing coat itself will be all that is required to enhance the appearance. Oil and varnish mostly produce a matt or satin finish while some of the synthetics such as the water-based Intergrain Seamaster or International two-part Epivar polyurethane create a similar attractive appearance to the wood.

TIP: NEVER LEAVE BARE WOOD EXPOSED TO THE AIR FOR TOO LONG BEFORE STARTING TO PAINT, AS IT WILL ABSORB MOISTURE.

Always apply clear finish or varnish with a new brush or one previously used for the same product; using a brush that has been used for paint, no matter how well it has been cleaned, is almost certain to result in tiny flecks of paint appearing at some stage. Also, pause every half-hour and clean the brush as drying varnish on the bristles will leave little lumps that will affect the final appearance of the job.

CLEANING UP

Good paint brushes are expensive, and since the best paint job can only be achieved using the best brushes, it makes sense to ensure that at the end of every paint job, the brushes are restored as nearly as possible to their original conditions. Many amateur painters think this is just a simple job of rinsing out the brushes in whatever solution is appropriate, but there is more to it than that, and saving money by taking care of brushes and rollers also involves a little time and expertise. Even more expensive is paint spraying equipment and once again careful cleaning at the end of a paint job is essential if the spray unit is to work effectively on subsequent jobs.

The agent used to clean the brushes must match the type of paint used. There are brush cleaning solutions, but these are expensive, and the cheapest and most effective solvents are:

- For acrylic paints—water
- For oil paints—mineral turpentine
- For resin-based paints—thinners

BRUSHES

Acrylic paint is removed from brushes simply by washing them thoroughly in water. Running tap water is preferable to static water, although a bucket of water can be used providing it is changed frequently as the paint contaminates the clean water. The bristles must be moved with the fingers to ensure that the water penetrates right into the brush—often, what looks like clean bristles on the outside conceals a mess of paint inside. Work the fingers back and forth through the bristles until no residue appears in the water, and when run under a tap, the water remains clean.

Acrylic paint can only be removed while it is wet, and frequently during a long painting job, the paint at the top of the bristles becomes dry and hard; then it is very difficult to remove. Soaking in water for a long period is the only way to soften this paint and get it out of the bristles. Indeed, if the brushes are to be used again within a day or two, they can be left in the water so that any hardened paint will have a chance to soften. Soapy water can also help and a dash of detergent in any cleaning solution will do no harm and may help considerably in the clean-up process.

Oil paint is easier to remove because it does not dry as quickly as acrylic, so there is less likelihood of paint hardening on the bristles. The first clean must be done in mineral turpentine and the bristles cleaned with the fingers as before. Once again, it is imperative to get all the paint out from the middle of the brush as well as the more obvious exterior

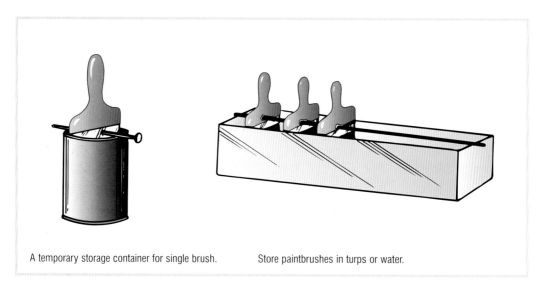

A temporary storage container for single brush.   Store paintbrushes in turps or water.

Cleaning brushes at intervals while painting prevents a build-up in the bristles and makes for a better paint job.

bristles, because once oil paint dries it will be almost impossible to remove. After cleaning with turps, the brushes must be dried as much as possible with a cloth or towel. They must then be cleaned in warm, even hot, fresh water with a liberal amount of detergent in it. After a thorough wash, manipulating the bristles as before, the brush is then rinsed in cold, clean water and dried.

Polyurethane paints require much the same treatment as oil paints, the only difference being that thinners are used instead of turpentine. The bristles must be thoroughly saturated in the thinners until all traces of the paint or varnish are removed, then dried and washed in hot detergent water to remove any remaining impurities. A final rinse in clear water should see them returned almost to new.

When cleaning any brushes, surgical gloves should be worn to avoid skin damage. This is, of course, not so important when washing with water, but certainly gloves must be worn when using thinners or turpentine. After the final wash, a towelling off with a dry cloth or towel will help the bristles dry quickly, ensuring that if the correct cleaning procedure has been followed, they will be soft and almost as good as new, ready for the next paint job.

ROLLERS

The same materials are used for cleaning rollers as for brushes, but the cleaning process requires a somewhat different technique. Instead of manipulating the bristles with the fingers, the soft lambswool (or plastic foam) is compressed by running the roller up and down inside the clenched hand. This squeezes out any paint in the material which, initially, will be quite a lot. As the roller becomes cleaner, the paint will give way to clean water (or turpentine, or thinners) until finally there is no paint residue left. In between squeezing, the roller is thoroughly immersed in the cleaning fluid and rolled around to ensure that it becomes thoroughly saturated again, then the squeezing process repeated.

Some schools of thought advocate rolling the saturated roller quickly on a flat surface, applying pressure to squeeze the paint from the lambswool or foam. While this may be

Because they absorb so much paint, rollers can be hard to clean, especially with anti-fouling.

effective, it will also be very messy, as the fast rolling will cause paint and cleaner to spray everywhere. If using this method, take care to protect the eyes and exposed skin. Where the roller is hard to clean, a long soak in the cleaning medium may be the only way to remove all the paint, especially where it has started to harden, even soaking overnight where necessary to remove stubborn residue.

Once the roller has been cleaned, firstly with the solvent and then the detergent/water solution, it can be dried with a towel and stood on end to drain off any remaining water.

SPRAY GUNS

Although the cleaning medium used will be the same as for cleaning brushes and rollers, the procedure for cleaning spray guns is totally different. Stage one is to fill the spray gun reservoir with solvent, switch on the power, and run the gun until the reservoir is empty. To avoid unnecessary waste (and cost) aim the spray into a bucket so that the solvent can be retained and used later, providing it is not too contaminated, for cleaning other bits and pieces. Then, the entire spraying system must be dismantled and small parts such as nozzles, measures and hoses placed in a bucket of solvent and cleaned, if necessary with a nail brush to get paint out of crevices and tight corners. Large pieces, such as the reservoir, can be cleaned by hand. Cleanliness with spray equipment is far more important than with brushes and rollers, for any contamination with dried paint left in the system can clog the nozzle and ruin the next spray job.

When every part is totally clean it can be given a final wash in the water/detergent solution if required, although some operators prefer to use just the solvent. The manufacturer's instructions should be followed at this stage and any lubrication or special requirements attended to before reassembling.

8

Sails

Well cut, well maintained sails not only look good, they perform better.

Just as motors need regular maintenance to keep them running well, sails also need regular attention if they are to be kept performing at their best. In both cases, a good maintenance program not only guarantees reliability in performance, but can also save a lot of unnecessary expense. The cost of replacing sails is high, and a sail that is abused or neglected will soon fall apart. Careful and regular maintenance can extend the life of both racing and cruising sails and thus reduce the overall cost of maintaining a boat.

There are numerous factors that cause deterioration of sailcloth and damage to sails. Among the more obvious are wear and tear, chafe, physical damage, such as occurs when the sail is allowed to flog badly, stretch (usually caused by using a sail in conditions too strong for its cloth structure), and chemical staining. Less obvious are factors such as the effect of UV radiation from the sun, excess heat, chemical impregnation from polluted atmospheres and fatigue. A regular check, especially during winter maintenance, is essential if problems like these are to be spotted early and rectified, so the sails can be kept in good condition and perform to their designed standard.

A MAINTENANCE PROGRAM

North Sails, perhaps the world's most prominent sailmakers, suggest a basic program of preventive maintenance to extend the life of sails which runs roughly along the following lines:

1. Check the sails regularly at least once a year, and more often if the sails come in for a lot of hard work. Seam stitching is the first place to look, for the old proverb of a stitch in time holds good with sails. Seams should be re-sewn when the first signs of chafe or wear appear, not left until the stitching gives way and causes further damage. Check for chafed areas and if necessary, provide protection in the form of doubled patches or covering for the object causing the chafe.

Sails must always be folded when not in use. The mainsail can be folded over the boom as it is lowered.

2. Keep sails clean. Apart from chemical staining from pollution in the atmosphere or in the water, stowing sails below decks can cause deterioration and aging apart from making the cabin smell musty. Although mostly impervious to dirt, modern synthetic sails can still stain and lose their pristine appearance very readily when not properly looked after.

KOOKABURRA

A simple, but effective mainsail cover.

3. Fold sails carefully when not in use. Nothing looks worse than a crumpled sail that has been stuffed randomly in a bag for some months, and such treatment does not help keep the cloth in good shape, either. Folding or furling after use keeps them looking attractive and helps extend the life of the sailcloth.

4. Keep sails covered. UV rays can play havoc with a sail that is left exposed to strong sunlight for some period of time. When sails are left on the boom or furled on the forestay while the boat is not in use they need to be covered, and the most common method is with a boom cover or, in the case of furled sails, a built-in leech and foot cover.

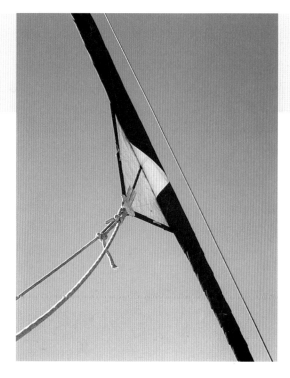

The leech and foot of a self-furling headsail should be fitted with protective material so that when furled, the sail is effectively covered.

SAILCLOTH

Sailcloth is a woven fabric in which the fibers run at right angles to each other. Fibers that run the length of the cloth are known as the 'warp' and those that run across as the 'weft,' also sometimes called the 'fill'. The shape and properties of a sail are determined by the way in which the sailmaker cuts his cloth, favoring either the warp or the weft so that when filled with wind, the sail will take up the shape he has planned, and perform to maximum advantage.

There is a wide variety of sailcloth material used in today's sails. Understanding the basic structure of the sailcloth can be of considerable assistance when carrying out maintenance routines, so a few of the more prominent sailcloths are listed here:

Canvas

Although still occasionally used, especially in some older traditional yachts, canvas has now been almost totally superseded by the modern synthetic cloths. While it served its purpose throughout the early centuries of sailing, the discovery of 'plastics' revolutionized the construction of sailcloth just as it revolutionized the construction of hulls. Synthetic material is basically lighter, stronger and requires far less maintenance than the old traditional materials. Canvas sails discolored quickly, were vulnerable to bad staining and would rot easily if not dried before being stowed away. They were also rather tough on the hands. Even with modern canvas material, the maintenance factor of canvas sails is high compared to those made of the synthetic material and the performance is not comparable.

Polyester

This is the most common of the modern synthetic sailcloths, being strong, durable and relatively inexpensive. The most widely known polyester fiber, Dacron, was developed by the Dupont company for use as a sailcloth. It is tightly packed, stable and is used both as a woven cloth and as a laminate. Woven Dacrons are preferred for taller, narrower sails, while the laminates are better for low aspect genoas. Terylene is another well known woven polyester sailcloth.

Nylon

One of the earliest forms of synthetic sailcloth, nylon suffers from a large stretch factor which makes it unsuitable for upwind sails. However, it is good for spinnakers and fuller reaching sails. Nylon is very vulnerable to UV and chemical degradation and therefore nylon sails are best stowed below when not in use. Never wash a nylon sail in a swimming pool or use chlorine as a cleaning agent.

Kevlar

Kevlar is made from aramid fibers that have a high resistance to stretch and a high breaking strain. It is reputed to be stronger than steel for its weight and five times more stretch resistant than polyester, which makes it an ideal material for racing sails. Its down side is that like nylon, it is susceptible to UV and in sunlight loses its strength twice as fast as polyester.

Mylar

Mylar is a film usually laminated to a polyester substrate and provides good strength for weight. However, the material is fairly fragile and must be used with caution, or damage and deterioration will reduce its life quickly. Factors that can adversely affect Mylar are UV radiation, flogging, over-tensioning the luff, and excessive wind speeds. It is also easily damaged by heat and solvents.

Its light weight and stretch factor make
nylon a popular cloth for spinnakers.

The different tones of cloth indicate the different types of sailcloth used in making the sail.

Spectra

This is a material made from highly processed polyethelene and is somewhat more expensive than Kevlar, but has a greater resistance to UV radiation and is very strong. It is more popular as a cruising sail than a racing sail because of its tendency to lose shape as the sail ages.

Pentex

Has a higher strength and lower stretch factor than Dacron, and is mostly used as a laminate with Mylar film. It is best suited to smaller racing yachts (below 12 m) and not usually provided in woven form.

CARE OF SAILS

From the sailcloth descriptions above, it is fairly obvious what factors cause most damage to sails. Prevention of such damage or wear and tear should be part of the day-to-day routine of sailing the boat, not just left to the winter maintenance period when repair work is carried out. Whether the sails are new or used, their life and performance can be enhanced by following a good 'care and prevention' plan whenever the boat is taken out for a sail, and whether it is cruising or racing.

Every sail is built for a maximum wind strength, and using it in winds above this will destroy it more quickly than anything else. Usually the wind speed is stamped on the

Racing sails come in for rougher treatment than cruising sails and therefore generally have a shorter life.

clew of the sail, particularly on racing headsails, but if it is not marked, it is important to find out from the sailmaker what maximum wind speed he recommends. Another killer of good sails is chafe.

The very nature of a sailboat and the way in which the sails are fitted makes it virtually impossible to avoid some chafe. The more obvious areas where chafe occurs are at the spreader ends, which must be well covered; a running backstay rubbing against the lee side of the main; and the foot of low-cut genoas being dragged across a deck or around shrouds. Leather should be used to cover chafe points where possible, otherwise tape around the offending fitting can provide a reasonable substitute. If this proves ineffective, it may be necessary to get the sailmaker to stitch a chafing patch on the sail. A regular check of the sail, as described earlier, will indicate any chafing before it has time to seriously damage the sail.

Of utmost importance when using any sails is to prevent them flogging by reducing the time they are flapping in the breeze. Flogging not only reduces the life of the sailcloth, it also wrecks the shape. This is particularly important with Kevlar sails which can be severely damaged even during a short period of flogging. Boats should avoid motoring into the wind with the sails flapping, and if rigging on the mooring or on the beach, the flapping time must be kept to a minimum. In heavy weather, reducing the sail before the wind gets too strong is wise, so the mainsail is not being constantly eased out, allowing the leech to flap at every gust, and genoa leech lines should be kept tight enough to stop fluttering in the leech. As mentioned earlier, avoiding UV damage by

This is no way to treat sails!

using covers if the sails are left above decks will protect the cloth and if stowed away, it is important to make sure the sails are dry and folded neatly in their bags.

TIP: AVOID FOLDING A SAIL ON THE SAME CREASES AS THIS WILL RISK WEAKENING THE SAILCLOTH IN THE AREAS OF THE CREASES.

If these methods are adopted, most synthetic sails will need little attention during the sailing season, and at winter maintenance time a routine check and repair of any parts showing signs of wear will be all that is required to have them ready for the next season.

TIP: TENNIS BALLS FITTED OVER THE ENDS OF SPREADERS CAN PREVENT CHAFE ON OVERLAPPING HEADSAILS.

However, if the summer has been a tough one, or the daily maintenance has not been up to scratch, there may be a few things needed during the winter overhaul to get the sails back to their pristine condition. Sails stowed away wet may have mildew or some other fungus which unless removed may stain the sail. Constant dragging across the deck, as with a low-footed genoa or a spinnaker when being handed, can also leave marks. While the boat is on the slip or on land for maintenance, it is a good time to take the sails ashore where they can be spread out and examined closely, then cleaned or repaired as required.

Allowing a sail to flog is a sure way
to reduce its effective life.

CLEANING

A lawn or large boat club rigging deck is a good place to work on sails because they can be assessed with an overall examination rather than just looking at small sections at a time, as is mostly the case on board. It is also a good place to clean them because both sides are accessible rather than just one at a time. The following is a winter check list that can be applied to sails while they are spread out ashore:

1. Check all stitching for any signs of wear or breakage. Unless you have a sailmaker's experience and also his machine, re-stitching means taking the sail to the sailmaker's loft. Particularly check the reinforcing at the corners of the sail as damaged stitching can sometimes be hard to detect in those areas. Also check the leech, as the leech flap can quickly damage stitching and the luff rope, if one is fitted.
2. Check the panels for any indication of chafe. This will be fairly obvious, and the next step is to determine what is causing the chafe. If it is not possible to cover the fitting with leather or tape, as described earlier, then make a note to tell the sailmaker to stitch a doubling patch before the sailcloth wears through.

Cleaning dirty marks from the sail is best done with warm water and a non-abrasive detergent.

3. If the sail needs cleaning, try to determine what caused the stain or mark and also note which sailcloth is involved. Different sailcloths require

Small boat sails need the same
attention as those of larger yachts,
especially racing sails.

A convenient way to look after sails is to take them home, wash them and hang them on the clothesline to dry.

different cleaners although all can be safely washed with a mild detergent.

4. Using warm water and the detergent (non-abrasive) gently remove all surface dirt and marks with a soft brush. Never scrub hard or use abrasive detergents as these may damage the sail surface. After each washing, flush away the detergent with fresh water and examine the results.

5. Ingrained dirt or stubborn marks may require a number of washes or the sail soaked overnight.

6. Mildew stains may be hard to remove with detergent, in which case a diluted bleach can be used or the sails can be washed in a swimming pool. If the mildew has got a good hold, the process may need to be repeated several times, after which the sail should be hung out in the sun each time, which hopefully will bleach out the marks a little more.

7. IMPORTANT:

   Never use bleaches with Kevlar or nylon sails.

   Never use acetone, M.E.K, solvents, gasoline or diesel with laminated sails.

8. After the final rinse in fresh water, hang the sails out somewhere to dry; preferably a washing line or rail where they can hang down and not become crumpled.

Masts, spars, and rigging

Like the engine of a motor boat, the mast, spars, and rigging are the power unit of a sailboat. As such, they need similar attention and care if they are to perform reliably and well. In racing boats, their performance is a major feature in winning races; in cruising yachts their performance is centered more on reliability and safety than on going fast.

MASTS AND SPARS

Most masts and spars these days are of extruded aluminum alloy; wood is rarely used and high tech material such as carbon fiber or titanium is mostly confined to performance racing craft. The type of alloy used varies according to the performance required and its resistance to corrosion. The extrusion, which is made by forcing the alloy through a die or extruding mold, also varies according to the type of yacht on which it will be used, and the type of performance required. Masts for cruising yachts, for example, will need to be of solid section with little or no bending characteristics. Masts used in racing, by contrast, may be required to bend into extraordinary shapes, although when this is the case, carbon fiber, titanium or some other medium will be used to give greater bending characteristics.

Modern sailors have few worries with rigging compared to their forebears!

Early wood masts and spars were mostly solid, although in the latter years, built wood masts were mainly a hollow section. Today's alloy masts are all hollow with a thin wall and ribbing or reinforcing inside the wall to give strength without adding greatly to the weight. Some are in round sections, some oval or aerofoil shaped to provide better airflow from the mast onto the sails. Spreaders, booms and other spars also tend to have an aerofoil section to again reduce wind drag and resistance. Masts may be stepped on deck or on the keel, and while there are advantages to both methods, stepping on deck is the most popular because of the ease of lowering the mast when repair or maintenance work is required. Also, if the mast goes over the side, it is less likely to damage the cabin or hull if it breaks away cleanly at the deck. Another advantage, especially in cruising yachts, is more open space in the cabin when the mast does not intrude down to the keel. However, the ability to bend into more advanced shapes favors the mast being stepped on the keel.

When a mast is stepped on deck—usually in what is called a 'tabernacle'—the cabin deckhead must be reinforced to take the load. One method uses a short steel pillar beneath the mast step which transmits the load down to the keel, but this intrudes on the cabin space and is less popular than the system that transmits the load through sturdy deck beams to the sides of the yacht where it is dispersed through the hull structure. Since they are subject to enormous stresses and strains in the course of transmitting the power from the sails into the driving force that moves the hull, masts and spars need careful attention and maintenance if they are to perform to standard. It is all too easy to lose a mast at sea, and the outcome can be inconvenient at best, life threatening at worst. But such problems can usually be minimized by a good maintenance program which ensures that the masts and spars are kept in good shape at all times.

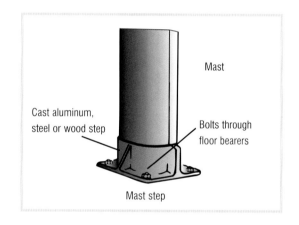

Mast

Cast aluminum, steel or wood step

Bolts through floor bearers

Mast step

CORROSION

As mentioned, some alloys are less resistant to corrosion than others although all aluminum alloys are generally less affected by corrosion from the elements than metals such as steel. Some masts are anodized to give them even greater resistance to this type of corrosion; the anodizing forms a protective coating that keeps the corrosive elements of air and sea from contact with the alloy itself. Painting is similarly used to prevent atmospheric corrosion.

But corrosion from the atmosphere is less of a problem with aluminum alloy than corrosion caused by the galvanic action between two dissimilar metals. Aluminum and copper, for example, if placed together in a salt solution (electrolyte), set up an electrical

The mast and rigging of a modern yacht should come in for a lot of attention at maintenance time, if only to avoid having to send a man aloft at sea.

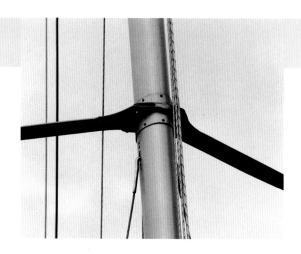

Like any fittings on a mast, the spreaders are a prime area for corrosion.

current which eats away the aluminium. Thus a copper fitting, screwed to an aluminum mast or spar in the salt-laden sea air, will create serious corrosion problems. Since brass, bronze and copper are three common metals used on board boats, and all interact with aluminum, the extent of the problem is obvious.

Prevention is always better than cure, and time and trouble spent in preventing galvanic action will be rewarded many times over in reduced maintenance costs, for once this type of corrosion gains a hold, it can soon reduce the strength of the mast or spar beyond its safety margin. Prevention begins by avoiding the use of fittings made of bronze, brass, copper or similar metals. Stainless steel or monel do not react so fiercely with aluminum so are far less likely to cause corrosion. Nowadays stainless steel is the most common metal for use with mast fittings. If a metal such as bronze must be used— some mast winches are bronze—then an insulating material must be placed between the fitting and the mast, and fastened with stainless steel bolts or rivets. If corrosion has already taken place, the only permanent cure is to remove the winch or fittings, clean away the corrosive areas, and providing the mast wall has not been weakened, re-fasten the winch or fitting after placing an insulation pad of tufnol, mica or some similar synthetic material between the two metals, and fastening with stainless steel fasteners.

TIP: METALS FROM THE MOST VULNERABLE TO THE LEAST AFFECTED BY GALVANIC CORROSION ARE: GALVANIZED IRON, ZINC, ALUMINUM, BRASS, COPPER, STAINLESS STEEL AND MONEL.

The mast step is another place that is vulnerable to corrosion. Often this is an aluminum casting and very vulnerable to galvanic corrosion. A mast step incorporated in the cabin roof or in the keel lay-up and covered with a layer of fiberglass is a good way of avoiding corrosion here. The mast cap, hounds, and spreader fittings must come in for close inspection when the mast is lowered, for all are vulnerable to corrosion and also virtually out of sight when the mast is stepped. Many a mast has been lost because corrosion at the spreaders got away before it was noticed and eventually ate into the mast wall. Winter maintenance time, when the mast is unstepped and taken ashore, is the perfect time for a thorough inspection of these areas, as well as similar vulnerable areas on the boom.

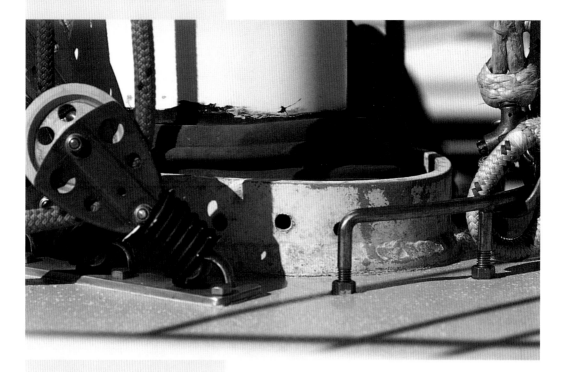

Because of the different metals used in the fittings, the equipment at the foot of the mast can create galvanic corrosion. Early signs are visible in this picture.

Corrosion usually shows up on an aluminum alloy as a white powder on the surface. While seemingly innocuous to the eye, the white aluminum oxide conceals the deterioration which is taking place beneath it and when the powder is removed the pitting of the metal will be seen. In the case of atmospheric corrosion this may not be serious and the slight pitting may only cause an unsightly appearance on the metal. If it allowed to persist, however, the pockmarks can get deeper and the appearance becomes more unsightly until eventually the corrosion will eat into the main structure of the mast wall and create a weakness.

Apart from preventing it from progressing to such a dangerous stage, there is really nothing much that can be done about corrosion that has started on an aluminum mast or spar other than to remove any source, such as dissimilar metals, in an effort to limit the damage. Restoring unsightly pitting is almost impossible, and the best tactic is probably to paint the mast or spar and thus lessen the appearance of the corrosion scars, although this again is never really satisfactory. A badly corroded mast or spar will most likely need to be replaced, if not for appearance then certainly for safety.

UNSTEPPING AND STEPPING A MAST

Most yacht owners unstep the mast as part of the winter maintenance schedule since the fittings at the top of the mast are every bit as important as those at the bottom. Even more so, perhaps, since a broken fitting aloft means sending a man to the top of the mast—a most uncomfortable exercise at sea—whereas fittings that can be reached from the deck are easily repaired, even when the boat is in a moderate seaway. So the benefit of checking out the mast and its fittings while the whole thing is lying on the wharf or on land is obvious and should guarantee that for most of the following season, at least, there will be no need to send someone aloft.

If the mast is stepped on the keel, there is only one way to lower it and that is to lift it bodily up out of the hull using a crane or gantry or some other lifting mechanism. The collar must first be removed as well as any securing points at the mast step and the crane secured to the mast ready to lift while the rigging is slackened back. Then the weight is taken and the rigging let go so that the mast can be lifted straight out, avoiding any risk of it swinging and damaging the cabin top.

Trailered yachts are designed to have their masts unstepped quickly and easily.

If it is stepped on deck and is not too tall, expensive cranes and gantries can be dispensed with and the mast lowered with a few good hands and a block and tackle. The boat must, of course, be in a secure position and unable to move and there needs to be an anchor point for the block and tackle well ahead of the bow. The tackle need not be particularly sophisticated although the ropes will need to be quite long. The weight factor is not as important as the angle; the farther forward the tackle can be taken and the higher it can be anchored, the better, since this will improve the angle when the mast is lowered. When the tackle is well secured to the anchor point, a wire is run from the mast head to the end of the tackle. Providing the forward lower shrouds are still in place the forestay or a halyard can be used as this wire connection.

When all is ready, the weight is taken on the tackle and the forward lower shrouds released. If the mast does not start to fall back it may need a little encouragement by pushing at the front or pulling on the backstay. The mast must still be held in the tabernacle to prevent the foot coming out as it leans back, and crew must be placed on either side of the boat holding the after lower shrouds to stop any tendency for it to swing to one side. As the tackle is eased back the mast can be guided down onto the deck, with the shroud crew taking the weight as it nears the deck, or a prop or crutch used to prevent the last sudden rush. This is where the angle of the block and tackle are important, for the higher the tackle can be located ahead of the bow, the easier it will be to lower the mast without any risk of it crashing down on deck. Once down it can be unshipped from the tabernacle, the remaining shrouds and stays released, and the whole outfit taken ashore where the maintenance work can be done with relative ease.

To re-step the mast the procedure is reversed. The foot of the mast is placed in the tabernacle (a hinged tabernacle makes life easier here), the after shrouds and backstays shackled on and the top of the mast connected to the purchase. It will be necessary to manually lift the mast until the weight of the tackle can take it, but from there on it should just be a matter of guiding it as the tackle pulls it up, until it is in position and the forward shrouds are secured, followed by the forestay. After tuning, the rig will be completely restored and ready for use.

STANDING RIGGING

Ropes are used for all kinds of purposes on boats. Steel ropes are used for rigging, safety rails and a variety of other uses where extreme strains are likely to be encountered. Synthetic ropes are used for everything from halyards and sheets to ski ropes, anchor warps and cordage. While modern ropes suffer far less from work and weather than did the older fiber ropes, nevertheless wear and tear eventually takes its toll and all ropes need attention and maintenance. Since they play such an important part in the safety of the boat, wise boat owners make a point of checking all the ropes on their craft every winter as part of the winter maintenance routine.

As a general rule, stainless steel wire rope is used for standing rigging on modern yachts. Some boat owners, particularly those that use their craft for cruising rather than racing, still favor galvanized plough steel wire, and indeed, old-fashioned though it may be, there are factors which justify its use. There are advantages and disadvantages with both so it is appropriate to examine these before discussing their maintenance and repair.

STAINLESS STEEL WIRE ROPE

This material is particularly popular with racing yachts, principally because of its great strength, which allows wire of smaller diameter to be used for rigging. Thinner wires means less wind resistance; an important factor in go-fast racing. Another advantage is its resistance to rust, a major factor in a salty environment where boats are very vulnerable to rust problems in any steel fittings. Apart from the obvious deterioration of rusting wire resulting in lower strength and possible stranding of the wire, the rust will make a mess of the sails causing them to deteriorate also, both in strength and appearance. But good quality stainless steel wire rope should not rust although constant contact during use will always leave marks of some sort on the sail.

The two main disadvantages of stainless steel wire are its higher cost and tendency to become brittle or work-hardened with time. This means that it can suddenly break with

Stainless steel wire rope is particularly
popular with racing boats because its
thin diameter reduces wind drag.

little or no warning; a nasty habit when the boat is used offshore. Stainless steel wire rope is usually laid up in the following forms:

- 1x19—consisting of a central strand around which 19 similar strands are laid in a spiral. This creates a stiff, non-flexible rope widely used for standing rigging.
- 7x19—which consists of seven strands, each made up of 19 smaller strands laid around one another to give a very flexible form of wire rope. This is the type of stainless steel wire used for rigging small boats and for running gear on larger yachts.
- 7x7—which is effectively a compromise between the two described previously. It has a seven-strand wire center around which six similar seven-strand wires are laid. It is a good all-purpose wire rope with a degree of flexibility but not enough for running rigging.

TIP: FIRST SIGNS OF DETERIORATION IN STAINLESS STEEL RIGGING WILL PROBABLY APPEAR AT THE TOP OF THE LOWER SWAGE.

GALVANIZED STEEL WIRE ROPE

As mentioned, this type of wire rope is rarely seen on racing yachts because of its lesser strength, greater bulk and tendency to rust with use. Although initially sealed from contact with the air by the galvanizing process, this tends to

In sailing conditions like these, the rigging comes under an enormous amount of pressure.

wear off with use and the mild steel of the wire strands then becomes exposed to salt air. Rust begins which, as described earlier, not only reduces the strength of the wire but also causes bad staining of sails, and rust stains are nearly impossible to remove from sailcloth. Because it has lower strength than stainless steel, galvanized wire used for rigging must be a heavier gauge and thus add weight and wind resistance to the rig. However, this is not a major consideration in cruising yachts which are not so concerned with wind drag so much as economy and reliability, for galvanized wire rope is much cheaper than stainless.

Apart from the saving in cost, one feature of galvanized wire rope that appeals to cruising skippers is the warning it gives before deterioration causes it to break. 'Whiskering' of the strands is a sure indication of deterioration of the wire, so the rig can be replaced long before it snaps and loses the mast and sails over the side. A test as to the stage the deterioration has reached can be carried out by bending the wire rope into a tight curve; fatigued or rusted strands will break almost immediately under this test, giving good warning that it is time the rig was changed.

A stainless steel turnbuckle with rod rigging, commonly found on racing yachts.

ROD RIGGING

One of the most efficient forms of rigging is the metal rod, used in some high performance racing yachts. Its advantages include greater strength for size, less windage, longer life and greater safety—

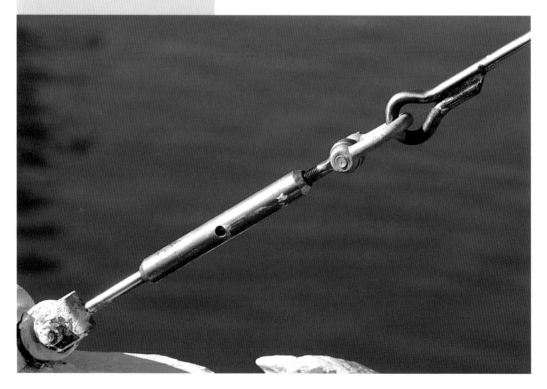

Handmade wire splices must be served or taped in order to cover the 'whiskers' on the strands.

all factors that are close to the heart of performance racing skippers. Cobalt steel and stainless steel are the most common metals used in rod rigging and as can be imagined, they are both very expensive rigging materials. The care and maintenance of rod rigging, which may involve the use of hydraulic gear to obtain tension, is beyond the expertise of most boat owners; it is a job for the experts and thus outside the scope of this book. Apart from which, the expense and sophistication of rod rigging restricts its use to only a few top line high performance racing yachts.

SPLICING WIRE ROPE

The days of splicing wire rope by hand are, fortunately, mostly a thing of the past. Only those who have experienced the blistering agony of laying up a Liverpool Splice with a large diameter wire rope will know the frustration associated with this art. Nowadays modern yacht rigging is spliced mechanically, thus saving much time, preventing many sore fingers, and avoiding much bad language! There are a number of modern methods that can be used to splice an eye in wire rope (the most common splicing practice), most of which require a powerful tool or machine, as each depends on high pressure. The tools for this work are expensive and for the once-a-year need to splice rigging, they are not worth purchasing, although smaller, hand-held tools are available which can be useful for many smaller wire splicing jobs around the boat.

The Nicopress System is probably the most common for use on small yachts and sailing dinghies for rigging and general purpose splicing, and it requires a relatively inexpensive tool not dissimilar in appearance (although very different in use), to bolt cutters. Used mostly for splicing eyes in light rigging wire, the system involves using a metal ferrule or nicopress sleeve which is clamped firmly around the wire. The basic procedure is as follows:

1. Choose the ferrule that fits snugly onto the wire. The ferrule metal must be of the correct type or it will create galvanic action when immersed in water. Copper is used for stainless steel wire and alloy ferrules for galvanized wire rope.
2. Thread the wire into the ferrule, make an eye and re-thread it back through. Avoid crossing the wires.

Nicopress splice.

3. Place a thimble of suitable size in the eye so formed, and pull the wire tight until it is firmly fitted around the thimble. Ensure that the thimble does not 'rattle' or it may drop out.
4. Using the swaging tool, clamp the ferrule firmly around the wire and apply pressure; the eye splice is complete.

This is very simple method of creating an eye splice in wire works equally well with stainless steel or galvanized wire rope. It is strong, probably stronger than a hand-made splice, and is much easier on the hands! For larger yachts, a common form of mechanical splicing is the rolled swage, probably the most common form of rigging splice used today. This needs special equipment so it is better to take the wire to a rigger's shop than purchase the expensive machines for the few jobs that will occur during the winter lay-up period.

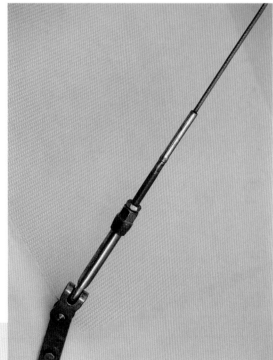

A machine-made rolled splice.

SETTING UP THE RIGGING

Raising and lowering the mast has been described earlier in this chapter, and this is a major part of the maintenance program as far as rigging is concerned. With everything down on the ground the work is made easy and more accurate than trying to do it afloat and sending a man aloft in the bosun's chair. Once the rig is back up, it then is fairly simple to tighten it up, although care is needed, because a lot of damage can be done to the hull and other parts of the boat by over-tightening parts of the standing rigging.

Where rigging needs to be replaced, it should be removed from the mast and careful note taken of which part of the rigging it is. While the rig may seem equally balanced when in situ, this is not always the case and mixing up the shrouds can cause some head scratching when the gear is re-rigged. Best to take off each shroud or stay individually and tag it so that the rigger, when he cuts a replacement for it, will be able to similarly tag the new piece and thus avoid frustrating mix-ups. If the rigging has to be replaced while the mast is still standing then it will be imperative to undo only one shroud or stay at a time, otherwise there will be a risk of the mast falling. Each stay can then be replaced with a new one and secured before moving onto the next. This is particularly important with permanent fore and backstays. It will be necessary to send a man aloft to undo the masthead or hounds fittings, and this will make the rig even more unstable. It is always best, if possible, to undertake mast and rigging maintenance with the rig down on deck or better still on shore.

If the wire shows no sign of deterioration, it will not be necessary to replace it. Stainless steel wire needs virtually no maintenance although a close inspection is important since, as mentioned, this type of wire gives little notice that it is about to break. Galvanized plough steel wire, on the other hand, will give plenty of warning with signs of rust or whiskering making it obvious where maintenance is required. At the same time as the wire inspection, a look at the fittings will indicate if any need attention. While fittings on deck such as turnbuckles will be visible all the time, masthead and crosstree fittings can begin to deteriorate without this being noticeable from deck level. With the mast down, a thorough inspection of the rig from top to bottom is the order of the day.

Once back up and secured in place, it will be time to set up or 'tune' the mast. First step is to ensure that it is sitting exactly amidships otherwise performance on one tack or the other will be affected. The shrouds can be set up by hoisting a pre-measured piece of rope to the hounds, then taking it out first to one gunwale then the other. If the mast is not plumbed in the center of the boat, the rigging screws or turnbuckles of the lower shrouds will need to be adjusted. Similarly, if the mast is bent higher up, the cap shrouds will need adjustment, while fore and aft trimming of the mast is done with the stays. But a word of warning; be very careful not to overdo the tension in the rigging. While it is important that the mast is correctly stayed and there is no slack in the rigging which will allow the mast to flop around, it is also important not to place too much tension in the shrouds and stays

Well set-up rigging means good
performance under sail.

Tuning the rig for performance racing is a skilled job.

or the mast may be driven down through the bottom of the boat; a very unhappy situation.

Tuning the rig of a sailboat for racing is a very specialized skill and requires detailed knowledge of the boat, her sails, her rig and her perfor-mance. Bending or raking the rig is an accepted part of tuning for racing, with adjustable or running backstays allowing the rig to be tuned each time the boat is raced, so tuning with high performance craft may be carried out throughout the racing season. How-ever, tuning a cruising yacht's rig simply requires the mast, shrouds and stays to be centered and tensioned. Since this type of boat will not be seeking optimum performance, the rig will get by with just a general tune-up when the maintenance schedule is over, and then probably a check on the rigging a few weeks later to counter any tendency for the wire to stretch. New rigging may stretch a little after the first strong blow, but other than this there is little likelihood of a cruising boat needing a major tune-up more than once or twice a year.

ANTI-CHAFE GEAR

Chafing is insidious, and what appears to be only a dirty mark on the sail can suddenly blow out where the stitching has been chafed through, unseen from the deck below. Any part of the rigging—or for that matter any part of the boat—which comes into contact with a sail can be a source of chafe, and since the sails cannot be protected, other than by reinforcing patches, prevention of chafe must be undertaken on the rigging.

Anti-chafe gear comes in many forms. The ends of the crosstrees can be covered with leather, plastic or even tennis balls to protect a wrap-around headsail, while lambswool, poly pipe or some similar anti-chafe material can be place around the backstays where they chafe the main if they cannot be tied off. Fitting anti-chafe gear where there are obvious signs of chafe is merely a question of ingenuity, using the most suitable material available and examining the sails for chafe marks. Winter time, when

Although not the most attractive, the plastic piping used on these lower shrouds provides a very effective protection against sail chafe.

the rig is down is the ideal time to do this, and it is well worth doing a sound job, even if it turns out to be a bit costly, in order to avoid having to send someone aloft to replace worn anti-chafe gear half way through the sailing season. While fine as a last resort, at least on cruising boats, a doubling patch on the sail is not a really good solution, and anti-chafe gear at contact points on the boat or rig are much better.

RUNNING RIGGING

Running rigging is basically the flexible wire or synthetic rope used to hoist and control sails. However, there are many other uses for ropes and cordage, so rather than separate them into different categories, all flexible wire rope, synthetic rope and cordage will be dealt with in this section no matter what its use.

FIBER ROPES

Traditionally, rope was made of vegetable fibers, mostly manila, hemp, sisal or cotton. Their advantages were few and their disadvantages many, so their use on modern craft has faded with the years. The big problem was their vulnerability to rot, and since ropes

Fiber ropes are not widely used these days as they are subject to rot.

on board any seagoing vessel are liable to be frequently saturated, fiber ropes required careful attention or their life span was shortened considerably. Stowing away wet ropes was a sure method to invite rot and since drying ropes after use was a tedious and often difficult chore, rot was a constant companion in the traditional rope locker. Indeed, the only real advantage in using fiber ropes these days is in economy because fiber ropes are cheaper than synthetic ropes, albeit only in the short term.

SYNTHETIC ROPES

Soon after World War II, synthetic ropes made their appearance on the maritime scene. Nylon was the first material to be woven into laid ropes, but as the softer braided ropes appeared, materials such as Dacron, Terylene and other synthetic materials were used. Today most ropes used on any form of seagoing craft are made from synthetic material. As a general rule, braided ropes, which are made up of a continuous plait, are used on leisure craft, especially yachts, where their pliability and ease of use make them popular as halyards or sheets. Laid ropes are also manufactured from the synthetic materials, although these are mostly used for larger craft where sizeable mooring ropes are needed. Anchor warps are usually nylon laid ropes because of the greater stretch factor of both the nylon and the laid warp, allowing a vessel to surge on her anchor line without putting undue or sudden stress on the anchor and plucking it out of the ground.

Running rigging on a modern yacht consists of synthetic rope and flexible wire rope of all types and sizes.

Synthetic ropes do not rot and therefore can be stowed away wet. They are impervious to salt air, humidity and other deteriorating factors, although they are affected by the UV rays of the sun, especially ropes made of polypropylene which can deteriorate rapidly in strong sunlight. Other than this, very little maintenance is required to keep synthetic ropes in good shape and appearance.

FLEXIBLE WIRE ROPES

These are used almost universally for running rigging such as halyards and running stays although they are also popular for uses such as liferails, topping lifts and strops. As a general rule, flexible wire rope consists of a series of strands (seven strands of 19-strand wire laid around one another is a popular form), while a rope core may be used to give more flexibility. Halyards that are wound onto a winch need greatest flexibility so that the strands are not over-stressed or flattened when running around the drum. A flexible wire rope spliced to a braided synthetic tail is commonly used for halyards, especially those that are pulled by hand, and there are many different combinations of wire to match the different requirements of vessels, particularly sailing vessels. Fatigue and hard use around blocks and winches tends to shorten the life of flexible wire rope so it is important that during the winter maintenance all halyards, braces, guys and the like are carefully examined for deterioration.

JOINING ROPES

Where ropes need to be joined, one of two methods can be used; splicing or knotting. Splicing is the more permanent method and where a rope needs to be lengthened or joined to another, a short splice or long splice can be used. An eye in the rope can be made by using an eye splice, or if it is only a temporary affair, it can made by tying a bowline or some similar knot.

Braided ropes are much more difficult to splice. Although it can be done by hand it requires a lot of time and expertise and most braided ropes are spliced by machine which means they must be brought ashore. Few boat owners these days bother to hand splice their braided ropes, they find it easier to make temporary joins with knots, particularly where an eye is required; indeed, the practice of splicing is becoming less and less common on modern boats.

One advantage of the synthetic materials is the convenience of being able to simply melt and fuse the frayed ends or strands with a lighted match so that they do not unravel or look unsightly. Fiber ropes had a nasty habit of unlaying rapidly when cut, with strands flying out all over the place until the ends had been 'whipped' with fine cordage. While the strands of synthetic ropes will also unravel quickly, if they are held together while a lighted match is used to fuse the ends together, this will secure them against unlaying and also eliminate the need for whipping.

Before cutting a rope a good practice is to place tape around the circumference of the rope on either side of the spot where the cut is to be made, so that when it is cut it will unravel only as far as the tape, and each end can then be fused with a lighted match prior to removing the tape. To make a good fusing, roll the melted ends of the strands together so they solidify as one, but do so with thick gloves as the melted synthetic material will stick to the fingers and can cause very severe burns.

A short splice in laid rope is made as follows:

1. Unlay both ends of the rope to be joined for a few centimetres.
2. 'Marry' the unlaid strands from each rope so they alternate with one another.
3. Take a strand of one rope and tuck it under a strand of the other rope, working against the lay.
4. Repeat this procedure with all three strands.
5. Continue the splice with over and under tucks until each strand is used up.
6. Turn the rope round and repeat the procedure with the strands of the other rope.
7. Cut off and fuse any loose strands.

A marline spike or something similar will be required to assist with tucking the loose strands under the laid strands. By 'dropping' one strand at a time as the strands are used up, the splice will be given a pleasant tapered appearance at each end.

A long splice joins the two ropes together without increasing the thickness of the rope.

1. Unlay both ends for some considerable distance back along the ropes and marry them alternately as for a short splice.
2. Taking two opposing strands, unlay one backwards and replace it with the opposing strand, effectively re-laying the rope with the opposite strand.
3. Continue this procedure until the loose strand is used up.
4. Carry out the same procedure this time working in the opposite direction.
5. Tie off the two strands at the end of the splice with an overhand knot and bury the knot in the lay of the rope. Tuck the ends of the strands into the body of the rope against the lay.
6. Repeat the whole procedure with the other pairs of strands.

When the splice is finished the ends of the strands, if still showing, can be fused and the whole splice rolled between the hands to smooth it out.

An eye splice is probably the most common form of splice used today. It is used to make an eye or loop in the end of a rope:

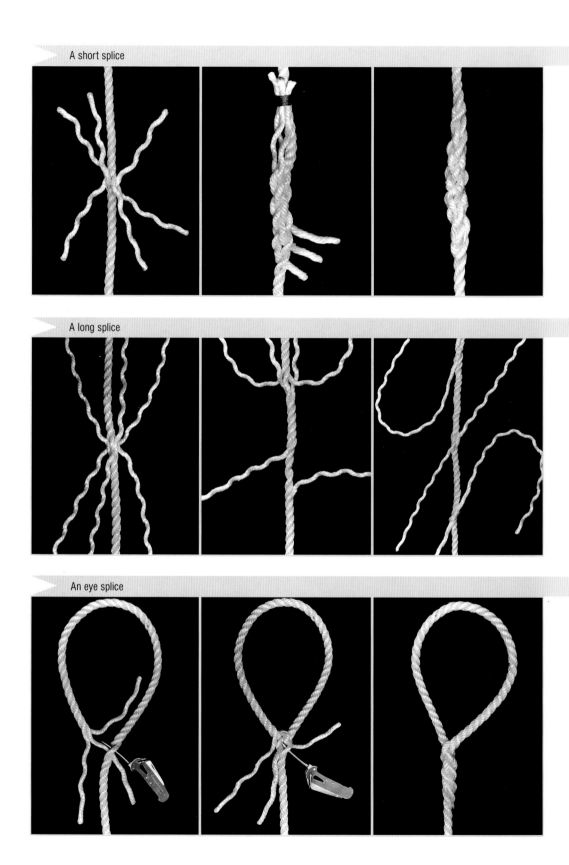

A short splice

A long splice

An eye splice

The essential boat maintenance manual

1. Form an eye or loop of the required size in the end of the rope and unravel the strands for a short distance back.
2. Using a spike, open up the strands in the standing part of the rope and thread one loose strand through one standing strand against the lay.
3. Repeat the procedure with the next strand.
4. Turn the rope over and repeat the procedure with the third strand.
5. Pull the strands tight and continue the splice with over and under tucking.
6. Taper the splice by dropping one strand at a time after a couple of tucks.
7. Trim off and fuse the ends of the strands, then roll the splice between the hands.

BLOCKS AND TACKLES

Winter maintenance time is the ideal time to check out and service the blocks and tackles on the boat. These are arguably the hardest working pieces of equipment on board and are subject to some tough treatment. By the same token they are often in locations where they cannot be closely observed at all times, such as the top of the mast, and can suffer considerable wear and tear without showing immediate signs. Since the failure of such equipment can result in serious damage, even life-threatening situations at sea, it is important that they are given close scrutiny during the annual maintenance checkup.

SHEAVES

The most important part of any block is the sheave, for this is the part over which the rope runs and therefore comes in for the greatest wear and tear. Modern sheaves are mostly of synthetic material or metal and may be incorporated in a traditional block system or recessed into mast or spar fittings. As a general rule, narrow metal sheaves are used for flexible wire rope and wider synthetic sheaves for synthetic ropes. Sheaves fitted into mast or spar inserts will probably be riveted into position whereas the traditional block and tackle arrangement is usually free moving and secured to the boat by means of shackles.

When replacing sheaves or blocks the most important factor in reducing wear is to fit the correct sized sheave (and block) for the size of rope to be used. A sheave that is too small for the rope will cause severe wear both on the rope and the sheave itself. A sheave that is too large will allow the rope to move around and also cause friction wear. Similarly, the size of the block is important; if the sheave does not fit tightly into the throat of the block there is a risk of the rope slipping between the sheave and the cheeks and fouling the rope or jamming—an all too frequent problem with masthead sheaves. If the sheave is too tight it will make hoisting and lowering heavy and put extra stress on the gear.

Maintenance of sheaves at the masthead, or anywhere above the deck line, is best done when the mast is unstepped. While it can be done by sending a man aloft in the bosun's chair, this is never the ideal environment in which to work, and often the result is a half-hearted job. With the mast down on the ground, the job is easier and there is

Blocks and tackles have many uses
onboard boats, especially work boats.

more opportunity to use the right tools. Some permanently fitted sheaves may need to be taken out of the mast or boom wall, which will necessitate drilling out the pop rivets and lifting out the sheave fitting before fitting a new one; a much easier job when done on deck than hanging unsteadily at the top of a mast!

Worn sheaves must be replaced, especially if they are at the masthead or well above the deck line. A halyard which has slipped off the sheave and jammed at the masthead can mean loss of time in a race and a dangerous situation when the boat is at sea and a blow coming on. Usually, the entire fitting is removed and replaced complete with new sheave, although it is possible with some fittings to just remove and replace the sheave, keeping the same fitting. Fortunately, wear and tear is fairly obvious with sheaves, because twirling them with the finger will immediately indicate if they are running true or have developed an irregularity. Since, as mentioned, such problems can lead to disaster at sea, even the slightest sign of damage to sheaves at the masthead call for an immediate replacement.

Free-moving blocks and tackles must come in for similar treatment; the problems that could arise with the jamming of a running backstay block in the middle of a heavy gybe would not be worth thinking about! Fortunately, most modern sheaves are self-lubricating or bushed to avoid the need for lubrication, so running aloft with an oil can is rarely necessary, and in any case, graphite is often a better lubricant than oil. Sheet tackles which incorporate blocks, such as main sheet gear, need to be checked although these are in regular use and mostly at or near deck level, so any deterioration will be more readily seen than with running gear aloft. Apart from the tackles themselves, maintenance time is a good time to check the fittings that secure them to the boom, mast or deck, for pop rivets can become corroded in use to the point where a sudden strain on the sheave will cause them to give way.

TACKLES AND PURCHASES

One of the most useful bits of gear carried on sailboats, and on many larger motor boats, is known as a 'Handy Billy'. It is a simple block and tackle arrangement that can be used for a multitude of purposes, from lifting a dinghy aboard to replacing damaged or broken rigging. As its name denotes, it is 'handy' for all sorts of things and like a bosun's chair, is kept in the locker of most medium and large boats for quick use when a need arises. Indeed, the term 'handy' could well be applied to any tackle or purchase, for the simple arrangements of a block at the top and another at the bottom can increase the lifting power and save a

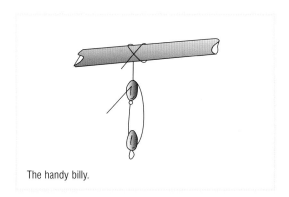

The handy billy.

The main sheet of a yacht is a typical example of the use of blocks and tackles to provide increased efficiency. The purchase system can be varied, but the mechanical advantage remains the same.

great deal of time and effort by making even the heaviest jobs easy to handle.

The degree to which the tackle can reduce the load depends on the number of sheaves involved and the position of the rope threaded through them. Most everyday tackles consist of two blocks, each of which may contain one, two or three sheaves. The 'Mechanical Advantage' (MA) of the purchase is the number of times the pull on the rope is increased.

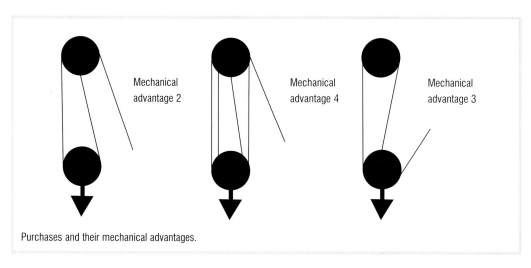

Mechanical advantage 2

Mechanical advantage 4

Mechanical advantage 3

Purchases and their mechanical advantages.

In other words an MA of 3 increases the effective strength of the person using it by three. The MA is determined by the number of ropes at the moving block, so a handy billy rigged with two single blocks and a downward pull would have an MA of two. If the pull were upwards from the bottom block this would increase the MA to three.

The diagram on the previous page indicates the MA of three convenient block and tackle arrangements.

THE BOSUN'S CHAIR

As mentioned earlier in this chapter, the bosun's chair is a useful piece of equipment that should be carried aboard every yacht. It provides a simple but effective way of enabling one of the crew to carry out work aloft without the need to hang on to mast or rigging and with reasonable safety. While it is an easy piece of equipment to make, it is not an expensive item to buy at the chandlery, consisting generally of a wooden seat or canvas sling in which a person can be seated. This is then shackled on to a halyard and hoisted on a mast winch to the point where work needs to be carried out.

Although impervious to most weather conditions, some synthetic ropes may be affected by sunlight and should be stowed below when not in use.

The main advantage of the bosun's chair, apart from eliminating the need to climb the rigging, is that it frees up both hands to work on the repair job. Securely held within the framework of the chair, the person aloft can use both hands without

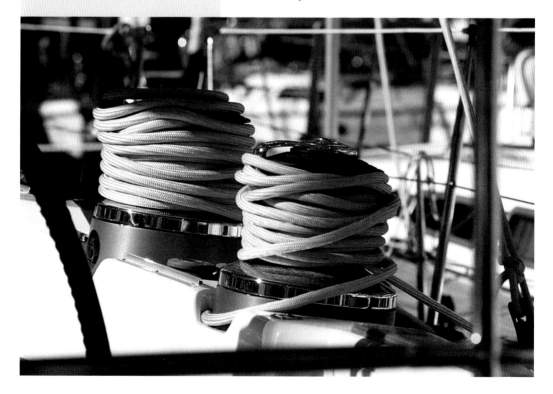

fear of a sudden lurch throwing him or her off the mast. If the chair swings too much it can be steadied by gripping the mast with the knees or tying off the chair to nearby rigging. It also enables a variety of tools to be carried in a bag attached to the chair.

The bosun's chair is usually kept in a locker below decks and needs little care and maintenance. However, bearing in mind that a person working aloft in the chair may be many feet above the deck, it is important that this useful piece of equipment is kept in good condition at all times.

TIP: BY PASSING THE BIGHT OF THE ROPE OVER YOUR HEAD AND UNDER YOUR LEGS, YOU CREATE A HALF HITCH ON THE ROPE WHICH ENABLES YOU TO RAISE AND LOWER YOURSELF IN THE CHAIR (PRACTICE THIS AT LOW LEVELS!)

Marine motors

Because of the huge range of motors available to boat owners these days, it would be impossible to deal in depth with every kind of boat motor in a book such as this. Manufacturers invariably provide manuals or handbooks with their motors and these should be used as the basis of all maintenance work. However, when a second-hand boat is purchased it often happens that the motor manual has been lost and there is nothing to provide details of servicing and maintaining the motor. This is especially the case with older craft, where the previous owner has become so used to the maintenance routine that manuals have become superfluous and any that might have once existed have long since disappeared. This chapter cannot obviously replace such detailed information on specific motors but is intended to give an outline of the basic procedures that are followed in general maintenance of marine motors.

Most boat motors fall into one of three main categories:
- Inboard
- Outboard
- Stern drive (or inboard/outboard)

These in turn also fall into three main categories according to their fuel requirements:
- Gasoline
- Diesel
- Two-stroke mix

While some may be air cooled, most are water cooled; some with fresh water, some using the ocean as their cooling medium.

INBOARD MOTORS

Inboard motors are used in almost every type of craft including large motor cruisers, medium-sized leisure boats and yachts, and can range from high speed turbo diesel engines to tiny single-cylinder 'putt-putt' gasoline motors. They are mounted in the hull

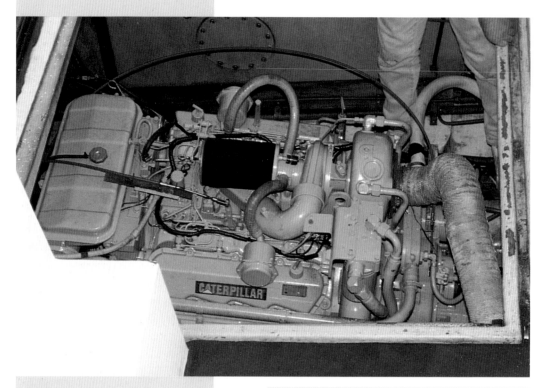

A typical inboard diesel installation in a small motor boat.

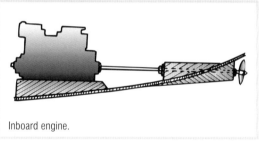

Inboard engine.

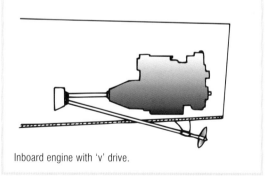

Inboard engine with 'v' drive.

and drive the boat through a single shaft (or twin shafts in the case of twin motors) which run through the stern gland to propellers at the after end of the hull, or via adaptations of the drive systems such as 'v' drive. Although some inboard motors are designed to run at high speeds, most do not reach the high revolutions of outboard motors, and as a result can use larger propellers which give greater thrust through a better 'bite' on the water. This mostly results in a slower hull speed but more power in the drive, a factor which can be important when punching against a big sea or when towing. Another form of drive popular with some boat owners is the jet drive, in which the inboard motor drives a water jet unit rather than a propeller. Almost all inboard gasoline motors are four-stroke engines and are water cooled.

Twin outboards provide speed and safety in offshore waters.

OUTBOARD MOTORS

These motors operate at high revolutions and are usually fitted to small, fast planing boats. While the propeller is much smaller than that of a slower-revving inboard motor, the high revolutions compensate for the small propeller and push the lighter hull at speed across the surface of the water, which makes it a popular motor for all sorts of sports activities including water skiing and racing. The outboard motor is totally self-contained and is mounted on the transom of the boat, usually connected by flexible hose to a separate fuel tank. These motors can be four-stroke or two-stroke; the former burning normal gasoline, the latter a two-stroke mix of gasoline and oil. Because they are located on the outside of the boat and the fuel tank also in the open, the hazard of carrying fuel inside an enclosed hull is avoided.

STERN-DRIVE MOTORS

Known also as inboard/outboards, stern-drive motors are a combination of both inboard and outboard power units. The motor itself is the inboard type, being contained within the hull, while the shaft exits through the transom rather than the underside of the hull, and drives the propeller through an adjustable outdrive which can resemble the lower section of a large outboard motor. The motor is usually located

A typical stern drive unit.

close to the stern, leaving more room inside the boat and making a more compact arrangement of the motor system than the conventional inboard drive. The benefit of the outdrive instead of direct drive is that the leg can be trimmed to improve performance and reduce the draft, since most boats with stern drives have planing hulls. The motor may be gasoline or diesel and usually provides a high revving performance to complement the planing hull, and for this reason, inboard/outboard motors are usually fitted in motor boats; rarely in yachts.

CARE AND MAINTENANCE

As with all motors, care and maintenance must be an ongoing procedure and not just a routine to be carried out when the boat is on the slipway or laid up on land for a winter overhaul. Most manufacturers require a regular routine check for their motors which is not dissimilar to that given to a car engine. The peculiar environment in which a marine motor operates makes it vulnerable to far more problems than a vehicle motor and unless properly looked after, a boat motor will experience a wide range of problems and be less reliable than motors in more amenable environments. Apart from the salt-laden atmosphere in which it has to operate, a boat motor is subject to infrequent use, often being left for weeks on end without being run or even turned over.

When a motor is left stationary for some time its protective oil runs down to the bottom of the sump, leaving vital working parts relatively unprotected and vulnerable. It takes only one small spot of rust or corrosion to start on a highly machined working part for trouble to begin and spread rapidly. It is a well-known maxim among engineers and mechanics that the worst possible thing for a marine motor is to leave it idle. Regular running, even for a few moments weekly, will keep everything operating smoothly and give the motor a considerably longer life span. So step number one in the maintenance of any marine motor is to run it at frequent intervals.

TIP: USE IT OR LOSE IT! LEAVING A MOTOR IDLE FOR A LONG TIME IS THE WORST TREATMENT YOU CAN GIVE IT.

Step number two is to keep an engine log book. This can be of great assistance to both the amateur and professional when the motor needs attention. The number of hours run, frequency of lubrication, oil pressure and water temperature changes and any problems encountered in use will all help diagnose any irregularities and indicate the health of the engine. With the aid of such a log book, for example, a gradual drop in oil pressure over a long period of time could indicate wear in the bearings or the spring in the relief valve losing its tension;

Regular maintenance is one way to avoid aggravating motor breakdowns when the boat is at sea.

problems which if spotted in good time can be rectified with little effort and cost, but which if allowed to progress could lead to damage of the main bearing and result in a very expensive repair job.

ROUTINE MAINTENANCE OF DIESEL MOTORS

As mentioned earlier, it would be impossible to provide in this chapter a complete run down on the maintenance of all the different types of boat motors, so the following routine for diesel engines is a general guide covering the basics, and is not intended to be used for any specific motor.

Weekly
- Check the water level in the header tank (if fitted). Check cooling system for leaks.
- Check sea cocks (open cooling systems).
- Check oil levels in sump and gearbox.
- Check lubricating oil pressure.
- Check battery condition and charging.
- Check engine temperature when running.

The cramped areas below decks often make engine maintenance a difficult operation.

Every 150 hours
- Check tension on belts and adjust where necessary.

- Check batteries and top up with distilled water where necessary.
- Check generator and batteries, clean contacts where necessary.
- Check fuel filter for any sign of pollutant or sediment.

Every 300 hours
- Check fuel system through including lift pump chamber and filters. Clean and renew where necessary.
- Check generator. Lubricate as indicated in the service manual.
- Drain cooling system (closed system) and refill with fresh coolant and filter.
- Check all systems for wear, signs of leaks or loose connections.

Every 1000 hours
- Remove injectors and send for cleaning.
- Check valve clearances.
- Inspect generator for signs of brush wear.
- Check lubrication of rocker shaft.
- Drain and clean fuel tank.

ROUTINE MAINTENANCE FOR INBOARD GASOLINE MOTORS

Standard inboard and stern-drive motors are mostly similar in design and therefore similar in their maintenance requirements. Most are four-stroke and therefore not unlike the motor of a vehicle on shore, indeed, some boats have modified car motors as their propulsion unit. General routine maintenance should be carried out along the following lines:

Weekly
- Check oil level in engine and gearbox.
- Check fuel lines for possible leaks. Check fuel filter bowl.
- Check header tank (closed system) and sea cocks (open system).
- Check battery charging.
- Check engine temperature when running.
- Check oil pressure.

Every 25 hours
- Check battery condition with hydrometer, top up if necessary.
- Check all fuel lines for leakage.
- Lubricate linkages and bearings as indicated in service manual.

Every 100 hours
- Pump out sump and replace with fresh oil.
- Check all electric leads and connections.

Every 250 hours

- Pump out gearbox and replace with fresh oil.
- Change the fuel filter.
- Change the oil filter.
- Change the air filter.
- Check fuel pump and carburettor, remove and clean where necessary.
- Empty fuel tank and clean before refilling.
- Check plugs and adjust gap where necessary.

Every 500 hours

- Clean and adjust contact points, adjust gap and lubricate distributor cam.
- Change spark plugs.
- Check ignition timing.
- Check battery, clean terminals, replace leads where necessary.
- Check generator.
- Check valve tappet clearance.

Every 1000 hours

- Call in a qualified marine engineer to check out the motor completely.

ROUTINE MAINTENANCE OF OUTBOARD MOTORS

Because of the compact nature and unique features of outboard motors which are not usually found in other engines, anything more than basic care and maintenance is outside the scope of the average boat owner. Much of an outboard motor is sealed against ingress of moisture, and the basic layout and design is different from normal motors because of the need for compactness and portability. Indeed, it is this compactness and portability which offers the safest and best routine for maintenance—transporting it to a qualified outboard mechanic. Of course, there are simple items of maintenance which can be safely carried out by boat owners, and these are included in this section. But modern outboard motors have become so sophisticated that even

Basic outboard maintenance can often be done at home.

routine motor maintenance, readily practiced with standard inboard engines, can be too complex for any but qualified engineers and mechanics to handle.

However, probably the most important part of care for an outboard engine

A well maintained motor means an efficient, safe boat.

is similar to that of any motor—starting and running it at frequent intervals. Outboards suffer perhaps even more than inboards from being left idle, and when the boat is not in use, the motor should be run for 10 or 15 minutes at least once a month. This can be done in the water or on the trailer providing that some sort of fresh water cooling is arranged. Most motor manufacturers have 'ear' systems where garden hoses can be clamped to the water intake of the motor to provide a flow of fresh water while the motor is run, but a large container, such as a garbage bin or oil drum will suffice providing it holds sufficient depth of water to cover the water intake when the motor leg is lowered into it.

Many of the later models of outboard motors are four-stroke and therefore use gasoline straight from the pump. Two-stroke motors use a mix of gasoline and oil (usually 50:1) and this may be mixed in the tank or fed from separate containers and mixed at the motor. Either way the use of correct fuel is obviously important and the manufacturer's instructions for each individual type of motor must be followed carefully or the motor will not perform correctly and may even be damaged. Similarly, some manufacturers recommend that when the motor has finished work the fuel should be disconnected and the motor run until it is dry, while others advocate stopping the motor with fuel still in the system. Once again the manufacturer's recommendations must be followed for each brand and model of motor. This is the sort of care that must be carried out by the boat owner and which will pay dividends in reducing maintenance, as well as improving performance and extending the life of the motor.

Greasing the linkages is a job that does not require an expert. Throttle and gear shift linkages from the remote control to the active part of the motor can be accessed and greased where required. Salt water soon dries out lubricated cables and linkages and routine maintenance of these with a good brand of marine (waterproof) grease will reduce the cost of having the engine serviced periodically. The propeller can be removed and the shear pins checked, and in the older and smaller models, spark plugs can be taken out and adjusted or fuel filters dismantled and cleaned. However, the sophisticated engineering of large, late model outboard motors prohibits anyone without the necessary expertise from doing more than making an external examination and keeping the motor clean.

TROUBLE SHOOTING A MARINE MOTOR

If an engine log is kept, as suggested earlier in this chapter, the degree of maintenance the motor will need when the boat is hauled out for her winter overhaul, will be easily determined. Apart from the number of hours run and the subsequent servicing required, the log should indicate any problems encountered during the running of the motor and what parts might need examination. Having the boat on shore or slipway will make it easier for the motor to be checked by an engineer or mechanic, and having details in the engine log of any previous problems will make his diagnosis easier. The following are a few of the more common symptoms of engine troubles and the checks that should be made to determine exactly where the problem lies before turning it over to the expert.

Diesel

Starter fails to turn engine:
1. Check battery.
2. Check switches, including solenoid.
3. Check cables and terminals.
4. Check that compression is off.
5. Check starter motor.

Engine turns but does not fire:
1. Check compression for possible piston wear.
2. Check that fuel tap is open.
3. Check that injectors have fuel, if not check fuel line.
4. Check possibility of an air lock in the fuel system.

Engine starts, runs, then stops:
1. Check fuel feed pipe and filter for possible blockage.
2. Check capacity of fuel lift pump for possible weakness.

A smoky exhaust is often a sign that the motor needs attention. This is particularly the case with diesel motors.

3. Check that breather hole in fuel tank is open.
4. Check for possible restriction in air or exhaust systems.
5. Check fuel lines for possible air lock.

Engine misfires or runs erratically:
1. Check fuel system for air lock.
2. Check air and exhaust systems.
3. Check fuel lines and filter for possible water pollution.
4. Check valve and pump timing.
5. Check atomisers.

Excess smoke from exhaust:
1. Check air filter and intake against restrictions.
2. Check fuel pump for possible defects.
3. Check valve and pump timing.
4. Check injectors.
5. Check compression.

One of the main problems that arise in diesel motors is poor compression. This can be felt by turning the engine by hand, when severe resistance should be felt. Poor compression can be the result of worn rings, worn liners or leaking valves, and will prevent the motor from performing correctly; in particular it will make for hard starting. Compression is vital to the efficient running of a diesel engine and serious loss of compression may mean a major overhaul to restore engine performance.

The color of the exhaust smoke can indicate problems with a diesel motor since, as a general rule, if the exhaust emits a lot of black smoke, it may be getting too much fuel in proportion to air. It can also indicate problems with dirty injectors or an overload on the engine. White smoke indicates too much air or moisture in the fuel mix, or perhaps even water in the fuel, while blue smoke may mean worn piston rings or liners. If the motor runs out of fuel while running, the entire fuel system will need to be bled through before it will start again. Service manuals describe how to bleed each specific motor.

Gasoline

Motor fails to start:
1. Check battery, leads, switches, distributor and the starter motor.
2. Check exhaust line for possible blockage.
3. Check that the correct fuel is being used and fuel line is not blocked.
4. Check there is a spark at the plug.
5. Check carburettor for blocked jets.
6. Check plugs to see if the motor is flooding.
7. Check air intake to see it is clear.
8. Check carburettor is not flooded (especially outboards).

Motor starts but backfires or stops:
1. Check the air/gasoline mixture (may be too lean or too rich).
2. Check for air lock in the fuel system.
3. Check for water in the fuel system.
4. Check electrics for cable leakage.
5. Check carburettor jets.
6. Check coil and condenser for possible failure.
7. Check timing.
8. Check plugs and distributor.

Overheating:
1. Check seacocks are open, check for blockage in cooling system.
2. Check for plastic bag sucked over intake skin fitting.
3. Check water pump.
4. Check timing.
5. Check oil level in sump.
6. Check for overloading which may be due to fouled prop shaft, incorrect propeller, binding, stern gland, weed or plastic bag on propeller.

ANCILLARY SYSTEMS

Motors have a great deal of ancillary equipment, including pumps, electrical systems, cooling systems, lubricating systems, and so on. Each of these systems is vital to the efficient running of the engine, so each must be given its own routine maintenance check. In some cases, such as with batteries, this must be done fairly frequently, but for most, the annual service during winter overhaul is sufficient to see the boat and motor through the year.

FUEL SYSTEMS

Fuel tanks should preferably be made of stainless steel, although good quality GRP tanks are acceptable. Galvanized or non-ferrous metals are not suitable as they tend to react with the chemicals in some fuels, particularly diesel. From the tank, one of two systems is used to feed the fuel to the motor; gravitational and pump. The gravitational system is common in small craft and requires the tank to be located somewhere in the boat above the level of the engine so that the fuel gravitates down to the filter bowl and motor. Large motors and outboards use a system in which the tank can be located anywhere and the fuel is pumped to the motor.

In both systems it is important that tanks, pipes and filters are readily accessible for cleaning or for

Some of the ancillary equipment on a diesel installation.

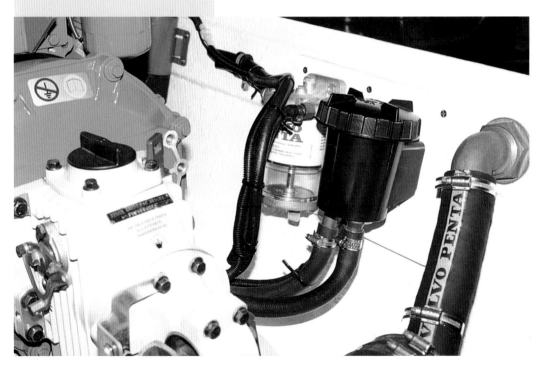

checking when problems arise. Fuel systems in boats suffer from impurities, often condensed water or sludge, and need to be periodically cleaned out. The tank in particular needs thorough cleaning, especially the sump, in which sludge and water will collect as it sinks to the bottom. A tap should be fitted to this sump to enable draining off of sediment and water at intervals and the fuel line take off should be about 10–15 mm above the top of the sump, never on the bottom of the tank where it will be open to any sediment sloshing around when the boat is moving. As an added precaution a strainer should be fitted over the end of the take off pipe inside the tank.

As well as cleaning the tank, the pipes should be blown through during the maintenance routine so as to remove any possible build-up of sludge or other material which will eventually restrict and even block the flow of fuel. Joints and terminals in the fuel lines should be thoroughly checked to prevent any fuel leaking out and air leaking in.

Next along the line is the fuel filter which is specifically designed to collect any dirt or water in the fuel before it reaches the motor. It is therefore a very important piece of equipment and needs to be checked at fairly frequent intervals, depending on the quality of the fuel being used. All fuel systems; diesel, gasoline and mix, need a filter and these can vary in shape, size and operation quite considerably, although the basic requirement of each is the same—to ensure that only clean fuel gets through to the motor. The most common is the filter bowl which, as its name denotes, is a glass bowl fitted into the fuel line at some point before the motor. Fuel from the tank flows into the bowl and is taken off by a pipe at the top. Some form of strainer is used to trap floating matter while any sediment or water sinks to the bottom where it is easily seen and removed, leaving only clean fuel to enter the take-off pipe at the top

A cartridge filter is another form of fuel filter, usually in the form of a plastic container inside which is a dispensable cartridge filter which screens the fuel as it passes through,

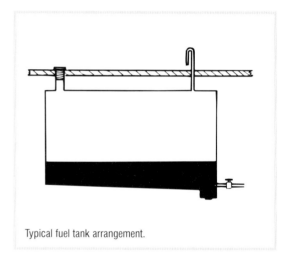

Typical fuel tank arrangement.

Cross section of fuel filter bowl.

Black soot around the exhaust pipe can indicate problems with the motor.

removing any foreign matter. This type of filter is not as successful in trapping water as is the bowl system, but its compact size makes it easy to fit and convenient to change at intervals. In all cases, putting the filter back together after maintenance must be done correctly, ensuring that it is fitted correctly and tightened up so there are no air or fuel leaks.

EXHAUST SYSTEMS

Most exhaust systems in boats are known as 'wet' exhausts because they are water cooled. Certain boats, such as some racing craft, may have air cooled exhaust systems similar to those on a car, but these call for the use of mufflers or silencers which are mostly cumbersome and too large to fit inside a boat. Fishing boats with big diesels and more room may have mufflers fitted, but most leisure craft use wet exhausts which act as mufflers and at the same time cool the exhaust pipes. The water comes from the engine's cooling system after circulating through the water jacket of the motor. Instead of being pumped over the side it is discharged into the exhaust pipe, thus cooling the exhaust pipe, often to the extent that it can be constructed of rubber or neoprene.

The most important factor in this type of exhaust system is to ensure that the water does not run back into the engine when it is stopped. A swan neck or air lock in the exhaust pipe between the water discharge pipe and the motor will ensure that the water

Model of a typical 'wet' exhaust system; note the 'trap' in the foreground.

cannot return back up the pipe either from the cooling water or sea water pushed back up the pipe from outside when the boat is moving in a seaway. The main section of the pipe from the motor to the swan neck must be of metal as it will get very hot. Iron is the most suitable metal as copper and brass tend to deteriorate rapidly when in contact with exhaust fumes and salt water. Just past the swan neck the cooling water discharge enters the exhaust pipe, so the remainder of its length to the

discharge point can be of almost any material, although flexible pipe is favored since it absorbs any vibration from the engine and prevents cracking of joints. Most modern boats use a trap or 'poop box' in the exhaust pipe between the motor and the skin fitting, which serves the same purpose as the swan neck in preventing water backing up to the motor. From the trap, the exhaust fumes exit through the skin via the exhaust outlet, which is always located above the water line.

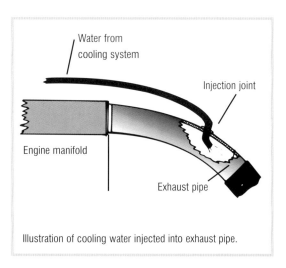

Illustration of cooling water injected into exhaust pipe.

TIP: TILTING AN OUTBOARD ABOVE HORIZONTAL CAN CAUSE WATER TO RUN UP THE EXHAUST AND DAMAGE THE MOTOR.

COOLING SYSTEMS

There are two forms of water cooling for marine engines: direct cooling and closed circuit cooling. While there may be a few marine engines that use air cooling, they are not common and the majority use one of the two water cooling systems.

The 'open' or direct water cooling system for marine engines—mostly

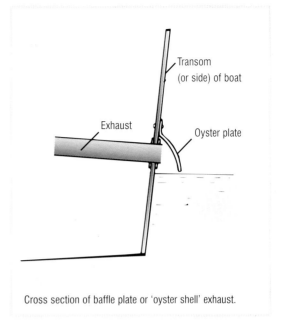

Cross section of baffle plate or 'oyster shell' exhaust.

smaller inboard motors and outboards, as large motors prefer closed systems—uses sea water pumped directly from outside the hull into the motor and then discharged again outside the hull, often through the exhaust. The water enters the hull through a skin fitting to which an intake pipe is secured on the inside and a strainer fitted over the outside. The first step in maintenance of this type of cooling system is to ensure that the strainer is kept clean and clear so there will be no blockage to the water entering the intake. If the boat is not used a great deal, marine growth can quickly reduce the amount of water entering the cooling system and this could lead to overheating of the motor. In use, items such as plastic bags can become caught and similarly block or impair the intake of water.

A seacock is inserted into the pipe just inside the skin fitting, often with a filter to further remove any foreign material that gets through the external strainer, so that in the event of a broken pipe in the cooling system, the intake pipe can be shut off before the hull begins to flood. While the system from here on will vary according to the design and manufacture of the motor, the next stage is usually a water pump attached to the engine which then pushes the water through the cooling system of the motor. Apart from the normal water jacket in the engine block that is standard with most internal combustion motors, the cooling system often incorporates a means of cooling the sump and gearbox oil, while the heated water at the end of the line may be used for domestic purposes on the boat.

The cooling water is then discharged back into the sea, mostly through a wet exhaust system described on pages 159–160 of this book. This uses the cooling water to both cool and muffle the exhaust before it is discharged back into the sea, thus completing the cycle of direct cooling. Maintenance is relatively easy since much of the system is inside the motor, but a check of all pipes, filters, pumps and connections should be

Some motors discharge their water through the exhaust, others through a discharge pipe.

undertaken at fairly regular intervals, especially during winter maintenance when it may be necessary to renew some sections.

The 'closed' system of cooling uses fresh water in order to avoid the corrosive action of salt water in the motor. There are a number of different methods used, one of the most common employing a series of pipes fitted under the hull of the boat as part of the system. Cooling water is fed into the motor from a header tank and recycled after cooling the motor, in a somewhat similar system to a motor vehicle cooling system. But instead of an air-cooled radiator, the heated water from the engine is passed out through the hull and into a series of pipes attached to the underside of the boat where it is cooled by passing sea water. The pipes then re-enter the hull and return the now cooler water to the header tank ready to start the cooling cycle again. In this way, only fresh water is passed through the cooling system, although the sea is used as a heat exchanger. Another system uses the header tank in the boat as a heat exchanger, the header tank being constantly filled with cold sea water pumped into the tank from outside the boat and the fresh water used to cool the engine recycled through the heat exchanger in the header tank. As with all cooling systems, maintenance is a question of checking the pipes and connections, although the outside hull pipes in the closed system can only be examined when the boat is out of the water. If sacrificial anodes are fitted in the cooling system to prevent corrosion, these will also need to be checked.

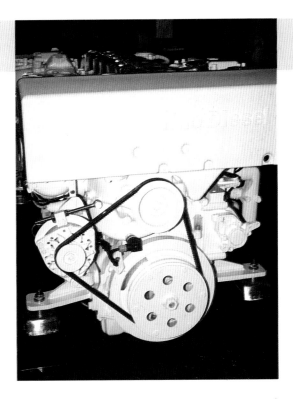
Big diesels usually have closed circuit cooling with large header tanks.

Outboard motors generally use the direct cooling system where sea water is pumped from an intake below the waterline on the drive leg, passed through the motor and discharged again from an outlet somewhere on the motor. The most important maintenance factor with this type of motor is to flush the system through with fresh water after use. Most outboards are made of aluminum and corrosion from salt water can play havoc with the narrow tubing of the cooling system. In addition, the impeller of the water pump, usually made of neoprene or some similar material, can become heavily coated with salt which dries out when the motor is not in use and becomes quite abrasive, creating wear on the synthetic blades of the impeller which will reduce its life considerably.

Most manufacturers have appliances which make flushing easy. One system uses a fitting around the intake—sometimes referred to as 'ears'—which, when connected to a garden hose, enables the motor to be run and thus flushed through with fresh water. Some boat owners merely place the motor in a tank or drum of fresh water and run it until the system is totally cleaned through. Whatever the method used, flushing through the cooling system with fresh water is essential if the motor is to be kept out of the water for any length of time.

LAYING UP A MOTOR FOR THE WINTER

Winter time is not usually conducive to boating and in colder climates most boats are laid up either on shore or at a mooring or marina. Wherever it may be kept throughout the winter months, if it is not used, the boat will be subject to deterioration in some areas. Since motors thrive on use, it follows that the equipment most likely to suffer from a long period of idleness is the engine and its ancillary gear. For this reason, it is essential to take special precautions before the boat is laid up to minimize any deterioration that may result from its lack of use. The best protection for any motor is to give it a run at frequent intervals, but that may not always be possible if, for instance, the boat is laid up on shore. Outboards can be run in a tank or with 'ears,' and where there is a closed cooling system it may be possible to turn the motor briefly without causing any problems, but direct cooling systems that have been drained mean no cooling is available and the motor must be turned by hand or started only very briefly.

When it will not be possible to run the motor at all for a lengthy period, the laying-up procedure must be followed. The procedure given here cannot be specific, of course, because motors vary so much and different manufacturers may prefer different procedures. But as a general guide, the following will offer protection to most motors when laid up for any length of time and is intended to take place before the boat is taken out of the water:

DIESEL MOTORS

1. Thoroughly clean all external parts of the engine.
2. Run the motor until well warmed through. Stop it and drain or pump the lubricating oil from the sump. Refill with the correct grade of fresh oil.
3. Change the oil filter and replace with a new one.
4. Change the air filter and clean out the breather pipe.
5. Drain the entire fuel system. Place in the empty tank at least 5 litres of special oil used for inhibiting fuel systems. The brands of oil and amounts to use will be listed in the service manual.
6. Prime the system and start the motor. Allow it to run for 15 to 20 minutes to ensure complete penetration of the inhibiting oil. Stop the motor.
7. Seal off the air vent in the tank and filler cap to reduce the risk of water condensation during lay-up.
8. Drain the entire cooling system. Dismantle the water pump and check the impeller, replacing it if necessary, and pack with grease or glycerine. Use ethyl glycol for a closed cooling system to reduce the risk of corrosion.
9. Remove the injectors or atomisers and send them to the workshop for checking and cleaning. Spray a small amount of lubricating oil into the cylinder before replacing the injectors. Rotate the motor for one complete revolution.
10. Seal off the exhaust. Change the gearbox oil.
11. Remove all belts and stow them away.
12. Remove batteries and take them ashore for charging throughout the winter.

GASOLINE MOTORS

The basic principles that apply to a diesel engine can also be applied to a gasoline motor where it is to be left idle for a long period of time. Like diesels, gasoline motors need to be protected against corrosion and other forms of deterioration if they cannot be run at regular intervals. If anything, a gasoline motor is more vulnerable because it has an

Outboard motors are easy to lay-up;
they can just be taken home.

electrical system which can be badly affected by the salt air. In very low temperatures the procedure for laying up is not dissimilar to that for a diesel but there are a few modifications:

1. Clean the engine as for a diesel.
2. Run the engine until warm. Stop it and pump out the sump, change the oil filter and air filter, empty the fuel and cooling systems and check impellers, valves, stop cocks, etc.
3. Remove the generator, starter motor, batteries and spark plugs and store ashore. Vaseline any terminals or electrical parts which may be exposed to prevent corrosion.
4. Place a small amount of lubricating oil or rust inhibiting oil and turn the engine briefly by hand. Change the oil in the gear box.

Obviously, not all factors will be covered by this program as different motors have different types of ancillary gear. But with this basic guide and a little common sense, it should not be difficult to ensure that any motor is well protected during the long winter months when it will not be used.

OUTBOARD MOTORS

By their very nature, outboard motors are almost always portable, either by removing them from the transom or by trailering the boat and motor into a garage or storage barn where they can be comfortably laid up out of the weather. If the cooling system has been flushed through with fresh water, as it should be after each use, and all exposed control linkages greased, there is little more that can be done to keep the motor in good shape through the winter lay-up other than giving it a run as often as possible. Most boat owners take advantage of this inactive period to run the motor into the dealer's workshop for its regular tune-up and service and this will take care of the remaining items that need to be checked before the motor is taken out of use.

The underwater areas

There are many ways a boat can be pulled out of the water for underwater maintenance. In areas with a large tidal range it can simply be landed on the bottom at high tide and the work carried out between tides. This is known as careening and is popular in regions where marina or boat shed facilities are not available. The use of marina facilities, such as slipway and cradle or lifting apparatus placing the boat high and dry on land makes the underwater maintenance so much easier and avoids the need to worry about incoming tides. Careening is mostly confined to simply cleaning and anti-fouling the hull between tides, and any major maintenance work is done at the winter lay-up on the slipway or on shore. Some marinas have sophisticated gantries to remove the boat from the water, others tow the boat up a ramp on a trailer-like cradle and 'park' it where required. Whatever the system, the advantages lie in the ability to take the boat out of the water at any state of the tide, as opposed to careening where the tide is the controlling factor, and keeping it out of the water for as long as is necessary—in some climates that means all winter.

SLIPPING

One type of slipway consists of a track, sometimes made of railway lines, up which a cradle is hauled by a winch until it is clear of the water. Sophisticated slipways can fit a number of boats along the track, others may have a 'shunting' arrangement which enables the cradle to be moved off the track and onto a working space, where it can be left, thus keeping the slipway clear for further vessels to be hauled out. Much the same applies with the other marina systems; with some a tractor tows the cradle up a concrete ramp and parks it in a working area, with others a gantry or crane lifts the boat clear of the water and then deposits it at the required spot. Whatever the system, the procedure is to remove the boat from the water at any state of tide, keep it out of the water while work is carried out on the underwater areas and then refloat it when the work is done. Dry land storage during the winter months is popular in many parts of the world, particularly in northern climes, not only to provide time for maintenance, but also to reduce the effects of the harsh winter climate on the boat.

The slipway cradle provides an even support all around the hull.

When landing a boat on a cradle or shore, or when careening on the sea bed, it is essential to ensure that excessive stress in not placed on any one part of its structure. The full weight of the hull and fittings is supported in the water by the flotation which places even stresses across the entire underwater area. Unless these stresses are similarly spread when the boat is lifted from the water, there may be distortion of the hull or damage to 'hot spots' where excessive pressure has been placed. The keel is the main member in the hull structure and as far as possible, all stresses on the hull should be evenly spaced along the keel when the boat is taken from the water. If the keel is supported in the centre and not at the ends, the forward and after parts of the hull will sag, creating a condition known as 'hogging'. If the hull is supported at the ends and not the centre, she will be subject to 'sagging' strains. Either of these situations can cause bad distortion to the hull, as can incorrect support of any other part.

Because of their long keel, motor boats are the easiest to land on either a slipway or shore.

Marina equipment such as cradles and hoists will have some form of mechanism which will distribute the load. Slings or cradle arms will support the hull at the sides and in the case of hoists or gantries, take the weight off the keel. When landed on a cradle or trailer, or on shore, beams are placed evenly under the length of the keel to ensure the weight of the boat is spread along the full length of the keel. Some boats can be landed without beams if the keel itself sits flat for most of its length—motor yachts and cruisers may have this type of keel. But fin keel

If shores are used they must be strategically placed to support the hull evenly. Pads may be necessary to avoid hot spots of pressure.

yachts have little to land on and thus the weight is borne down on one small part of the keel, and almost certainly this will require additional support—in the form of shores—under the bow and stern.

When the boat is to be slipped, she is floated into position either in the cradle or trailer at the bottom of the ramp and secured in such a way that as the cradle is hauled out the weight is evenly placed. Again, most commercial marinas are equipped to cater for all shapes and sizes of boats with cradles that have adjustable arms or base to ensure that every boat is well supported. With a hoist or gantry the same applies, with the slings being placed around the hull to spread the weight evenly as she is lifted from the water. Slings provide the closest thing to the natural support of water, although an unsupported keel can create stress points as it hangs between the main slings, but generally, slings with broad canvas supports are close to the best support a boat can have when lifted from her natural element.

With the boat out of the water and in position either on the slipway or on land, it is time to check that she is sitting properly and not placing undue stress on any part of the hull, yet allowing access to all underwater areas for maintenance work. If she is not sitting correctly on the beams or chocks, wedges hammered between the keel and the chocks will enable adjustments to be made. Similarly, it is important to ensure that the boat does not fall off when workers scramble aboard, and props or shores tucked under the rubbing strake or sponson may be necessary to stop her falling sideways when people are moving around on deck. A ladder will also be necessary to provide access to the deck.

CAREENING

This is the oldest method used for cleaning a boat's underwater areas, and dates back to the earliest days of shipping when hoists and slipways were not available. With the older sailing ships it was known as 'hauling down' as the hull, once landed on the bottom and exposed by the receding tide, was hauled over onto its side to allow access to the underwater areas. A halyard, or some other rope secured high on the mast, was taken ashore and tied to a tree or some other convenient point, and winched tight. The ship was pulled down onto one side so that maintenance crews could get right underneath the hull.

Although big ships no longer practice this method of cleaning the underwater areas but instead use dry docks, careening is still used by many yachtsmen and other boat owners, particularly when the boat's bottom has become fouled and there is no marina or slipway within reach for pulling her out of the water. It is also, of course, a much cheaper exercise than hiring marina facilities. It is a simple process and one that can be used by any boat owner providing the tidal conditions are conducive. The boat has to be landed on the bottom in shallow water and propped up so that as the tide recedes, the underwater areas of the hull become accessible for cleaning and maintenance.

TIP: CAREENING IS ILLEGAL IN SOME COUNTRIES DUE TO ENVIRONMENTAL LAWS. CHECK WITH LOCAL AUTHORITIES BEFORE LANDING THE BOAT ON THE FORESHORE.

The only restriction is that work must be done between tides, which are roughly six hours apart at the top of each tide, although where there is a low rise and fall, the actual time the hull is clear of the water may be much less. Areas with a high tidal range and a sandy or muddy (not too muddy) bottom are ideal as they not only provide good working time out of the water, but also a soft landing for the keel. A wise precaution is to select a fairly sheltered position, for strong winds can blow the boat over when she is precariously perched on the keel with her entire hull out of the water.

Much the same precautions are required for careening as for supporting a boat on land. The ground must be level and able to support the keel evenly along its entire length. As mentioned, sand is good although a sandy bottom can be uneven in places. Mud is ideal, but not very pleasant to work in. If the bottom is not entirely flat it may be possible to place a few beams or chocks across the sand to level out the landing place and ensure that the keel has a good base on which to sit. These will also raise the keel off the bottom a little and allow maintenance work to be carried out underneath sections of the keel. Wood beams or railway sleepers are ideal for this if they are available, but if the boat

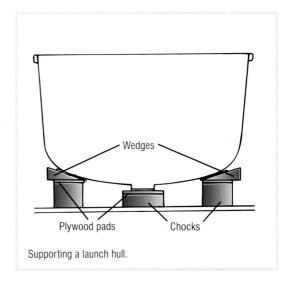

Supporting a launch hull.

Different shaped keels require
different support when careening.

is being careened in some distant creek or remote island, tree branches or rocks might be the only alternative. At all events, a smooth, even landing bed must be prepared at low tide and the boat secured into position over it prior to landing on it.

There are a number of different ways in which the boat can be careened. Tied up to a wharf or pier is a useful arrangement because the pier provides good support for the grounded vessel and holds her upright. It will be necessary to tend the mooring lines as the tide drops to keep her snugged up against the pier as the level of water falls and she takes to the ground, after which she can be securely tied to the pier. Some popular rivers and boat harbors have piles driven into the sea bed at spots which dry out at low tide and these can be used in the same way as the pier or wharf. Two piles are usually placed fairly close together to provide support for the boat, and mooring lines hold her against them while the tide drops. Flat bottom boats or boats with long flat keels, such as motor yachts, may be able to just sit on the bottom, although they will need some support to prevent them heeling onto the bilges when the water drops.

In remote areas where there are no maritime facilities, the boat must stand on her own, and once again this is fairly easy with flat bottomed or bilge keel boats, but can be a problem with a keel yacht. With no pier or piles to provide support, the boat will fall over on its side when the keel takes the ground and this can be disastrous, as the incoming tide will not be able to lift her and she will almost certainly fill with water before she floats. One system for preventing this is to use shores (sometimes called 'legs') or

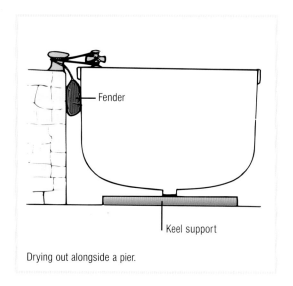

Drying out alongside a pier.

Make sure the hull is securely braced before the tide falls away, or the careening exercise can become a nightmare.

props on either side to hold the hull upright as the tide falls. At least two wooden props should be cut to a length a little longer than the height from keel to gunwale. As the tide drops and the keel takes the ground on the prepared bed, the props are secured in place on either side to shore her up. When the water has fallen right away, an inspection will indicate if more props are needed to ensure that she is well shored up.

As mentioned, the one major drawback with careening is that the tide will return fairly soon so the time to work on the boat is restricted. By securing her firmly in position with mooring ropes, she can hold over the bed and thus land again with each ebb tide, but this will mean readjusting the props each time to ensure that she is held securely when she lands on the hard again. Fortunately, some anti-fouling paints can be wetted fairly soon after being applied, so if a program is worked out whereby the hull is scraped, cleaned and repaired on one low tide, and the anti-fouling put on quickly before the last rising tide, careening can be as successful—albeit a little more staggered—as the same job carried out on a commercial slipway.

ANTI-FOULING PAINTS

Without doubt the underwater areas of a vessel require more maintenance than any other section. This is partly because of the constant attack by marine growth on any

Boats with retractable keels can be
landed on shore or taken out of the
water on a trailer.

immersed surface, and also because some types of anti-fouling use a 'wasting' action which reduces the thickness of the anti-fouling consistently and it therefore has to be replaced at regular intervals. This is quite a normal procedure and since the amount of anti-fouling removed is small, the need to repaint will not occur for some months. The wasting takes place all the time but can be exacerbated by the movement of the boat through the water. This is not a bad thing because each time a layer of anti-fouling is washed away, a fresh coat appears to ensure that marine growth still cannot attach to the hull. There is a running argument among sailors as to whether using the boat is good or bad, from an anti-fouling point of view. One argument says that using the boat washes away the top layer of anti-fouling and therefore shortens its effective life, the other says that leaving the boat stationary on the mooring reduces the potency of anti-fouling because new biocides are not coming through as the old is not being washed away.

TIP: TRAILERED BOATS DO NOT NEED ANTI-FOULING AS THEIR TIME IN THE WATER IS INSUFFICIENT TO ATTRACT MARINE GROWTH.

There are two main types of anti-fouling composition—the 'eroding' type and the 'hard' anti-fouling. As the name denotes, the eroding type tend to lose layers of the paint, exposing new layers of fresh biocides to withstand the attack of marine growth, while the 'hard' or ablative products, again as the name denotes, can withstand the washing action of water passing the hull, and indeed can be scrubbed without affecting the performance. The hard anti-fouling is particularly useful for high speed or racing vessels as not only does it withstand the effect of the water washing past at speed, but it can be cleaned by rubbing off any slime or growth without reducing the thickness of the coating, thus enabling racing craft to have a spotlessly clean and polished hull each time they race. Its anti-fouling properties come from the fact that the hard surface is porous and packed with biocides which leach out on contact with water and prevent marine growth from attaching to the hull.

There is a school of thought, mainly among cruising skippers, that some hulls, particularly steel, aluminum and fiberglass hulls, do not need frequent anti-fouling but can simply be scraped clean at intervals. Speed is not the object with such craft and the reasoning is that since these synthetic or metal hulls can withstand the damaging effect of borers or other such water borne pests, the only problem created by marine growth is a reduction of speed, and this can be overcome by scraping off. To a certain extent this may be true, but over a long period of time certain types of marine fouling can damage the substrate of a fiberglass hull, and rust or corrosion can set in on a metal hull. However, there is no question that anti-fouling is essential for wood boats. Teredo worms, unless checked, can literally eat away the planking of a wood boat. A heavily encrusted boat will sit lower in the water and therefore respond more slowly to

A clean underwater surface means maximum performance.

maneuvers, increase fuel bills and compromise the safety of the boat in heavy weather conditions, so a coat of anti-fouling paint is really a good investment with any type of craft.

MARINE FOULING

Different waters in different parts of the world, and even in different parts of the same coastal region, can experience different degrees of marine fouling. The main factors affecting marine growth are water temperature, salinity, pollution and even sunlight. Boats moored in fresh or brackish rivers will experience different degrees of growth to coastal harbors that are flushed by sea water each day. Climate changes such as excessive rainfall can also create different conditions of growth, as can the amount of use the boat gets. There are three principal forms of marine fouling that occur in most waters of the world:

Animal

Barnacles, coral and other marine animals, mostly in larval form, seek a base onto which they can cling while feeding on the nutrients that float around in the currents, and the most ready platform is the static hull of a boat. Marine worms feed on wood that is constantly immersed.

Weed

There are numerous forms of vegetation that live in the water and cling to static objects as seen by the appearance of rocks at low tide. If a boat remains in one place for long,

Coral creates a crust around the hull that slows the boat and is hard to remove.

it is certain to attract marine weed of some type, even in colder climates.

Slime

Slime is caused by tiny single-celled algae which produce a syrupy-type medium in which they settle. Once established, they can grow quickly and create quite a thick layer, which does not wash off when the hull moves through the water.

PREPARING AND PAINTING THE UNDERWATER AREAS

The first step in cleaning off the underwater areas is to remove any marine growth clinging to the hull, and this is best done as soon as the boat is hauled clear of the water. While it is still wet, slime, weed and a certain amount of barnacle and coral growth is much easier to remove than after it has dried out. A high pressure hose is the most useful cleaning tool initially, although a certain amount of care is needed to ensure that it does not also damage the hull. High pressure water can rip wood fibers from planking and gouge caulking, tear off loose or damaged fiberglass and damage weakened areas of gel coat, so unless the hull is in top shape, the water jets should be used sparingly. However, there is no question that this is one of the more labor-saving methods of getting rid of marine growth clinging to the hull, and when combined with a scraper for the more stubborn fouling, should clean the underwater

The scourge of wood boats, marine worm can literally eat its way through a wood hull skin.

areas to the point where a moderate hand sanding will prepare the surface for a new anti-fouling coat.

TIP: TAKE CARE WHEN USING A POWER SANDER TO REMOVE OLD ANTI-FOULING AS A TOXIC DUST WILL BE FORMED THAT CAN BE DANGEROUS WHEN INHALED. USE WET HAND SANDING WHERE POSSIBLE.

If the composition of the old anti-fouling already on the hull is not known, it is probably best to remove it completely before repainting with a new anti-fouling product. Unless the new is compatible with the old, it is likely to blister or flake off while in use. Similarly, any old anti-fouling that is in poor condition must be removed and bare spots touched up with primer before the new coat is applied. Aluminum hulls and fittings must not be anti-fouled with products containing copper as corrosive electrolytic action will be set up between the two dissimilar metals. In some parts of the world, marine authorities prohibit the use of certain anti-fouling materials on environmental grounds.

Since anti-fouling can create problems because of these factors, it is always best to check with the manufacturer of the paint to ensure that it is compatible with the hull and the use for which it is intended, and with waterway authorities to ensure that it is environ-

Tough marine growth that cannot be washed off with high pressure water will need to be scraped or sanded off.

mentally safe. International Epiglass provide an excellent advisory service offering advice on all types of marine paints and paint problems including anti-fouling products. Another factor that must be taken into consideration is the drying time for newly painted underwater areas, for some anti-fouled hulls need to be immersed in the water soon after painting, while others need the paint to be dry. If the job is not done correctly, the anti-fouling is likely to peel off with use and that means not only an immediate attack by marine growth and a costly repainting job, but also the chore of having to pull the boat out of the water again.

Apart from the mess, the toxic chemicals in anti-fouling composite make it essential to wear protective clothing when sanding off the hull.

When the marine growth has been removed and the hull cleaned off, the condition of the hull should be checked for damage or any flaking areas of the previous anti-fouling. Then the surface can be sanded off with a wet and dry abrasive, keeping the surface wet to prevent dust developing. If there are any bare patches and the hull skin is exposed, a primer will be required before the anti-fouling coat is applied. At least two coats of primer followed by at least two coats of anti-fouling will

High pressure water hoses make relatively light work of cleaning the underwater areas providing the growth is removed before it has dried.

be necessary to give the hull good protection; in waterways where heavy growth is experienced, even three coats may be necessary.

Anti-fouling paint can be applied with a brush, roller or spray gun, although spraying requires the use of special equipment. Before commencing the paint job, check that the new paint is compatible with the old and stir it thoroughly, for the heavy compounds in the mixture often sink to the bottom of the can. Probably roller application is best, especially where there are large areas to be covered, although a brush will be necessary for curved areas and corners, as is the case with any type of roller painting. Because of its thick consistency, the composite is often quite heavy and painting can be tiring on the arms when two or three coats are required. The appearance is not critical because the finish will be underwater and will not be seen, but it is important that all areas of the hull receive a good thick coating, especially any areas where high turbulence may be experienced, such as the leading and trailing edges, the keel, waterline and rudder. These are areas where the extra flow of water causes faster eroding of the anti-fouling material.

Propellers and sometimes rudders may need special treatment as the nature of their action tends to wear the anti-fouling more rapidly than on the hull. A number of coats of hard anti-fouling after several coats of primer, to give it a good bond, is the best method to follow. Sacrificial anodes must not be painted as this will interfere with their ability to provide protection against galvanic action, similarly, some manufacturers do not like their depth sounder transducers heavily coated as this may interfere with transmission and reception of the sonic wave. A very important factor in achieving good results with any anti-fouling paint is to ensure the right immersion time when the job is completed. In all cases follow the manufacturer's instructions as these vary from brand to brand and even within the same brand from paint to paint.

TIP: THE CORRECT COLOR OF THE ANTI-FOULING PRODUCT WILL NOT APPEAR UNTIL SOME WEEKS AFTER THE BOAT IS BACK IN THE WATER.

A badly fouled hull slows the boat's speed and increases the fuel bills.

Putting the boat back in the water simply means a reversal of the docking or slipping procedure, and will be handled by marina staff if the work is done in a boat yard. Floating off the boat when careened should not be difficult either, although it is important to ensure that she is properly afloat before removing the shores. If she is still standing on the keel when the props are removed, she is liable to heel over and damage the bilge, a mishap which can be particularly disastrous with a keel yacht, since she may fall right over onto her side and fill with water before there is any chance of floating her.

Cleaning up painting tools can be an onerous chore after slipping as anti-fouling paint is a thicker, heavier mix than most paints. The cleaning medium will be indicated on the paint can and may vary between water, mineral turpentine and

Ideal for applying a thick coat of anti-fouling over the large underwater surfaces, rollers have become a favorite tool on slipways.

thinners. Many boat owners consider anti-fouling brushes and rollers beyond restoring for use with other paints and simply clean them as best they can, keeping them for future use only with anti-fouling.

CAULKING AND SPLINING A WOOD HULL

The caulking material, usually cotton or oakum, is firmly hammered into the seams.

Anyone who has owned an old, planked wood boat will know of the problems with leaking through hull planks. Even new carvel or clinker boats can run into leaking problems, but it is mostly the older, well used craft that are at risk, where the wood in the hull skin has either dried out and opened up, or become saturated, or else been stressed and strained in use. Vibration from a motor can cause leaking seams in a motor boat while the stresses passing down the mast and rigging into the hull, when under sail, can also strain the planks and allow access to the sea. Since most older boats have chainplates secured to the hull planking, it is obvious that the stress of holding the mast up under a press of sail will sooner or later work the fastenings or the planks to the point where they are no longer watertight.

Another common cause of leaking planked hulls is grounding. No hull is meant to be supported unevenly and grounding on an uneven bed, quite apart from any physical damage, will stress the planks to the point where the caulking is moved and leaks will appear. In small boats the problem can appear through keeping the boat out of water, for the planks shrink when dried out, and although they may swell again and close the gaps between the planking when returned to the water, there is still a strong chance that the planks will not close completely and the water will get into the hull.

Whatever the reason, it is a fact of life that an old planked hull will be liable to leakage problems which no amount of paint or putty will cure. There are, however, two methods which, if properly carried out, can considerably reduce, if not totally prevent any leaking through the planking seams. Caulking is the usual procedure carried out when a carvel hull boat is built. Splining may also be used in the construction of the hull, but more often it is carried out on old hulls to cure serious leaking problems. Caulking uses a soft material, such as cotton, forced between the planks and sealed with some form of composite. Splining follows the same procedure but involves the use of a shaped wood strip (spline) forced between the planks and glued into place.

TIP: IT IS ESSENTIAL THAT CAULKING AND SPLINING SHOULD BE DONE WITH THE HULL COVERED AS ANY DAMPNESS WILL SWELL THE PLANKS AND REDUCE THE EFFECTIVENESS OF THE WORK.

Before commencing new caulking it may be necessary first to remove old caulking; much depends on where the leaking is located. If it can be pinpointed to one section of a seam it may be possible to just caulk that section and marry it to the old caulking still in place on either side. If the leaking is widespread, the old caulking will need to be removed and replaced with new. Cotton is probably the best caulking material and this can be obtained in strands, one end of which is pushed into the end of the seam. A caulking tool, which is not unlike a narrow hammer, is used to hammer the caulking home firmly into the seam, working along the seam and hammering the cotton caulking hard into the seam until it is below the level of the planking. When the full seam or the repaired length has been caulked, the seam is sealed with a glue compound. Since there

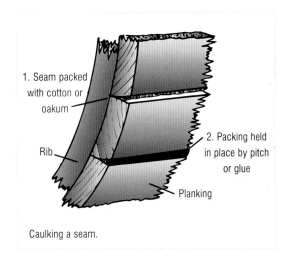

1. Seam packed with cotton or oakum

2. Packing held in place by pitch or glue

Rib

Planking

Caulking a seam.

Caulking hammer and iron.

are many types of compound available, and new products are being released all the time, the advice of the marina or chandler should be sought on which to buy.

Splining uses a shaped and fitted strip of wood hammered between the planks to prevent leaking. It is rather more involved than caulking but many wooden boat

owners believe it is more permanent and more secure than using caulking cotton. In this case all the previous caulking will need to be removed and the seams between the planks shaved and shaped to match the shape of the spline. The most common is a simple 'v' in which the edges of the planks must be bevelled back with a chisel to create a 'v'-lie seam which matches the bevelled edge of the wood strip. This is the critical part of the operation for unless the spline fits snugly into the seam with edges fitting snugly, the job will not be totally successful. Of course, a complete match will be a practical impossibility, but modern glues can usually fill small gaps that might occur here and there.

Once the planks and spline are prepared, a good marine glue is applied to the edges of both and the tapered spline hammered into the seam. If the job has been done well, the result will be a totally waterproof seal which must be left to cure, then the excess spline planed away flush with the hull of the boat. Treatment of the underwater section of the hull will

take care of any leaking while the boat is static, although some owners like to spline the whole hull to give full waterproofing at all times. Needless to say, this procedure also adds greatly to the strength of the hull. Primer and a coat of polyurethane will finish the job and restore the hull to its original condition.

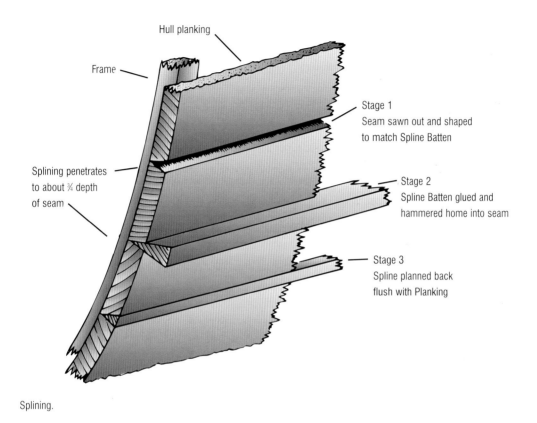

Hull planking

Frame

Stage 1
Seam sawn out and shaped
to match Spline Batten

Splining penetrates
to about ¾ depth
of seam

Stage 2
Spline Batten glued and
hammered home into seam

Stage 3
Spline planned back
flush with Planking

Splining.

THE UNDERWATER FITTINGS

With the boat out of the water it is an opportune time to check everything which is not normally visible: the underwater fittings. Since protrusions from the underside of the boat tend to create drag and slow the boat, there are usually only a minimum of essential fittings, but all are important and must be checked while there is an opportunity to examine and, if needs be, service them.

THE PROPELLER

The propeller is a vitally important part of the boat's propulsion unit, and it can be vulnerable to a number of problems, not least of which is galvanic action. Propellers are often made from brass or bronze while the shaft is made of steel, and here is the classic situation where dissimilar metals immersed in an electrolyte set up an electrical current

Underwater metal fittings, such as the propeller, must be protected from galvanic action. Note the sacrificial anode adjacent to the shaft.

which eats away the anodic metal, in this case the bronze, with galvanic action.

Any galvanic action in this area will almost certainly result in the propeller becoming severely pitted as it is eaten away, and unless prevented, will reduce its efficiency to the point where, theoretically, it could disintegrate altogether. This is prevented by placing on or near the propeller a 'sacrificial anode,' which is usually a bar of a more vulnerable metal such as zinc, which attracts the electrical current away from the propeller. Gradually the galvanic action eats away the zinc bar until it is totally destroyed—hence the name 'sacrificial'. One of the most important tasks when inspecting the propeller is to ensure that these zinc anodes are in place and if almost eaten away, replace them with new ones, thus preventing galvanic damage to the propeller blades.

This picture illustrates the destructive effect of galvanic corrosion.

The propeller, shaft and stern tube can only be checked and maintained when the boat is out of the water.

Physical damage can also affect the performance of a propeller, and it is not uncommon to find, when the boat is pulled out of the water, that a blade may be chipped or bent as a result of hitting something in the water. If the damage is slight, it may be possible to file it smooth—the propeller is cast so it cannot be straightened—but if it is serious, the propeller must be removed and taken to a workshop to be ground out. Outboard motors, because of their high speed revolutions, are vulnerable to propeller damage from striking objects in the water, or striking the ground when running onto a beach. They are easily removed and either repaired or replaced.

THE SHAFT AND STERN GLAND

Repacking the stern gland is mentioned here because it is directly associated with the propeller shaft. It is not usual to 'draw' a propeller shaft unless some physical damage has bent it or there is some problem that requires it to be machined. Since the only time that this can be done is when the boat is out of the water, checking the shaft falls into the inspection routine for any underwater fittings and in particular those in the propeller area. Although it will vary from boat to boat, most propellers are attached to the shaft with a large nut and a spline key at the outboard end and with a flange at the motor end. It may or may not be necessary to remove the shaft to repack the gland; preventing excess leaking can usually be fixed by tightening the nut on the stuffing box.

If the shaft has to be drawn, the nuts on the inside flange must be undone and the flange taken off, then the shaft slid backwards through the stern tube until it is clear of the boat. The nut on the shaft must then be removed, taking care not to lose the spline key, at which point the shaft should be free and ready for the workshop. The stern gland and stern tube are both readily accessible with the shaft and propeller out of the way, so it is a good time to check the bearings and the stuffing box.

RUDDER FITTINGS

Most modern rudders are blade or balanced rudders projecting down through the bottom of the boat where they are secured by collar or bearing. This is usually accessible from the deck or cockpit, or in the case of motor boats, through the after hatches. Older craft, especially some older yachts, still mount their rudders on pintles which again are usually visible from the deck level, even though they may be partly under water. As a result, checking the rudder mountings while the boat is out of the water is a fairly routine task and any wear and tear or damage should be readily visible.

ELECTRONIC FITTINGS

The main underwater fittings for electronic gear are the pods for sounder and sonar, if fitted, and the impeller for the speed and distance indicator. These come in a variety of shapes and sizes and there is little that needs to be done when the boat is out of the water other than check for physical damage—especially if an impeller is used for the speed log. It is wise not to coat these fittings too heavily with anti-fouling composition as it can impair their function, indeed some manufacturers insist that depth sounder transducers are not painted at all on the bottom, so it would be worth checking to make sure which applies.

Other underwater fittings are mostly water intakes or discharges for servicing motors, ancillary engine gear, galleys and toilets. They should be examined to see that skin fittings and strainers are clear and clean before being anti-fouled.

LAYING UP THE BOAT FOR WINTER

Although boats in tropical and sub-tropical climates may be in use all year round, in most countries winter time is lay-up time. All boats require maintenance at some stage in the year and whether this is done in summer or winter is immaterial. But since most boat owners prefer to use their boats to their fullest extent in summer, it is during winter that most come in for maintenance and overhaul. A good place to do this is on the slipway or shore where the boat can be landed for a few weeks or, if the climate makes it necessary, for the whole winter. Laying up is not an idle time for boat owners, indeed, where the winters are fairly short, it can be a hectic time getting the boat cleaned up and maintained ready for the next season.

The hull must be carefully braced and supported so that it will not suffer distortion during the long winter lay-up period.

In climates where winter fishing, sailing and other boating activities are out of the question and the boat will not be used for some time, it must be prepared for the lay-up otherwise the equipment will deteriorate while out of action. Engines, for example, thrive on work and deteriorate rapidly when left idle for long periods, so if they cannot be started and run during the winter lay-up period, then steps must be taken to prevent corrosion and other destructive influences from taking place. Details on laying up motors is provided in Chapter 10 of this book.

Sails, masts, spars and paintwork can also suffer problems during lay-up and all need some sort of preventative treatment if they are to be in good shape for the next season. Usually, the laying up procedure is run in conjunction with the winter maintenance work, so there will always be someone working around the boat to keep an eye on things and watch for any deterioration. If, as is the case in regions where winters are severe, the boat will be for the most part totally closed up and laid up, then the following steps are the minimum for keeping the boat in good shape through the cold period:

1. Take ashore all linen, clothing, blankets, curtains, etc. and send them to the laundry or dry cleaners before stowing them somewhere warm and dry. Also take ashore all crockery, cutlery and domestic items as well as any food and drink left aboard from the previous season.

2. Remove and store ashore sails, ropes, dodgers, gas cylinders, batteries, navigational instruments, charts, safety gear, boathook, anchors and deck gear. Check each item for signs of deterioration then stow somewhere clean and dry.

3. Vacuum and if necessary wash lockers, cup-boards, etc., with special attention to the galley area. Wash down all painted and fiberglass surfaces and allow to dry. Spray the entire interior with deodorant or air freshener, leaving the boat closed up overnight for these to work.

4. Pour a detergent or de-greaser into the bilges, pump out then repeat with fresh water. Ensure that all areas in the lower section of the hull are clean and dry. Open up portholes, ventilators, etc. on fine days to air the boat thoroughly. If the boat has to be permanently closed up without ventilation, place moisture-absorbing crystals at points around the interior.

5. Check the deck gear for anything that may need lubricating or covering against severe weather, such as winches, windlasses and cockpit instruments.

It is important to provide total protection from the weather for the laid-up boat, but equally important to allow good circulation of fresh air.

Where winters are particularly severe, it is often preferable to store the boat permanently on shore. Small boats can be easily put on a trailer and run into a garage or storage barn. But most larger craft must be stored in the open with covers to protect them from the wind and weather. This is no real

Like other parts of the boat, motors
need careful attention prior to laying
up for the winter.

problem and providing the covers are adequate and correctly secured to keep the water out, they should be sufficient to protect the boat through the harshest of winters.

What can be a problem, however, is storing the boat on land for a long period of time. A boat is designed to be supported by an even pressure of water around her entire underwater hull area. Out of her natural element and propped up in a cradle or with chocks, the hull can be subject to stresses and strains, especially hot spots, which her hull was not designed to take. This is a particularly serious problem with fiberglass hulls, where prolonged pressure from incorrectly placed supports can result in the hull becoming distorted.

It is important that good support is given to areas subject to heavy weight, such as the keel, motors and the overhangs of bow and stern. Where the vessel has a broad beam, such as with motor boats, support under the bilges is vital to prevent the hull sagging. Ideally a cradle that supports the hull in a number of places is the way to avoid most problems; chocks may be fine for a brief period, but over a long time these can apply serious upwards stresses and hot spots where they hold up the hull.

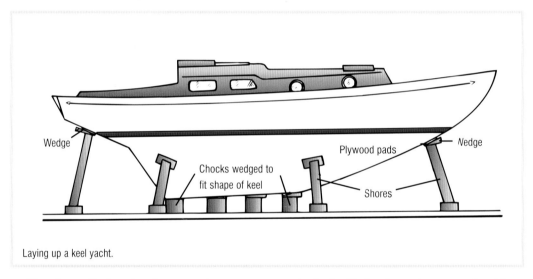

Laying up a keel yacht.

Good ventilation is also very important, particularly if the boat is covered with a 'cocoon'-like overall cover. Fresh air must be allowed to circulate through the boat otherwise condensation will form and result in a wide range of problems, from dry rot to mold to all kinds of corrosion. It is wise to land the boat so that she is slightly down by the stern, as this will ensure that rainwater will run off straight away and not lie in puddles where it might eventually seep into the interior.

12

The main causes of maintenance problems

The term 'maintenance' can cover a multitude of sins, since the factors which cause maintenance can be many and varied. Physical damage as a result of an accident, wear and tear due to constant use, weather effects and the ravages of the sea are just some of the causes, and there are others, some of which could be 'localized' to a specific geographical area, such as a polluted waterway, or result from a specific usage. For this reason it would be very difficult to encompass in one book all the main causes of maintenance problems.

Running aground can create major maintenance problems.

Most maintenance problems are related to the type of material from which the boat is built. Wood is the most susceptible, with fiberglass and metal less vulnerable, but which nevertheless have their own unique problems. Other factors can create or retard the need for maintenance, such as the degree of care given the boat when in use. A boat which is kept under cover most of the time is less likely to suffer from the ravages of the weather than a boat which swings to wind and tide and which is constantly exposed to the elements. A boat which is kept out of the water will not require anti-fouling. And motors which are run regularly are always less prone to problems than those which are merely turned over once or twice during the winter lay-up period.

So although there is always maintenance of some kind required, no matter what material the hull is constructed from and no matter whether the boat is permanently in the water or kept in the garage for most of the year, the cause and cure of these problems can vary considerably. It is not possible to cover all such problems in a book of this nature, but the principal causes of maintenance problems and how they can be countered, are covered here.

OSMOSIS

Osmosis is a 'disease' of modern fiberglass boats; mostly those which are permanently kept in the water. Usually it occurs when water enters the structure of the fiberglass through the gel coat or is previously trapped inside during the lay-up process. The water reacts with chemical components in the manufactured hull, creating pressure spots which cause blisters beneath the gel coat. Such blisters, if left untreated, may eventually crack and this allows ingress of even more water and eventual destruction of the hull. Impurities in the laminate or gel coat will sometimes result in osmosis in fairly new hulls and this becomes obvious within two or three years of the boat being launched.

TIP: WATER CAN ALSO CREATE OSMOSIS FROM THE INSIDE OF THE HULL. BILGE WATER CAN CREEP BY CAPILLARY ACTION INTO THE LAMINATE AND THROUGH TO THE GEL COAT WHERE THE BLISTERS FORM. KEEP YOUR BILGES DRY!

Older fiberglass boats suffer mostly as a result of being kept in the water and osmosis is more noticeable in boats kept in fresh water than those moored in salt water. This type of osmosis takes some time to develop as the water has to permeate through the gel coat and into the laminate so that boats which are taken out after use, either on a trailer or propped up on land, are unlikely to suffer this problem. However, another form of osmosis is caused by incorrect laying up of the hull in the mold, or laying up under humid or similarly unsuitable drying conditions. The locked-in moisture may take some time to appear as blisters, but sooner or later it will make their presence known, and if the hull has been kept in the water such problems may be exacerbated.

The area affected is mostly the section of the hull below the waterline, and since many anti-fouling paints are permeable they do not offer any protection from osmosis. Unless treated at an early stage, the water in the osmotic blisters can spread throughout the lamination of the hull GRP causing serious, even terminal damage; at worst the hull can begin to delaminate. Modern gel coat resins are more resistant to osmosis, although it is still not unknown even in quite recently built craft. Among other things the quality of the resin used will have an effect on whether or not a boat is affected and to what extent, so if the boat is new and has not been in the water for long, the boat builder may need to have some answers ready. But whatever the cause, it is a wise precaution to check the surface of the hull each time the boat is hauled for underwater maintenance to ensure there is no sign of the insidious plague developing.

The most obvious signs of osmosis infection is the appearance of blisters on the gel coat surface or under the anti-fouling. These may be small, and indeed may merely be blemishes resulting from poor manufacturing practices, but all blisters should be treated as suspect and tested to determine whether or not osmosis exists. Pricking the blisters with a pin will allow the fluid inside to run out. The osmosis fluid is quite distinctive, having a pungent odor and a greasy or sticky feeling when rubbed between the fingers.

The only cure for osmosis is fairly dramatic; the blisters must be ripped open and the trapped water released. This is done by sanding back the gel coat or in serious cases, peeling or 'blasting'—a job for professionals. The hull must then be extensively washed and dried to ensure that the pockets created by the osmosis are completely clean and dry, as well as drying out the laminate in the surrounding area where dampness may have seeped through capillary action. Hot air fans, heat lamps or any form of drying heat— but not, of course, naked flames—should be used for some period of time to make quite certain that the hull skin is absolutely dry, for when the repair job is done, any moisture still trapped in the cavities will create a weakness behind the new skin and lead to another bout of osmosis. The drying process may take some weeks, even months, depending on what heat is applied; a suitable moisture meter will indicate the remaining presence of any moisture in the laminate.

With the cavities, the adjacent laminate and the gel coat around the infected area completely dry, the damage must now be repaired. The pockmarked cavities must first be checked for total cleanliness and the surrounding areas sanded back and treated with a solventless epoxy prior to filling. Several coats of a solvent based epoxy primer will create a waterproof barrier over the 'wound,' which is then ready for the filler. As a general rule the damage is fairly limited and it will not be necessary to rebuild the laminate; a good epoxy filler will do the job adequately. If the cavity is large and needs fresh laminate to ensure a sound job, it is best turned over to the yard as this is a specialist job. The filler must be worked right into the corners of the cavities to ensure that there are no air bubbles trapped anywhere, and then allowed to dry, when the surface can be wet and dry sanded flush with the surrounding skin.

A further treatment with solvent based epoxy primer will create a second waterproof seal, after which at least four coats of good quality epoxy paint such as Interprotect will finish the job. The anti-fouling composition used on the underwater sections is not suitable on its own since, as mentioned, many anti-fouling paints are permeable and therefore the damaged area will not be fully protected. If the osmosis is confined to a limited area then localized treatment of the repaired sections, as described, will be sufficient before applying the new anti-fouling. If the osmosis has spread well across the hull, it may be worthwhile considering a total removal and repaint of the underwater skin to not only cure the current problem, but also prevent further osmosis.

TIP: THE USE OF A SOLVENT-BASED PRIMER CANNOT BE SEEN AS AN ALTERNATIVE TO THOROUGH DRYING OF THE HULL. WATER TRAPPED BEHIND THE PRIMER CAN LEAD TO THE OSMOSIS RE-OCCURRING.

DRY ROT

Contrary to most opinions, dry rot is not confined solely to wood boats. While wood is the material affected by dry rot, the problem can be found as much in wood fittings in small fiberglass power boats as it can in the hull of an older type of yacht. Indeed,

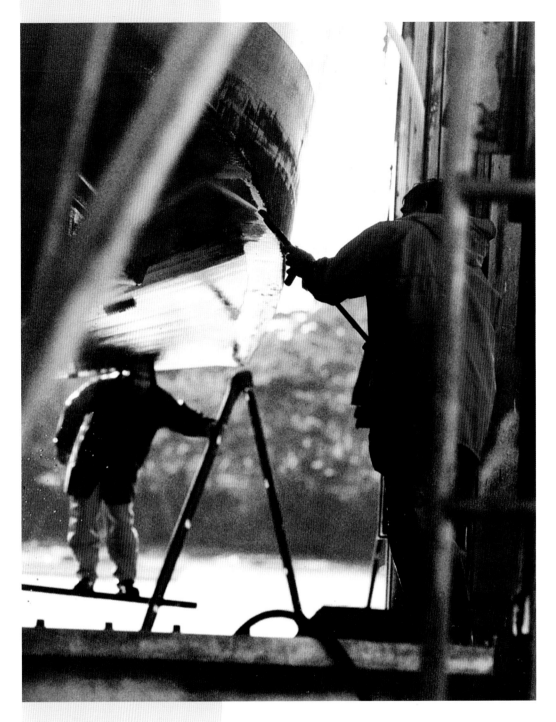

Osmosis blisters can best be seen
when the hull has been hosed off
and is still wet.

it is more likely to be found in fittings and furnishings, for dry rot depends more on dampness and humidity than it does from saturation by salt water. So much so that in the days gone by, when the decks were invariably made of wood, many skippers insisted on washing down each morning with salt water to decrease the risk of dry rot in the decks.

Dry rot is the deterioration of wood due to the growth of a fungus. The fungus is not readily visible to the eye and can therefore be hard to detect. Indeed, one of its most insidious features is that often by the time it is visible, it has created irreparable damage or damage requiring major surgery. Outwardly a piece of wood may appear untouched, but behind the pristine surface, the interior of the wood will have disintegrated into a powdery hollow which will collapse the moment it receives a blow or any strain is placed on it. Apart from the damage to fittings and furniture there is an obvious danger if dry rot attacks a structural member of the boat's hull. This is just one good reason why a surveyor should be called in before a second-hand boat is purchased; his skills (and hammer) can detect dry rot problems which may be totally concealed to the inexperienced eye.

Dry rot may not become apparent until the outer surface of the wood has been removed.

The mold created by the fungus may give off a distinctive, musty odor and it is this smell pervading the interior of the boat that can indicate the presence of dry rot, especially if the boat has been closed up for some time. To detect and locate

the dry rot, if it is not visible to the eye, a small hammer or tapping device can be used. By tapping the outside surface of the wood, a change in the sound will be detected, indicating the presence of dry rot. Prodding with a screwdriver or knife will reveal just where the soft patches are and how extensive the damage. The fungus will spread quickly unless treated, through spores given off and carried through the air until they settle on unaffected wood. Mostly, the rot begins in a moist, humid environment such as the interior of a closed boat where lack of ventilation allows the spores to disseminate through the unmoving air.

Rainwater is often the culprit, as dry rot is caused by fresh rather than salt water. A small boat that is trailered home and closed up with a cover while still damp after being out on a rainy day, or leaks in a cabin roof of a larger vessel battened down and left on a mooring—these are the sort of conditions which encourage the dry rot fungus to develop, especially if the ventilation is poor. It will grow on any piece of wood, be it the panel of a dashboard, interior furniture or the hull itself, and often the first indication of its presence is the collapse of the affected wood. Once it has taken hold it will most likely require surgery to remove it, and if it is not removed quickly it will spread through all the wood in the boat.

There is no cure for dry rot once it has gained a foothold, for the deterioration of the wood fibers is complete. The affected wood must be cut out and replaced with clean wood, which has preferably been impregnated with anti-fungus chemicals. Prevention is the only answer to this scourge, and it is always better than cure. By using treated wood initially, drying out the boat after a wet trip, and ensuring that it has a good flow of ventilation, the risk of dry rot developing can be minimized. This is particularly important in tropical or sub-tropical areas where the dampness and humidity of the wet seasons create ideal breeding conditions for the fungus. When in use, the air inside the boat will be moved around by the vortex action of the boat moving through the air and the wind blowing across doorways and hatches. But when tied up to the marina, swinging to a mooring, or wrapped under covers on a trailer, there is little movement of air and any dampness will encourage an attack of the dry rot spores. Adequate ventilation is the only answer.

WET ROT

Unlike dry rot, this problem is unlikely to affect fiberglass or aluminum boats, and indeed is mostly confined to wood vessels that are kept permanently in the water because for wet rot to exist the fibers of the wood must be permanently saturated, resulting in them disintegrating into a spongy mass. Any type of wood—but particularly the soft woods often used in boat building—left lying in water for a long period of time will eventually rot. When the hull of a boat is unprotected by suitable coats of paint or experiences permanent leaking in some area, the woods will eventually become saturated and rot will set in. Fortunately it is readily spotted and does not have the insidious nature of dry rot, and if caught early, can often be cured without any major effort. But if the wood continues to be saturated and the rot allowed to continue, it will eventually disintegrate.

Although it is fairly visible, some concealed areas of the boat, such as the bilges, may experience rot through being permanently damp and not checked. If the damage is severe, then the rot will need to be cut out and replaced by new wood, but in its early stages wet rot can usually be tackled by drying out the wet fibers and treating the wood providing its structure has not been weakened. Wet rot does not spread in the same way as dry rot, being mostly confined to the sections of wood that are saturated. It appears as a dark stain which will show on the surface from the time the wood first becomes wet, although it can be harder to spot when it creeps beneath a painted surface. But even then the signs soon become apparent as the paint begins to peel off and the adhesion between the wet wood and the paint is broken.

Prevention is again an important factor and the boat owner who checks his boat for any leaks, particularly rainwater leaks around hatches, at the deck line, or anywhere that rainwater might sneak in, will be ahead of the problem and spot any dampening of the wood before the rot has a chance to take hold. Maintaining an overall good paint coat and waterproof covers will also help ensure that any wood is kept dry and free from the risk of rot.

TIP: MODERN WOOD IMPREGNATION CAN OFTEN REDUCE OR PREVENT ROT. CHECK WITH YOUR WOOD YARD AS TO WHICH IS THE BEST WOOD TO USE FOR REPAIR AND FITTING OUT WORK.

PREVENTING CONDENSATION

No matter what the material of the hull and deck, when a few people sleep on board a boat, a problem arises with condensation. It is probably worse in metal or fiberglass boats than wood, but when the nights are cool and the hatches are closed (even partly) moisture gathers on the underside of the deck and the sides of the hull and runs down, often soaking bedclothes, furnishings and carpets. On warm nights when the hatches, doors and windows can be opened it may not be such a problem, but such nights are the exception rather than the rule other than in the tropics, and in any case, leaving hatches open all night is inviting an even worse problem when heavy rain or thunderstorms are in the vicinity.

But while dampness in bedding and furnishings can be an inconvenience, a far more sinister problem can arise when the boat is subject to frequent condensation, and that is dry rot. Dry rot thrives on damp, humid conditions, and nothing is more conducive to such conditions than a boat that has been subject to condensation. People sleeping on board is perhaps not as bad as keeping the boat totally covered for weeks on end while on a mooring or at a marina. The damp atmosphere inside the boat will condense into

Wet rot causes the fibers of the wood to disintegrate.

water on cold nights, and be fired up again during the day when the sun warms the topsides and deck areas. The cycle will lead to any wood in the boat becoming saturated with moisture and this can easily lead to dry rot.

The answer lies in good ventilation. If the boat is lying at a mooring, good ventilation is easy to achieve since she will weathercock (unless the tide is strong), and therefore always lie bow to wind. Ventilators can be set for this condition so a flow of air is maintained at all times, and this will either disperse the humidity inside the boat, or dry it out as soon as it forms. Berthed at a marina, this practice will also help keep the boat dry and ventilated, but she will not weathercock to the wind so some ventilators may need to be set in different directions to counter changes in wind direction. Big windows or large ventilators will help, but these are not always possible in small craft, particularly sailing craft where large hatches, doors or windows do not suit the structure of the boat.

A good cover will protect the boat but allow good ventilation to prevent condensation causing dry rot in the wood furnishings and fittings.

Big motor cruisers often have large welldecks with doors that are under an awning, and these allow a good flow of air without ingress of rain or any other water. But small power boats and sailing craft are by their very nature restricted to fairly limited openings and even with the hatches and doors ajar, there is often insufficient ventilation to

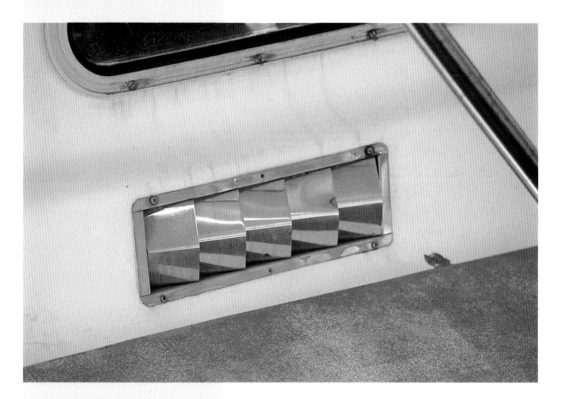

A neat stainless steel ventilator.

prevent condensation inside the hull. Ventilators are also small in these craft, so apart from rigging an awning over the cockpit which enables the main companionway to be left open, there is little that can be done to increase the ventilation when overnighting or when the boat is left at a marina berth.

Experienced boat owners who spend a lot of time sleeping on their boats find it is often worthwhile lining the interior with an absorbent paint composite. This is the system that has been used on large steel ships for generations and although more sophisticated air conditioning equipment takes care of the problem in most seagoing vessels these days, this is usually somewhat impractical and too expensive for small boat use. Anti-condensation paint is usually a composite of normal paint with granules of cork impregnated through it. When painted on the cabin sides the cork acts as an insulator, preventing the moisture-laden interior air from coming into contact with the cold side of the hull where it will condense. Materials other than cork can be used and the sides and ceiling of the cabin can be physically insulated with any type of insulating material, but for simplicity and low cost, the anti-condensation paint is hard to beat, yet quick and easy to apply.

STAINED OR FADED FIBERGLASS

A good quality gel coat will shed dirt and grime without too much effort and everyday marks should be easily cleaned off. However, a poor quality, aged or porous gel coat will

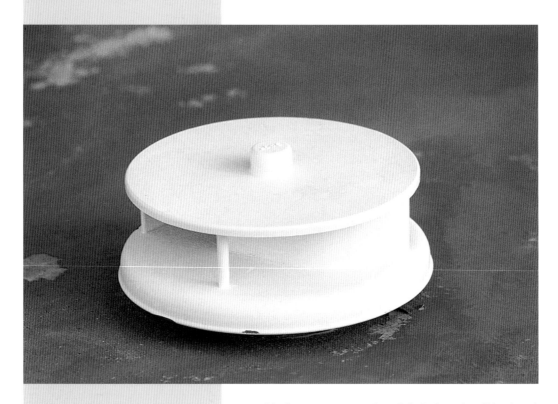

There is a wide range of ventilators available for small craft, most of which allow the passage of air but not water.

quickly become stained and faded and will be hard to keep clean. Much the same applies to a badly weathered gel coat where the effects of wind and sun have reduced the original gel to the point where it becomes stained. The UV effect of strong sunlight is particularly detrimental to the exterior appearance of GRP, while stains caused by contaminants such as oil and chemicals floating in the water, or in the atmosphere, are often hard to remove as they tend to permeate into the surface. All these factors contribute to the loss of appearance of a fiberglass hull and the yellowing or fading of colors.

TIP: FADED OR DULLED GEL COAT CAN BE RESTORED BY SPRAYING WITH A TWO-PACK EPOXY RESIN.

Cleaning a GRP hull and removing the day-to-day marks from a sound gel coat surface is simple and is dealt with on page 16 of this book. Attempting to remove heavy stains is not so easy, and can be impossible if the stain is badly impregnated into the hull skin. Sometimes frequent washing with detergent will remove oil that has adhered to the outside of the hull around the waterline, where most of the problems occur. Some fiberglass cleaners or laundry bleaches can be used, although care must be taken with these as the gel coat can be further damaged and if used, they should be washed off

Rust stains in the gel coat can be
hard to remove.

The great thing about small boats is that you can take them home in order to do any cleaning or maintenance chores.

immediately. With even more stubborn stains, thinners, acetone or carbon tetrachloride can be tried, but these are a last resort and must be used with great caution and immediately washed off after use, as they may compound the problem by creating stains of their own.

TIP: MOST FIBERGLASS STAINS ARE CAUSED BY CHEMICAL POLLUTION IN THE WATER OR THE ATMOSPHERE. IF POSSIBLE, AVOID KEEPING THE BOAT IN WATERWAYS SUBJECT TO THESE PROBLEMS.

When all else fails, it will be necessary to resort to abrasives such as cutting polish, scouring creams or even wet and dry sandpaper to remove stubborn ingrained stains, but this will result in surface damage and loss of the high sheen of the original gel coat. Much will depend on the type of polish used and this in turn will depend on how much the surface has deteriorated. A harsh 'cutting' polish will restore the appearance but skim off a thin layer of the gel coat and make it more porous in doing so. If the surface does not require such robust treatment, then a softer or less abrasive polish should be used. There are special fiberglass polishes available and these should be used after consulting the chandlery proprietor on which would be the most suitable for the job at hand. Car polishes can be used to the same effect as can some metal polishes, but it is important to check that these are compatible with fiberglass and are not too abrasive or they may create more problems than they cure. Once the gel coat becomes porous it is far more vulnerable to impregnation by the chemicals that cause discoloration and stains.

Having made the decision that the surface is too far gone for restoration without damaging the surface, it is time to bring in the cavalry in the form of a bath brick or wet and dry sandpaper. This is the last resort for stains and discoloration for it will mean a paint coat to restore the damage to the gel coat. However, if the hull is so badly stained that it has resisted all attempts to restore it, then the chances are it is going to need a paint job anyway. Unfortunately, this sort of damage is usually in a limited area, such as around the waterline, but it will necessitate painting the entire hull, since patches of paint on the damaged areas will not blend with the remaining surface and stand out, giving an appearance almost as bad as the discoloration. Some boat owners are prepared to live with the loss of the shiny gel, leaving the hull with a dull but clean surface, and the only problem with this is that the first harsh clean is the thin edge of the wedge, for losing the protective covering of the gel coat means that the hull will become more vulnerable to weathering and staining. A full paint job is the only real means of restoring the hull to its original appearance.

Colors in fiberglass, as in paint, tend to fade in sunlight.

LEAKS

DECK LEAKS

One of the most common and insidious problems in boats of all shapes and sizes, is a deck leak. Whether it is just through a weakened rubber seal of a hatch or damage from an accident, it needs to be fixed and fixed securely. Nothing is more aggravating at sea than having a steady drip of water in the cabin, saturating bunks and cushions and making life below decks uncomfortable. Apart from the obvious discomfort and the possibility of water getting into electrical equipment and ruining it, fresh water leaking into a boat where there are wood furnishings is liable to set up dry rot even if it thoroughly dried out on the surface. Fixing such leaks should, of course, be done before the boat puts out to sea. A boat bouncing around in a seaway is not the place to work on such problems, even if they are more apparent and the source more readily located in those conditions. A hose can usually be substituted for a sea in this case and a good wash down at the marina will soon indicate where the leaks are.

While aesthetically pleasing, laid decks, unless well maintained, are often subject to consistent leaking.

Although leaks are less likely in fiberglass and metal hulls than they are in wood hulls, nevertheless they can be experienced in any type of boat. Nothing is more aggravating or more difficult to fix than insidious leaks which are not

enough to endanger the boat, but sufficient to make the interior damp, the furnishings wet, short out light circuits or just generally make life below decks miserable. Hatch covers, by their very nature, are prone to leaks, as are mast collars, stern glands and other fixtures where there is an opening in the hull. Wood boats suffer most since joins, such as those in a laid deck, are vulnerable because the swelling of wood when wet, and shrinking when dried out, makes a permanent seal almost impossible.

Leaks are usually quite easily fixed since there are very effective sealing compounds available on the market today. But finding the source of the leak can be another thing, since leaks have a nasty habit of occurring in hidden spots, then running along and behind other fittings to make their presence known in some other part of the hull, often quite some distance from the actual leak itself. This is particularly the case with deckhead leaks, such as around hatch coamings and windows, or through laid decks where the water may be spotted running down the side of the boat a long way from the point where it gets in. So a degree of detective work is necessary, either making examinations and notes when the leak is active, or using a hose to simulate weather on the outside, while stalking the leak on the inside.

Deck leaks should not be a problem in fiberglass boats since as a general rule the hull is laid up in one piece, as is the deck, and then both are bonded together. If a leak does occur it could indicate a serious problem such as a crack in the laminate or

A damaged rubbing strake or sponson can cause leaking between the deck and the hull.

a break in the bonded join between hull and deck. Of course, it could indicate less serious problems such as a leak around a hatch coaming, ventilator or mast, but either way, the first step is to locate exactly where the leak is and determine whether or not it needs major repairs.

If the leak is under a wood trim, such as around the sponson, rubbing strake, toe rail or a hatch cover, the wood may need to be removed to get at the problem. While sometimes pumping sealer into the leaking area from the inside may solve the problem, a more satisfactory job will always be achieved by applying the sealer from the outside, since that is where the water will come from. Fastenings of wood trim sometimes work loose and if these are the cause of the problem, fixing the leak may simply be a matter of drawing the fastenings, filling the cavities with sealer and replacing the fastenings. But if the fiberglass has cracked either in way of the fastening hole or if the join between hull and deck is opening, it will be necessary to first fix the damage, and this will almost certainly mean removing the trim or sponson.

Filler is mostly all that is required to repair a minor crack in the gel coat and laminate, but a serious crack or significant damage may require the fiberglass structure to be rebuilt. Full details of carrying out either form of repair is provided in Chapter 2 of this book. When the repair has been carried out it will then need to be sanded back and restored to its original appearance. If it is under the wood trim, this will need to be done before the trim is replaced.

HATCH LEAKS

No matter how well a hatch is fitted, and no matter of what material it is constructed, under certain conditions it is likely to allow some water to get in. The join between the coaming and the hatch itself is very hard to seal against all the elements, particularly in boats which go offshore and experience big sea conditions. Not only is there the constant immersion in water, which can occur with sea or rain, but in a seaway when the boat takes a wave aboard, there is the impact of the water crashing against the hatch, which can force water through seals that are quite watertight under normal conditions.

Wood hatch covers are the most vulnerable because, as mentioned, there is movement in the wood itself as it swells when wet and shrinks when dry, but warping and other damage can also render fiberglass or metal hatch covers vulnerable. Indeed, it can be expected that in heavy weather even the most secure hatch cover could allow a little water here and there. If the hatch cover is old and worn or deteriorated, then the leak will probably be in need of immediate attention, possibly even before winter maintenance time, but certainly at that time when all hull openings must come in for attention, if the boat is to be dry and comfortable during her next season's work. Removable hatch covers can be taken ashore and obvious areas of damage or distortion sanded or planed or sections replaced to make them fit snugly.

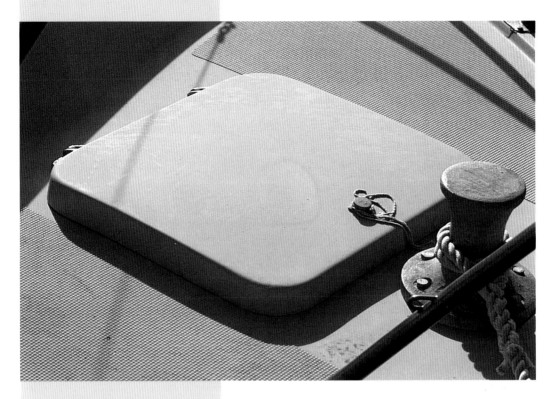

A tightly fitting hatch cover with a good seal should withstand most weather and sea conditions.

The coaming too, may need attention, particularly if the wear and tear of ropes and gear being hauled through it have worn grooves or chafed it out of shape so that it does not fit firmly into the hatch cover. When the best possible job has been done to reconstruct the shape of the coaming, a strip of rubber, about 1/4" thick should be glued around the top of the coaming (or if it is wide enough on top of the coaming), to provide a seal at the most vulnerable point. A second strip should be glued (and screwed if necessary) onto the deck tight up against the base of the coaming. When the hatch cover is landed and screwed up tight, it should then squeeze down on the two rubber strips and create as near to a watertight seal as is possible. A good strongback is a simple way of ensuring maximum pressure on the hatch to prevent leaks.

Sliding hatches are a nightmare as far as leak prevention is concerned. Their moving parts mostly prohibit rubber strips being used to seal

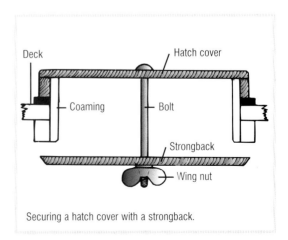

Securing a hatch cover with a strongback.

Like hatches, windows must have their seals carefully maintained if they are to keep the water out.

around the hatch, and similarly even sealant can only be used in places where there is no movement. Unless a sliding hatch has been made watertight when originally built, there is little that can be done to prevent any water getting in, and it is also difficult to repair the inevitable wear and tear which occurs when the hatch cover is constantly slid back and forth.

13

Vulnerable electrics

Modern leisure craft are equipped with a great deal of electrical equipment. Apart from the navigation instruments which can include Global Positioning Systems (GPS) radar, compasses, depth sounders and radio transmitters, most larger boats carry domestic equipment in the form of refrigerators, CD players, computers and television, even air conditioning. All of these can demand a considerable power supply, and allowance must be made when fitting out or equipping the boat not only for the electrical units themselves, but also for the power source that will service them. Most yachts and small motor boats will rely on batteries, with solar cells or wind charging gear, but most larger vessels are equipped with a full 120 or 240-volt supply from generators as well as the 12- or 24-volt supply from the batteries.

BATTERIES

Navigation systems rely heavily on a stable power supply, so a constant and reliable power source is essential. Since most small craft use 12- or 24-volt current, their supply comes from batteries. In any craft, but particularly in small boats, a bank of batteries is an important feature and needs careful maintenance if the power supply is to be maintained. Depending on the number of instruments, lights, heaters, and domestic appliances, a heavy drain may be placed on the batteries, especially when several units are running at the same time, so it is important to ensure that the number of batteries in the bank is sufficient to cope with the demand and also any excess which could arise if equipment, like bilge pumps, need to be used for any length of time. The marina electrician will advise on the number of batteries required to meet the needs of the equipment on board and these must be installed together with a main switch and fuse box. Spill-proof marine batteries should be used and the area in which they are located must be well ventilated to carry off any fumes or gases.

Maintenance of batteries usually only requires a regular check on the level of the electrolyte with an occasional check on its specific gravity. A hygrometer should be carried on board so that checks can be carried out wherever the boat is berthed or even when she is at sea. When a battery is charged for the first time it is filled with acid of the correct specific gravity, but due to evaporation when in use, the liquid in the cells is

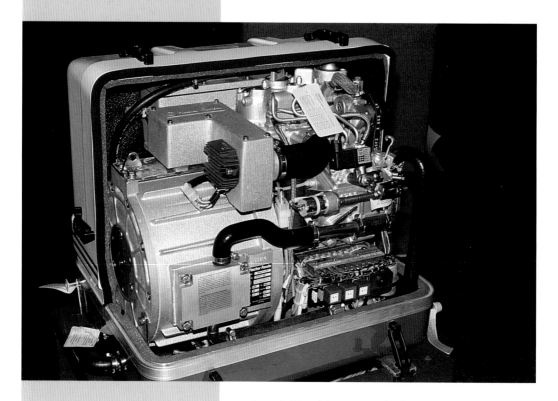

Portable generators are ideal as a small boat power unit and as a battery charger.

reduced. For this reason the battery should never be topped up with acid, but with distilled water to replace that lost during use. A container of distilled water to top up the batteries should be kept aboard, as topping up can be a quite frequent routine in warm climates. As a substitute for distilled water, rainwater may be used, but tap water should be avoided as it may contain chemicals which will affect the liquid already in the cells. Salt water must never be used. A reading of 1250–1280 on the hygrometer indicates a fully charged battery and a reading below 1150 indicates a discharged battery. Some hygrometers read off the state of charge against a color code in which, naturally, the red zone usually indicates a flattened battery.

The battery caps should be removed and the level of the liquid examined through the filler holes if there is no indicator system attached to the battery. The plates should always be covered by the electrolyte and any signs of the top of the plates appearing above the surface indicates the battery needs topping up. A jug or long spout, small watering can is useful for this job, and any liquid spilled on the battery should be wiped clean before it affects terminals and leads. A battery which is not in use will gradually lose its charge so a wise skipper will keep a spare battery fully charged and ready in case the main battery becomes discharged or collapses. A flat battery should be recharged as soon as possible; leaving it completely discharged for any length of time will cause the plates to deteriorate, making recharging slow and uncertain.

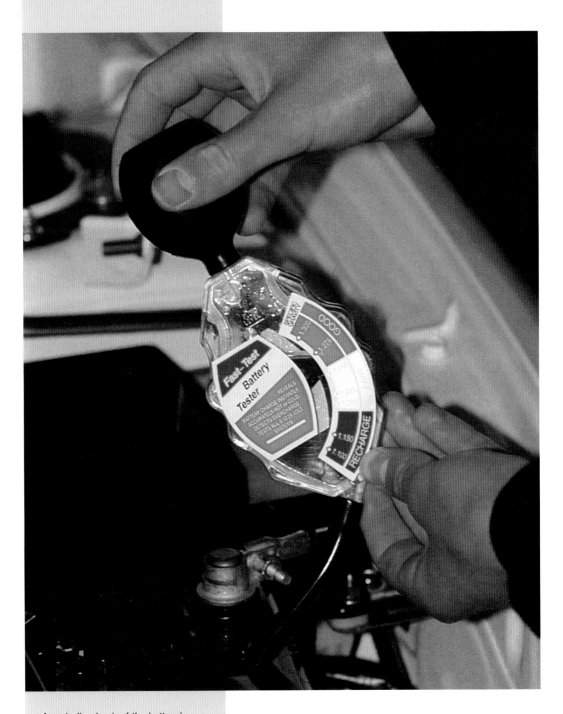

A periodic check of the battery's specific gravity with the hygrometer indicates whether or not it is holding its charge satisfactorily.

Apart from the electrolyte, attention must be given to keeping cables and terminals in good order.

The terminals should be kept clean and coated with Vaseline or grease to prevent corrosion, as the salt atmosphere on board a boat can play havoc with copper or brass fittings. The battery case can be cleaned using a solution of one pound of baking soda to five quarts of water. Rub this all over the battery case, but take care it does not get into the electrolyte. Cables must also receive attention since they are the main link between the batteries and the instruments or lights, and since they are made of metal, they are vulnerable to salt air corrosion. The wiring should be examined throughout the boat at maintenance time, with particular attention to the insulated covering of cables. Any cracked or chafed wiring should be replaced and any sign of deterioration in connections noted. In particular, areas such as where wiring penetrates through decks or bulkheads should come in for attention as the insulated covering of the cables can be worn or chafed in these spots. The fuse box, too, should be part of the maintenance check on batteries and wiring, for like any electrical fittings, it is subject to corrosion in the salt-laden atmosphere of a boat. Small, compact generators are available and easily installed if not already filled. These make ideal charging units for the batteries.

NAVIGATION LIGHTS

Because they are constantly exposed to the sun, sea and weather, and because they are often in a position where they are vulnerable to knocks or bumps, navigation lights can

Navigation lights must be checked during maintenance to ensure that the screening and range are correct.

come in for a lot of wear and tear in the course of a season of hard racing, cruising or fishing. It is an important part of the maintenance routine in the off-season to check out not only the wiring and bulbs, but also the alignment of the lights and their screens. This not only ensures that the boat will be readily seen at night and not give other boats a misleading signal as to which way she is heading, but also conform with maritime law and thus avoid the risk of a fine.

The basic requirements for navigation lights are simple; they must be of such a color and so screened that the light when seen from another vessel, gives a clear indication of the direction the boat is travelling and also indicates any special activity that may be taking place, such as anchoring. The colors follow the standard coloring for all navigational signals—red to port (left) and green to starboard (right). White is usually used as an all-round signal. Thus when two vessels are maneuvering at night, each will be able to determine what the other is doing and in which direction it is heading. On a dark night in a narrow channel this can mean the difference between passing safely and colliding.

TIP: IN SOME MARITIME COUNTRIES, NOTABLY PARTS OF THE USA, RED AND GREEN COLORS ARE REVERSED ON NAVIGATION BEACONS. HOWEVER, THE COLORS OF THE BOAT'S SIDELIGHTS REMAIN THE SAME THROUGHOUT THE WORLD.

The international regulations require all vessels under way to show the red and green sidelights, while vessels under power less than 50 m long must show a white light above the sidelights. Sailing vessels can carry their lights at the masthead or on deck or even on their pulpits whereas power boats usually carry their sidelights on deck and the white light on a short mast above the flybridge or cabin. There is no hard and fast rule as to location providing the screening and color of the lights conforms with the international rules. The screening of the lights is an important factor in maintenance, because as mentioned they can easily be knocked and sometimes displaced out of the correct alignment. A yacht which has her lights mounted on the forward pulpit, for example, will find them very vulnerable to misalignment by simply bumping a pier or pile with the pulpit while berthing. Maintenance time is the time to check these things.

The red and green sidelights are screened in such a way that they can be seen from right ahead to a point 112.5° down each side. The screens are usually part of the structure of the light, sometimes even part of the vessel, in which case they are less likely to be displaced. But when mounted on rails, or in rigging, or even on the side of the cabin, there is always the risk that a knock will push them out of alignment. The white light used when under power is carried above the sidelights on a short mast or cabin top. This light covers the same arc as the sidelights but illuminates both side of the vessel rather than just one side. In other words, the white light covers an arc from right ahead to 112.5° on both sides. Because of its high position, this light is less likely to be displaced than the sidelights.

A white stern light usually mounted on the transom, stern rail or rear of the cabin awning, completes the arc formed by the other lights. In other words it shines from right astern to 67.5° on either side. With this arrangement it becomes obvious to each vessel where it is in relation to another and which way the other is heading. Obviously, the correct screening is vitally important to the safety of the vessel.

CHECKING THE SCREENING

This can be done on the marina or against a pier—anywhere that the boat can be held firmly in position. There are many ways it can be carried out but probably the simplest is using the hand-bearing compass. The procedure is as follows:

1. Read off the heading on which the boat is secured.
2. Calculate the 112.5° bearing on, say, the starboard side of the boat by adding 112.5° to the boat's heading, and holding the hand-bearing compass over the light, sight up a prominent object on the shore not too far away that lies on that bearing.
3. Send one of the crew away to stand beside that prominent object and switch on the navigation lights. He should be able to see the green light at that point but if he moves to his left the light should disappear. The white steaming light over the green should also disappear and the white stern light should appear.

4. Repeat the exercise on the other side of the boat, subtracting the 112.5° from the boat's heading to get the port side bearing. This time the red light and the masthead light will disappear and the stern light appear as the observer moves to his or her right.

On small craft, of course, the screening can never be totally accurate, so a certain degree of tolerance will be necessary, but providing the screening produces a reasonably accurate cut-out of the lights when the observer moves off the bearing, it will be acceptable.

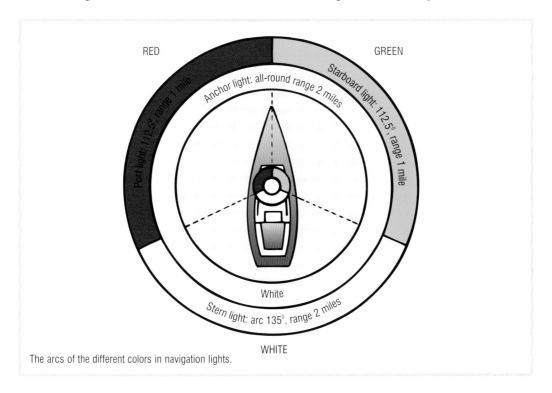

RED   GREEN

Anchor light: all-round range 2 miles

Starboard light: 112.5°, range 1 mile

Port light: 112.5°, range 1 mile

White

Stern light: arc 135°, range 2 miles

WHITE

The arcs of the different colors in navigation lights.

CHECKING THE WIRING

The wiring is the most vulnerable part of the navigation light system, particularly in old boats. In modern craft it is mostly sealed inside the outer skin of the boat or passed up the inside of the mast (in the case of yachts), but in older boats, where the wiring is taken outside to the lights, it can be subject to a lot of wear and tear. A visual check along the length of the wiring, where possible, is the only way to ensure that it is in good condition. Particularly check the insulation to see it is not worn, chafed or cracked, and check places where it passes through the deck or cabin to ensure there are no leaks. Damaged insulation will require replacing of the cable, but leaks can usually be taken care of with a plastic sealant.

CHECKING THE RANGE

This is a more difficult exercise and perhaps one that is not as essential as checking the screening. In boats between 39' and 164' (12 m and 50 m) in length the masthead light should be visible for 5 nautical miles, and for boats under 65' (20 m), 3 miles. The sidelights and stern light should be visible for 2 miles. For boats under 39' (12 m), the masthead and stern lights should be visible at 2 miles and the side lights at 1 mile in clear weather.

There is really only one way to check such ranges and that is in practice either with another boat or with a person on shore. However, it would be unlikely that the range of a light, providing it were burning brightly, would be sufficiently weak to attract the attention of the maritime authorities. And since a collision can only occur when boats are close to each other, a few feet in the range of a light should not make any difference to the risk with small craft. Assuming the lights, when fitted, were a reliable brand and specifically designed for the job, the best maintenance procedure to ensure that they show over the required range is to keep the glass clean and always use the correct bulb.

OTHER REGULATION LIGHTS

In day-to-day use, most small boats are likely to use only one other form of navigation light and that is the anchor light. This is an all-round white light which must be located high in the fore part of the vessel and be visible at a distance of 2 nautical miles.

TIP: NORMAL CABIN OR DECK LIGHTS SHOULD BE SCREENED TO PREVENT LIGHT THROWING FORWARD OF THE STEERING POSITION; THE REFLECTION ON THE FOREDECK CAN DESTROY THE HELMSMAN'S NIGHT VISION.

NAVIGATION EQUIPMENT

As one of the major safety factors on a boat, the navigation equipment must come in for regular checking, and no time is a better time than when the boat is in for winter maintenance and overhaul. The type of navigation gear can range from a basic magnetic compass to full electronic instrumentation including GPS and electronic charts. Every boat that puts out to sea must have a compass, and for offshore fishermen a depth sounder (also known as a fish finder) can be important to find the reefs or locate the schools of fish. Extended cruising along the coastline requires additional equipment in the form of charts (electronic or otherwise), a speed and distance log and perhaps radar, while boats heading out over the horizon on ocean-crossing ventures need the lot.

THE COMPASS

The basic navigational instrument, the compass, comes in a range of shapes, sizes and forms. Most boats carry a simple, liquid-filled magnetic compass although more elaborate craft may fit an electric (fluxgate) compass. The latter are very sophisticated instruments and outside the range of the average boat owner to service and maintain; a

After any maintenance work on board, the compass must be checked to ensure that the deviation has not changed.

specialist must be called in when they need servicing. But for the most part, the everyday magnetic compass can be serviced and maintained without the need for an instrument maker although much, of course, will depend on the make and sophistication of the compass.

The main problems that arise in the use of a magnetic compass are twofold:

1. Physical damage or wear and tear. A common problem that arises when the compass has been in use for some time is the appearance of a bubble in the damping fluid. This can upset the reading of the compass and must be removed. Some manufacturers make it easy for a handy person to do this by providing a filler cap on the underside of the bowl. The compass must be inverted and the screw cap removed, then the bowl topped up with the fluid specified by the manufacturer—usually an alcohol mix—until it is full to the brim, then the screw replaced and the compass bowl returned to its normal position. If the type of compass does not allow for topping up the fluid, it will have to be taken ashore to an instrument maker.

2. Other forms of wear and tear can be scratches on the glass, physical damage to the bowl or glass, or losing a needle from beneath the card. Problems of this nature require the attention of an instrument maker or the manufacturer as they are too technical to be handled by the average boat owner.

Accuracy of the compass is particularly important when navigating close inshore.

Magnetic errors can sometimes occur as a result of changes to the boat or its equipment since the original magnetic corrections were tabled, and these errors must be recalculated and the compass recalibrated or the errors drawn up in a new table. The principle error is known as 'deviation' and comes about because metal and electrical fields in the boat create a magnetic field which disturbs the compass and induces an error. For instance, loading the boat with cans of food and drink for an extended trip can cause deviation of the compass; the metal in the cans creates a magnetic force. Fitting a new winch or some other object close to the compass can also cause this error, as can changes in the wiring on the boat. It follows, then, that if the boat has been up for a winter overhaul and has had any extensive changes made to her fittings, a check of the compass is important to ensure that before the boat puts out to sea, there will be no deviation errors. Checking the errors and listing them in the deviation table is easy. Removing them from the compass requires an expert.

TIP: KEEP ANYTHING METAL OR ELECTRICAL (PORTABLE RADIOS, MOBILE PHONES) AT LEAST THREE FEET FROM THE COMPASS WHEN IN USE OR STRAY MAGNETIC FIELDS MAY AFFECT THE COMPASS.

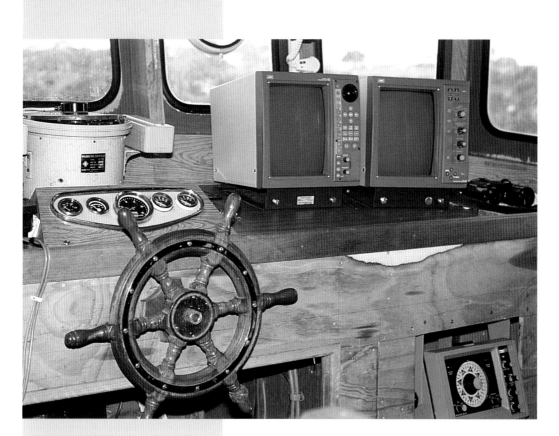

Maintenance time is a good opportunity to check and calibrate all electronic instruments.

Swinging for deviation

The procedure for checking deviation errors is simple, and easily handled by any boat owner. Specialist compass adjusters can be called in, and will be necessary if the compass is badly out of kilter or in need of major work, but the initial checking is not difficult and the errors can be compiled into a table. They can be removed from the compass, but this requires the services of a compass adjuster, so most boat owners simply compile a table of the deviation errors so that they can be applied to the compass when it is in use. The procedure, for checking and tabling the deviation, known as 'Swinging the Compass' is as follows:

1. Draw up a table with the major compass headings (the cardinal points are popular) in the first column, and leave the second column blank for the deviation encountered on each major heading.
2. Take the boat out into the water and line up two objects in transit (one behind the other) and obtain the magnetic reading of the transit bearing from a chart of the area. This is found by applying the chart variation to the true bearing read off the chart.
3. With the two objects in transit, set the boat's heading on North and read off the transit bearing on the compass. The difference between the bearing on the compass and the magnetic bearing is the deviation affecting the compass when on a North heading.

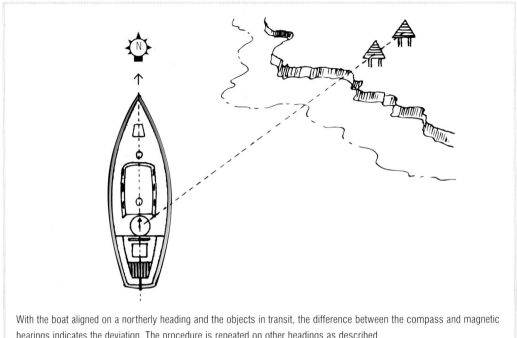

With the boat aligned on a northerly heading and the objects in transit, the difference between the compass and magnetic bearings indicates the deviation. The procedure is repeated on other headings as described.

4. Since deviation changes according to the direction in which the boat is heading, the procedure must be repeated holding the boat on the transit bearing and swinging her bow onto each of the cardinal points listed in the first column. The deviation obtained on each heading is listed against that heading on the deviation card.
5. The result will be a table of the deviation on all headings around the compass which is kept with the navigation gear for reference when the boat is at sea. As a general rule the deviation is not significant in fiberglass or wood boats, but metal boats, especially those with steel hulls, may encounter large deviation readings due to the magnetism in the steel. When this occurs, or for any case where deviation is high, a compass adjuster should be called in to reduce the deviation to manageable levels.

OTHER INSTRUMENTS

Electronic equipment such as the GPS (Global Positioning System) may need calibrating from time to time and this can be done at the end of any repair or major maintenance work and before the boat is taken out to sea again. A good time is immediately after the winter maintenance has been completed, when the boat is taken out onto the water to check compasses, motors and the like to ensure that the lay-up period has not caused any problems. As a general rule, maintenance, repair to and adjustment of any sophisticated electronic instruments should be carried out by a qualified person, although routine checks can be done by the boat owner to avoid calling in an expert unless there is a significant problem. Most charts and/or sailing directions

With so much electronic equipment
aboard, modern boats need a good
power supply and wiring system.

The sextant is still an important navigational instrument and must be checked and calibrated periodically.

provide a GPS check point close to the harbor entrance where the accuracy of this invaluable instrument can be checked to within a tolerance of around 300 feet or so.

TIP: NAUTICAL MEASUREMENTS ARE IN NAUTICAL MILES, NOT STATUTE MILES. ONE NAUTICAL MILE EQUALS 1.15 STATUTE MILES

Likewise, many harbors have a measured mile and a few runs along this will enable the distance log to be calibrated, bearing in mind that since it is distance being measured, no allowance for tide run need be applied. On the other hand, if the speed log is being checked, the run of tide (obtainable from tide charts) will need to be taken into consideration. The sounder can be checked out by anchoring over a spot of known depth. The depth is read from the chart and adjusted for the tide height at that time, and the reading off the sounder compared with this figure. Because the sea bed can change considerably after storms or a big tidal runoff, checking the depth sounder should take place over a number of different locations at a number of different depths.

Radar can similarly be checked by comparing the monitor with a chart of the area, and range rings, distance measurement readouts, bearing indicators and the like can all be checked at the same time and in the same spot. Electronic charts can be compared with traditional paper charts, although errors in these are rare and it is more a case of ensuring the chart is up to date with any recent 'Notices to Mariners'. A quick chat on air with maritime radio stations on different frequencies will indicate the state of the radio equipment and RDF or similar equipment can be checked using a nearby homing beacon.

A day out on the harbor, after the winter maintenance routine has been completed, will ensure that all equipment is checked and ready for sea so that unexpected problems will not be encountered halfway through the first offshore passage!

GROUNDING THE ELECTRIC WIRING

Because of the damp environment in which a boat operates, any form of electrical fitting requires special treatment. Instruments, lights and other electrical equipment which are made specifically for boats will mostly be waterproof when supplied, but the power to operate them must be conveyed through the boat, sometimes internally, sometimes externally, and then connected. This is the vulnerable zone, for although new boats will usually have their electrical wiring already installed, when changes to the system need to be made, or new equipment wired up, or even old systems subject to routine maintenance, it is often necessary to renew the wiring or install new circuits. While the fitting of the new wiring is not a real problem, ensuring that it cannot be affected by the salty atmosphere or sea water, can create a few headaches.

And it is not just a matter of putting in the wiring where required, it may be necessary to ground the wiring and the instruments to prevent static electricity building up;

A particularly large copper ground plate is required for the extensive electrical equipment carried aboard this boat.

particularly when the wiring is in the vicinity of fuel tanks or outlets, or the main engine. This is particularly the case in dry atmospheric conditions, where static electricity can build quickly and where a single spark during refuelling can blow the vessel and her occupants sky-high. Newly built boats will almost certainly have their electrical circuits grounded when they are delivered, but second-hand boats, especially older craft, may need to be checked to ensure that the wiring has not deteriorated and the system is properly grounded.

All metal parts connected to the engine and in particular the metal parts of the fuel system must be electrically bonded, or connected together, and grounded, usually to a plate outside the hull under the waterline. Many shipwrights prefer to ground to a metal fitting in the hull such as the propeller shaft or skin fittings, but this can lead to corrosion through galvanic action and a reasonably sized plate (depending on how much electrical equipment is hooked up), makes for a better grounding terminal. The grounding circuit should be connected to one terminal of the electrical supply, usually a battery.

Wiring, both for the grounding circuit and any electrical circuit to fittings in the boat (they must of course be separate), needs to be of good quality to resist wear and tear and weathering, and thick enough to reduce voltage drop. Where batteries are the main source of current, a single battery will produce 12 volts of power, while two batteries connected in series will produce 24 volts of power. Batteries connected in parallel will not increase voltage but will have an increased capacity. Boats with generators may produce a power of any voltage; a common arrangement with large vessels where considerable power is required to operate air conditioners, refrigerators and other power-hungry equipment. When a low voltage system is used, thick wiring is more important to avoid heating and voltage drop than with higher voltage systems.

Wiring must be well secured so that it does not become loose or chafe as the boat moves in a seaway, and as much as possible it should be invisible. With wood hulls the cable can be tacked securely into place using electrical clips and brass screws. The problem becomes more difficult with metal boats, although with aluminum, self-tapping screws or pop rivets can be used where the situation permits. Fiberglass hulls can also be tap screwed in some areas, but perhaps the best method here is to glass the wire in. The hull, in way of the wiring, will need to be cleaned of any paint and the cable tacked temporarily in place. Then a strip of fiberglass tape can be run over the cable and secured into position by saturating with resin. When dry this will make a secure and watertight bond that can be over-painted to match the color of the surrounding structure.

When taking a wire through the side of an exposed bulkhead, such as when running cables out on deck or into the cockpit, a fine hole should be drilled through the bulkhead to match as nearly as possible the diameter of the cable and the wire threaded through it. The hole is then sealed with a weather-tight sealer and the cable on the inside of the hole run vertically up the bulkhead on the interior of the cabin. The whole section of cable on the inside is then covered with the weatherproof sealer thus ensuring that it is highly unlikely any water will get into the cabin no matter what happens on the outside. This system is particularly useful when fitting wiring to navigation lights, mast fittings, electric winches, and so on.

SOLAR CHARGING PANELS

A useful addition to the electrical system of any boat is a set of solar panels. Unobtrusive and easily maintained and not all that expensive initially, solar panels provide a great means of keeping the batteries charged while the boat is not in use. This is particularly the case with boats that are left swinging at a mooring where there is no means of plugging into a shore supply, as there is on a marina. Batteries can deteriorate quickly if they are run down and left uncharged, and in any case, it is always good to have the batteries fully charged at all times so that when the boat is to be used, starting the motor, using the electric bilge pump, or switching on the electronic navigation gear is quick and simple.

An electrician should be consulted when installing solar panels to ensure that the most suitable type are fitted to match the battery bank and the charging system. As a general rule they are fitted to the cabin roof in the case of motor cruisers or large yachts, and to a hatch cover on smaller craft. Where permanent fitting is not possible

Solar panels are ideal for small boats which rely on batteries for their power supply.

or not convenient, they can be mounted on a board that can be placed out in the cockpit or on the deck when the boat is left on the mooring, and taken inside when the boat is in use. A length of cable will provide the electrical link between the cells and the batteries, and this can be fed through door vents or wherever is convenient. This is quite a good idea in fishing boats and small yachts where the cells could be damaged if permanently fitted in a place where there is a lot of activity going on. Once in place and hooked up to the batteries, solar panels need little in the way of maintenance; mostly a routine check of the wiring a terminals, and a wipe down of the perspex on the cells occasionally to remove salt or dirt.

A BASIC LIGHTNING CONDUCTOR

Most yacht masts these days are aluminum and therefore effective lightning conductors in their own right. The problem lies with what happens to the lightning when it reaches the bottom of the mast. Neither fiberglass nor wood are good conductors of electricity, so the lightning will come to a sudden halt when it reaches the deck. But lightning doesn't like sudden halts and it will blast its way through deck, cabins, hulls or whatever to reach its ultimate goal—grounding in the water. A metal hull will give it good conductivity but will probably light up like a Christmas tree and electrocute everyone on

An efficient but somewhat
unattractive lightning conductor on
the hull of a restored historic vessel.

board. So whatever the construction material of the hull, to be safe in a thunderstorm a boat must provide an easy passage for the lightning directly from the mast to the sea.

Motor cruisers have the same problem even without a tall mast. Radio, GPS and other antennae will attract a close lightning strike like bees to a honey pot, and similarly, if it finds its passage obstructed by a fiberglass hull, the lightning will blast its way through anything in its way to ground itself in the water. While it is true that lightning strikes damaging vessels are fairly rare, it does happen, and having a fitted lightning conductor on the boat can provide considerable peace of mind when a thunderstorm is crackling all around.

TIP: PEOPLE GET KILLED BY LIGHTNING STRIKING A GOLF CLUB OR UMBRELLA. IMAGINE WHAT HAPPENS WHEN IT STRIKES A MAST!

Lightning will always follow the path of least resistance to ground which in the case of boats means the sea, so protecting the boat against damage from lightning merely means providing a conductor that leads directly into the sea. In the case of yachts, a wire from the foot of the forestay and down the stem to the water will be fairly unobtrusive and well away from where crew or passengers might be. Not quite so easy with a motor cruiser since the antennae are likely to be on the flybridge around the midships area. Many modern cruisers will have built in conductors, but if not it is a wise and inexpensive exercise to fit one and enjoy the confidence of knowing that whatever else might strike the boat, it won't be lightning.

The conductor should not be taken into the interior of the boat as the lightning can create all sorts of problems and all sorts of damage on its way through to the ocean. The alternative is an unsightly metal strip running across the cabin roof and deck, then down the side of the hull, which would be aesthetically repugnant. One solution is to rig up a temporary conductor for use only when an electrical storm is in the vicinity. This can be done quite simply by fitting a heavy gauge metal strip with an electrically compatible connection at one end to match a similar fitting at the foot of the mast or the forestay or, in the case of a motor cruiser, the base of the antenna. When the storm develops, the metal strip is simply clipped on and the other end dropped in the water, thus providing a complete and easy path for the lightning to take directly to the water.

Since boats vary greatly the aesthetics of fitting a lightning conductor will also vary and whether a 'portable' conductor is kept in the drawer, or a neatly hidden ground wire built into the hull structure, will be a matter of personal choice. The only important factor is that a direct path from somewhere high on the boat to the water is in place when the celestial fireworks get close.

14

The safety gear

Without doubt, one of the most important parts of the winter maintenance procedure is checking the safety gear. This is not a difficult task, and it usually involves merely inspecting the various items to ensure that they have not deteriorated since the last inspection. Items, such as life jackets, are sometimes stowed away in a locker and neglected to the point where mold or rot can begin to cause them to deteriorate and therefore to be unsafe.

As with all emergency equipment on a boat, it is vitally important that everything is kept in constant working order so that it is usable if the need arises. A thorough check of the safety equipment should therefore form part of the maintenance routine during the winter lay-up.

Winter time is the time to check the safety gear, and in particular life jackets, for any signs of deterioration.

LIFE JACKETS

Depending on the material they are made of, life jackets may suffer mold or rot as a result of not being properly dried and then put away damp. They should be taken out, and aired or dried, and there is no better time to do this than while the boat is on land or in the slipway where there is room to spread them out in the sun. A check on the life jacket's ancillary gear, such as strobe lamps, whistles, and the like, should be carried out, and at the same time the locker should be cleaned and dried thoroughly in readiness for re-stowing.

Although fitted with a long-life battery, EPIRBs must still be periodically checked to ensure the battery is not running down.

EPIRBS

Perhaps one of the most important pieces of safety equipment for boats that put out to sea, EPIRBs (Emergency Position Indicating Radio Beacon) usually have a test switch which can be used to check that the batteries are still functioning properly. Such a test must be brief and under no circumstance must the unit be operated fully. Personal EPIRBs should be checked at the same time.

LIFE RAFT

An inspection of the exterior of the life raft will indicate any damage or deterioration which might need attention. As with the EPIRBs, a full test cannot be carried out by operating the raft, but most manufacturers provide a maintenance service in which a qualified person checks the raft at regular intervals.

GRAB BAG

Most large yachts and motor boats have a grab bag which contains emergency equipment to be 'grabbed' and put aboard the life raft in an emergency. Since this may need to be done in a hurry, the grab bag is prepared with food, water, tools, signalling equipment and any other possible requirements that might be needed if the crew has to take to the raft. Winter maintenance time is the ideal time to open the grab bag and inspect all the equipment,

During maintenance routines, always check the release mechanism of the life raft.

update food and renew fresh water (unless carried separately), and generally prepare the bag for the next year of sailing.

FLARES AND ROCKETS

Even the smallest fishing boat heading offshore must carry flares and other signals in case of emergency. These vary from country to country, even from state to state, but basically consist of signalling equipment suitable for calling for assistance both in the daytime and at night. Pyrotechnics have a limited lifespan so the expiration date needs to be checked and the flares and rockets replaced if necessary. A check that the boat is carrying all legal requirements is also worth while at this time; small open boats must carry a bailer or bucket, sometimes a spare motor, oars, anchor, compass and the like. Such boats are also required to carry adequate flotation which should be checked as described on page 248 of this book. Whatever the size and type of boat, a check that the safety gear complies with the legal requirements can be carried out at this time.

Considered by many sailors to be the most vital piece of safety equipment for inshore waters, the anchor and warp should receive regular attention.

ANCHOR AND WARP

Although not solely used for safety purposes, the anchor is nevertheless one of the most important pieces of safety gear carried on the boat. When the

chips are down and the boat has no motor or no mast and a lee shore is looming up close astern, the only thing that will prevent disaster is the anchor. And to work effectively, an anchor requires a long warp, preferably with chain at the anchor end. And old adage says that the longer the warp the safer the anchor, so it is worth carrying spare rope in case in an emergency the fitted anchor rope needs to be extended. Winter time is the time to check the fittings at the anchor, especially the shackles, the warp and spare warp, and in particular ensure that the end of the warp is shackled securely into the anchor locker.

LIFE RINGS

Larger vessels will carry life rings fitted with ropes or lights that can be thrown over the side when a person is in the water. There are many different types of equipment used for this, and since it is carried on deck, any deterioration can be easily spotted. A routine check that strobe lights are working and the ropes are secured properly may be all that is required during the winter maintenance period.

Life rings must be stowed, ready for uses with attached ropes and strobe lights.

RADIOS

An important piece of equipment when an emergency arises, the radio is used almost every day, so any problems will show up during use and

anything more than a routine check after the boat is returned to service—as described earlier in this chapter—should not be necessary.

FIRE EXTINGUISHERS

Again a vitally important part of the safety equipment on a boat, and again one which must come in for attention at winter overhaul time. Fire extinguishers in the confines of a boat's cabin should be dry powder or similar, any toxic fumes from an extinguisher will extinguish the crew before they extinguish the fire! Some extinguishers will need to be recharged each winter, some will last of a couple of seasons. All should be checked at least once a year to ensure they are correctly charged and not in any way damaged.

Different maritime authorities require different safety equipment to be carried, so it would be impossible to cover all such equipment in a book like this. Then there are certain areas of the world where special emergency equipment is required, and different rules are applied to different sizes and types of craft. Suffice it to say that the winter lay-up is the ideal time to ensure that like all other equipment on the boat, the safety gear is up to standard and ready for use when the next season commences.

THE STEERING GEAR

Since the safety of a boat depends to a great extent on her ability to maneuver, the steering and control mechanisms can be considered in the same category as other safety gear. And when the boat is undergoing her winter overhaul it is important to ensure that the steering and control systems are checked and lubricated, for generally speaking, that is the only time they are given a substantial examination. There is a wide range of steering gear available for boats, and many variations on the basic themes. Thus individual systems may vary slightly, but as a general rule one of five steering systems is used for boats:

- Direct steering with a tiller.
- Wire and pulleys.
- The Morse system of steering cable.
- Hydraulic steering.
- Propeller steering—outboard motor.

Tiller steering is the simplest of all. It will be found on a few small motor boats but is universally popular with small to medium sized sailing boats. The tiller is directly connected to the rudder and therefore any movement of the tiller by the helmsman is immediately transferred to the rudder and causes a change in the direction of the boat. Maintenance of the tiller steering system consists mostly of ensuring that there is no play, either in the tiller or the rudder, which would indicate wear. If the rudder is a balanced type, any movement will probably be the result of wear in the collar and, as with

Many racing skippers, even on large yachts, prefer the direct response of tiller steering to that of a wheel.

wear in the pintles of a transom-hung rudder, will need to be rectified before it becomes worse and interferes with the boat's steering.

The wire and pulley system is still used in some small craft, although it has been mostly replaced by more modern systems. Wires which run over small pulleys around the boat, mostly under the gunwale, connect the wheel to the rudder. As the wheel is turned, the action is transferred to the rudder through the wire moving over the pulleys. Maintenance is important with this steering system since the wires are vulnerable to rust as well as chafe, particularly in the vicinity of the pulleys. The pulleys, too, may need to be lubricated unless they run on nylon bushes. However, as a rule the whole system is easily inspected and any wear and tear can be spotted early and rectified before it interferes with the steering of the boat.

The Morse system is the most widely used steering system with small motor boats and is also used in different adaptations for throttle and gear controls. It consists of a single, fairly heavy duty flexible wire which can be curved around a reasonable radius and is operated by a rack and pinion at the wheel and a rod connection to the rudder or outboard motor. Maintenance is essential with this type of steering as the cable is encased in a sheath and therefore needs lubrication to prevent it from rusting or drying up. In most Morse systems, the steering lever at the stern has a cap which enables grease

The complex control centre of a high profile racing yacht. The steering system is hydraulically operated by the large wheel.

to be pumped in and contained so that as the steering gear is used, the lubrication moves along the length of the cable inside the sheath. At the steering end it is also sometimes possible to lubricate through the links between the cable and the wheel.

Hydraulic steering is very common on larger vessels, particularly motor boats. There are many types of hydraulic steering systems but basically all work on the principal of small tubes transmitting the movements of the wheel to a ram which is in turn connected by hydraulic pipes, to the rudder stock, quadrant or tiller. As far as maintenance is concerned, inspection of the system should be made at intervals to ensure there is no leaking of the hydraulic oil in the tubes or at the connections. But repair or replacement of any part of a hydraulic system requires expert knowledge and should be turned over to the marina engineers. The steering system of any boat, but particularly a large, high speed vessel, is one of the most important parts in ensuring her safe navigation, and therefore should only be handled by experts.

Propeller steering in small craft is almost universally achieved through an outboard propeller, either through an inboard/outboard mechanism where the drive leg turns, or with the popular outboard motor where the whole motor turns. But while in both cases, the actual steering is carried out by the propulsion unit, transferring the movements of the wheel to the motor is carried out by one of the systems described earlier; either hydraulic or Morse steering. Maintenance of the propulsion unit is of course a job for a qualified mechanic, but maintenance of the rest of the steering mechanism is as described for each individual system earlier in this chapter.

CONTROL SYSTEMS

As mentioned earlier in this section, adaptations of the Morse and hydraulic systems described for steering control, are also used for throttle, gear shift and other controls on many boats, in particular, larger boats. All should come in for a thorough inspection at maintenance time, and any maintenance work required should be carried out as described for the steering systems.

BILGE PUMPS

Because of the enormous number and variety of bilge pumps on the market, it is impossible to deal in specific detail with the care and maintenance of this important piece of equipment. Some pumps are worked by hand, some are mechanically driven and many are electrically operated. A useful pump is the type that is controlled by a float switch, which automatically starts the pump when the water in the bilges rises to a pre-set level. Probably the most basic is the device used in many small sailing craft where the vortex action of the water flowing past the hull sucks out any water inside.

Because of the environment in which they work, almost all bilge pumps are subject to problems and all need regular maintenance. Rubber diaphragms and synthetic impellers are subject to damage from small, sharp objects or from corrosive liquids which have somehow got into the bilge, while most are prone to blockage every now and then from solid lumps of material that get into either the hose or the mechanism of the pump. Such a blockage or failure of the pump can be annoying at the best of times, but it can be disastrous in an emergency. When the hull is holed or water has come aboard in quantity, the bilge pump may be the only means of keeping the vessel afloat, so it is imperative that it is kept in good working order in case such an emergency arises.

Maintenance of bilge pumps consists mainly of keeping all the parts clean and in working order. With this in mind, most pumps are easy to dismantle and clean. A routine check on all working parts and frequent checking of the intake and hose, to ensure no foreign matter is lodged in the pipe, will ensure that it is ready if an emergency occurs. A strainer on the end of the intake hose will keep out large foreign objects and the strainer should be as large as possible to enable it to keep working even if a section becomes partly clogged with rubbish. Similarly, a large diameter hose will reduce the risk of a blockage occurring.

Manufacturers' instructions concerning oiling, greasing and cleaning should be closely followed with the whole system totally stripped down for inspection and repair during winter maintenance. Impellers and diaphragms can usually be dismantled by undoing a few nuts or clips, and the hoses should be secured with well greased hose

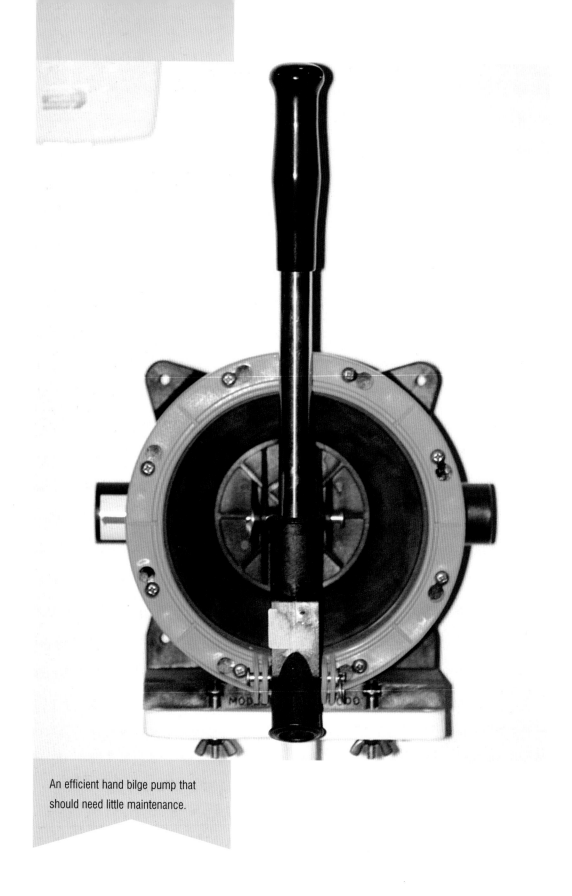

An efficient hand bilge pump that
should need little maintenance.

clamps which can be easily undone if a serious blockage occurs. These hose clips should be of lightweight metal, preferably stainless steel, so that they do not rust and jam.

But perhaps the most important factor in terms of pumping bilges lies not so much with the pump as with the bilge itself. No pump can be expected to function properly when the bilge is full of foreign matter. A paper tissue can block a bilge pump so it is small wonder that it will not work efficiently when the bilge has everything from wood shavings to oily cotton waste floating in it. A clean, uncluttered bilge is not only a sign of a healthy boat, but it is also a guarantee that when an emergency arises, the bilge pump will work adequately.

GAS AND SAFETY

LP gas is the most widely used utility for galley cooking on board small craft. It is convenient to use and bottles can mostly be filled in any port, but there is a potential for danger in having gas on board, and care in fitting and use of a gas system is important. In many countries there are strict regulations concerning the installation of gas bottles and piping and it may be necessary to have the system fitted by a licensed plumber. Indeed, this is a good option whether required by law or not, since a faulty gas system in a boat can lead to extreme danger, and the few extra dollars spent in getting it fitted professionally may well save the boat and its occupants from an unpleasant experience, even a disaster, at some future date.

While gas is a useful cooking fuel on board boats, the pipes and fittings must be carefully checked to prevent any risk of gas leaks. Bottles must be stowed in a special compartment.

The cylinder should be located either on deck in the open air or in a separate locker with openings at deck level to allow drainage outboard, for gas is heavier than air and will run out onto the deck through ports left at the bottom of the locker. The gas bottle must be well chocked and secured to prevent any movement which might fracture the pipe. The stern of the boat at the back of the cockpit or welldeck is a popular spot, well away from any source of flame or

A well maintained stove and gas system is less likely to encounter problems.

spark from the galley and the engine. A regulator must be fitted into the feeder pipe, which should be led into the cabin through a hole high in the bulkhead and made waterproof if it is open to wind and weather. The pipe must have at least one coil in it before leaving the locker, so that any vibration or movement will be absorbed by the coil and not fracture the pipe. Access to the bottle must be easy so that the gas can be turned off at the bottle when not in use. Under no circumstances must the pipe between gas bottle and galley stove be led through the bilges, as any leakage will cause gas to collect in the bilges, creating a virtual time bomb. Neither should it be hidden behind quarter berths or lining, as it needs to be accessible for checking and repair in case of a leak.

Copper piping is preferable, with a minimum number of joints, and secured to prevent any movement which may cause it to fracture or leak. A flexible hose of approved standard provides the connection between the galley end of the main pipe and the stove. Some boat owners like to fit a second tap at this point, but this is not recommended as the temptation on a cold night to turn the gas off at this tap, rather than crawling out to the bottle, can be overwhelming but is not good practice. The gas should always be turned off at the bottle. A gas detector placed in the bilge is good insurance that should there be a leak in the gas system it will be quickly identified.

FIREPROOFING

Without question, one of the greatest hazards on board a boat is fire, especially in large motor boats and cruising yachts where quantities of highly flammable fuel are carried. But even in yachts with small auxiliary motors, there is still enough fuel to start a serious conflagration and there are other flammables such as gas and cooking oils, kerosene for lamps and perhaps in the tool locker, resins, paint and methylated spirits. Whatever the cause, a fire on board when the boat is at sea creates an extremely serious situation, for apart from being out of reach of fire engines, if the fire cannot be stopped, there is nowhere for the occupants to go to get out of danger; they must stay with the boat. And if the fire gets out of control and they can no longer stay aboard, they must take to the rafts and hope for rescue.

So prevention is always better than cure with fire on board, and while it goes without saying that every boat must be fitted with the correct firefighting equipment, it should also be fitted with fire preventative materials as far as possible. Even in a steel or aluminum hull, where there is less flammable material than in a wood boat, there is sufficient to create disaster if a fire breaks out. One step is to reduce the risk as far as possible, in the first place by keeping to a minimum fittings or material that are combustible, and secondly to use fire-retardant materials where possible. Taking care with gas fittings, as described earlier in this chapter, and in particular ensuring that fuel tanks are correctly vented and warning systems fitted in the bilges are also ways in which fire risk can be minimized.

Cabin insulation and soundproofing should be carried out with material that is non-flammable and where possible a fireproof bulkhead (firewall) fitted in places where highly flammable material is stored, such as the engine room or fuel tanks. In most cases, especially with large motor craft, this will have been done when the boat was built, but in small craft or older vessels, it might be a good idea during winter maintenance to give some thought to enclosing or sealing off areas which are a high fire risk, and enclosing them with non-flammable materials.

One of the latest and most useful developments in this area has been the production of fireproof paint. Paint itself is usually very flammable, and to be able to remove this risk and at the same time coat areas of the boat with fireproof paint is a great step forward in preventing fires at sea. One of the earliest manufacturers to introduce such a paint is National Maritime Products (ANZ) Pty Ltd, whose fire retardant paint 'Firefree 88' is claimed to repel any form of fire or heat for at least one hour—and one hour is more than sufficient time to put firefighting practices into effect or time for help to arrive. The paint is non-toxic and has a water base, so it is easy to apply and equally easy to clean up; a major plus in making seagoing safer.

When used in conjunction with other fire-inhibiting materials and fire prevention procedures, such a paint could reduce the risk of fire on board considerably and provide the boat owner and his passengers with greater peace of mind when they are out on the ocean and many miles from help or rescue.

Deck paint with sand or pumice dust makes an efficient non-skid surface.

NON-SKID DECKS

When the deck of a boat—particularly the foredeck —gets wet this can create a hazardous situation for anyone moving around or working, as the deck can become slippery and dangerous when the boat is moving in a seaway. It does not apply as much to laid decks, where the wood will provide some grip for deck shoes and the caulking between the planks, which is often raised or depressed a little, also gives a better footing. But with fiberglass and painted steel or aluminum decks, some form of non-skid surface is essential, for once wet, these decks can be like skating rinks. It is hard enough at sea to maintain a footing on a wildly pitching deck at any time, but if there is nothing to provide a grip for deck shoes, then the chances of a serious accident or losing a man overboard are very real.

Many fiberglass boats have a non-skid surface molded into the deck when the vessel is built, and this may be adequate. The mold surface is patterned so that when the deck is laid up, the pattern is reproduced in the surface of the laminate or the gel coat, thus creating a tread or grip which provides a footing. But some boat builders tend not to worry too much about non-skid surfaces, and in any case, wear and tear can soon cause the pattern of the molded tread to wear smooth, so some additional non-skid protection is required. Like smooth fiberglass, aluminum or steel decks without a non-skid surface are effectively death traps for crew working on deck in a seaway. Even if the boat is not intended to go to sea, non-skid deck surfaces are essential, for without a grip for shoes (or bare feet) passengers or crew walking around a wet deck can break a leg or slip over the side at the least movement of the hull. Like a bald tire on a car, the smooth deck surface when wet prevents anything from getting a firm grip.

Non-skid deck paint is the most widely used material for providing good footing on a wet deck. This may be a specially made paint or just a normal deck paint composition which has been mixed with an abrasive, gritty substance such as pumice powder to provide the grip. A method that has been used for untold years but which is still widely used both in commercial and leisure craft today, is the use of sand, scattered over a freshly painted deck or mixed into the paint, to provide the non-skid surface. If the sand is evenly spread across the deck while the paint is still wet it will provide a first class non-skid surface and probably work out to be much cheaper than commercially sold composites. The sand should be fine, since coarse sand will lose its adhesion to the paint with wear and tear and this will defeat the purpose of the exercise. Although perhaps not the most attractive from an appearance point of view, it is unquestionably one of the most effective, and is used on commercial craft such as tugs, fishing vessels, even ocean-going freighters, as well as small leisure craft.

Molded non-skid decks can create an attractive pattern.

TIP: WHEN USING SAND FOR NON-SKID DECK SURFACES ENSURE THAT IT IS FINE SAND, IS CLEAN AND HAS BEEN WASHED TO REMOVE ANY SALT.

Another system, and one which perhaps looks a little neater, is to lay strips of non-skid material across the deck areas. This material comes in a wide variety of colors and usually has adhesive backing which means that once cut and shaped as required, the non-skid material is simply pressed into place on the areas of the deck where it will be most effective. It has a roughened surface that provides good grip for deck shoes and even bare feet when wet, and providing a good quality is used, should last for some time. In any case, it can easily be replaced when worn by peeling off the old material and attaching new material in its place.

Matting, or marine carpeting can also be used, and is a favorite with tuna fishing boats where the soft carpet prevents the landed fish from bruising. The matting is cut to shape and glued to the deck, providing a safe working environment for the crew and a quite attractive appearance for the boat.

SMALL BOAT BUOYANCY

Owners of small boats such as centreboard sailing dinghies or outboard powered fishing boats, will be constantly aware of the importance of buoyancy should the boat capsize or be swamped. In the case of plywood sailing dinghies like the Mirror, the problem is not so acute since even if the boat is totally filled, being wood it will not sink. However, fiberglass will sink, as will aluminum, and boats made of these materials are reliant on the fitted buoyancy to keep

Specially made carpet can provide a good non-skid surface and also enhance the appearance of the boat.

them afloat in the event of a mishap. Regulations now require all power boats to be fitted with adequate buoyancy but there is no specification as to the life of the material used, and certain types of foam can deteriorate either with age and damage, or through coming into contact with certain liquids or chemicals. Maintenance routines should cover this important aspect to ensure that if the boat does become waterlogged, there will be adequate buoyancy in good condition to keep her afloat as a survival platform.

Air has been used in the past for buoyancy in some small boats, but this is never really adequate. Tanks can leak, inflatable bags can be punctured and there are many other ways in which buoyancy tanks filled with air can lose their effectiveness when called upon to keep the boat afloat. Plastic foam (styrofoam) is the most commonly used buoyancy material, although some manufacturers use other types of chemical foam. Some foams can be sprayed into the buoyancy cavity where on contact with the air they expand to fill the compartment, others come as blocks which can be cut to any shape and fitted into the boat's hull, or merely strapped beneath thwarts. The type of material is not important, it is the effect it has on keeping the boat and payload afloat that determines if it is effective.

It is important that the buoyancy in a small boat is kept up to standard against the possibility of mishaps like this.

A routine maintenance check on an older boat may show that the buoyancy material has deteriorated and needs replacing. This can be a problem, mainly depending on where the buoyancy has been placed and how well it has been secured. For example, if it was sprayed in and expanded to

fill a tank, removing it will be a long and arduous task, scraping it out handful by handful or else removing one side of the tank. On the other hand, if it consists of blocks of foam simply strapped under thwarts, replacement will be no problem. However, it is important in all cases to measure the volume of the buoyancy material before removing it, in case it disintegrates into powder while being removed, so that the same amount can be obtained to replace it. The state of the buoyancy will be indicated by its color (should be white) and condition (should be firm and not crumbly). If there is any doubt, it should be replaced, for this is a major part of the boat's safety equipment.

Other than with styrofoam blocks secured beneath the seats or in lockers, the easiest and perhaps most effective way of replacing old foam is to use the expanding foam spray. The amount of space required to be filled and the amount of foam required to fill it can be calculated and the appropriate number of cans of liquid or spray foam purchased. The foam will quickly set when in place so it is a wise move to have everything ready and not have any hold-ups once the procedure is started.

15

A few fitting out ideas

Maintenance work on boats invariably means repair or refitting, not just to the hull, deck or motors, but also to the interior equipment. As with a house, there is always something to be done in the galley, the salon or the heads when renovation time comes around, and most of this work can be done by the average handyman using the average handyman tools. Tools and fastenings have been covered elsewhere in this book, but as far as interior furnishings are concerned there has been little mention of methods.

SIMPLE JOINERY

Since most interior furniture is wood, regardless of the hull material, a basic knowledge of joinery can help make the difference between a pro-fessional looking job, and something that will not enhance the boat's interior appearance.

HALF LAP JOINT

The simplest form of joining two pieces of wood together is to nail, screw or glue them, but this is neither attractive nor efficient. Jointing makes for a more solid join as well as giving the work a more attractive appearance. The basic joint is the half lap joint which is widely used in all forms of joinery. It is strong and easy to make and gets its name

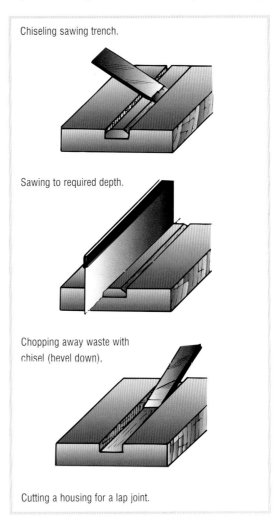

Chiseling sawing trench.

Sawing to required depth.

Chopping away waste with chisel (bevel down).

Cutting a housing for a lap joint.

from the fact that half the width of each wood is used, recessing one half into the other to restore the full width. The procedure for cutting the rabbet is as follows:

1. Mark the wood to be lapped, making sure the alignment is correct.
2. With a light saw or knife, cut lightly along the lines.
3. Use a chisel on the inside of the groove to cut a groove into which a tenon saw blade can be inserted.
4. With the saw cut each marked line down to the half width point.
5. Pare away the wood between the saw cuts with a chisel then fair off the recessed section.

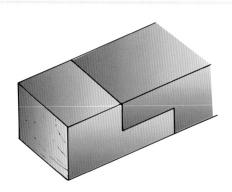

THE STRAIGHT HALF LAP
Closely resembling a scarf, this joint holds together the butt ends of two pieces of wood, making them virtually one long piece.

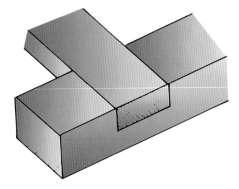

THE TEE HALF LAP
Again a common joint, this time for corners. Simpler than, but not as strong as, a dovetail joint, this provides the basic joint for gluing and screwing or dowelling.

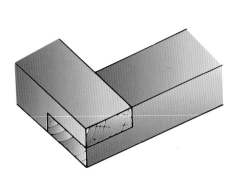

THE CORNER HALF LAP
Commonly used in all types of joinery, this joint can be used for cupboards, drawer framework etc.

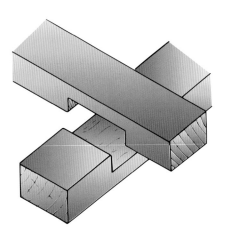

THE CROSS HALF LAP
For strength in structural cross members this joint is ideal. Also used widely for construction of cupboards and other large interior fittings.

Straight half lap

This joint holds together the butt ends of two pieces of wood, effectively making them one long piece.

Tee half lap

A common join used for all manner of joinery, particularly strong for corners.

Corner half lap

The sort of corner joint used in many applications such as windows, picture frames, etc.

Cross half lap

A very strong corner joint used for large interior fittings where strength is important.

SINGLE DOVETAIL

A difficult joint to make, but considerably stronger than most joints, this is the sort of work gradually becoming less favored by amateur carpenters, probably because its strength can nowadays be replaced by using a good glue.

MORTICE AND TENON

Strongest of all joints, the mortice and tenon uses an interlocking action to give it enormous

Neat wood work can add to the appearance of even small boats.

robustness. It is a very difficult join to make because a great deal of careful chiselling is required. Instead of the half thicknesses used in half lap joints, the mortice and tenon uses one-third thicknesses, combining each one third section to make up the full thickness of the wood when the joint is brought together.

FITTING A HANDRAIL

In the course of the summer sailing season, it is not uncommon to identify the need for a feature that is not fitted but which could prove very useful—such as a handrail. Many a boat owner has discovered in the course of climbing around the outside of the cabin on a motor boat, or scrambling to get forward when a yacht is pitching in a seaway, that a handrail would make life a little easier, but there just is not one there. Handrails are easy to make and fit (they can be purchased ready made if required), so a note is made that when the boat is in for her winter overhaul, fitting a handrail should be on the list of things to do.

The handrail can be cut from a template with a bandsaw, then planed, sanded and finished to match the part of the boat on which it will be mounted. The choice of wood will be important if it is not to be painted; teak is possibly the best although hard to work, but it can be left unvarnished or treated with a clear polyurethane, whichever suits. If it is to be painted, a less expensive wood such as Oregon can be used. Holes for through bolts need to be drilled between the hand grips and countersunk so the head of the bolt can be covered with a dowel.

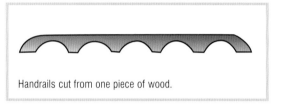

Handrails cut from one piece of wood.

Fastening the rail in place requires special attention because it is possible that heavy loads may be placed on it with crew working forward and hanging on as the boat moves in a seaway. If it is not well secured, the fastenings may pull out under severe strain, creating a life threatening situation for the person hanging on to the rail. If it is secured through a fiberglass roof or bulkhead, a solid pad must be placed under the nut in order

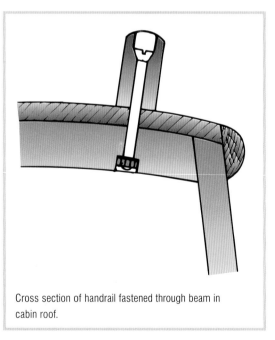

Cross section of handrail fastened through beam in cabin roof.

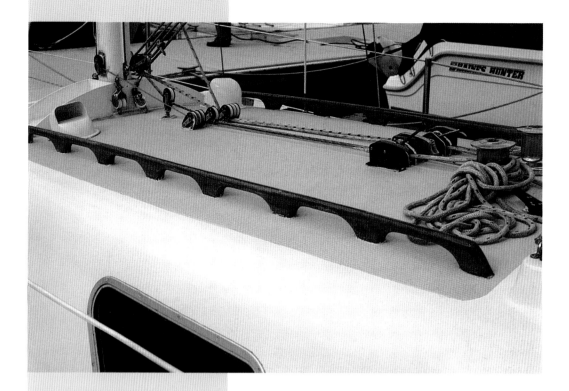

Wood handrails can add to the appearance of a fiberglass cabin.

to spread the load. This pad can be plywood or metal or even made up with a few extra layers of fiberglass. Making a secure fastening through GRP is described in more detail on page 84.

In wood boats the bolts should be secured through a beam, whereas most metal panels will have sufficient strength that a pad is not necessary. The surfaces between the rail and the bolts should be coated with a heavy sealant to prevent any possibility of leakage, then the bolts tightened up and covered with a dowel or filler.

SELF-LOCKING DRAWERS

One of the most essential features of a boat's interior furniture is prevention of doors flying open and cupboards and drawers emptying out when the boat pitches or rolls in a seaway. Apart from damaging the wood work, nothing is more frustrating than picking up the spilled and sometimes broken contents of drawers than have fallen open with the movement of the boat. There are many remedies, but most involve the use of catches or hooks or bolts, none of which add much to the aesthetic appearance of the cabin furniture, however practical they may be. Also, human nature being what it is, invariably hooks are left undone or bolts not secured as the boat heads out to sea.

The simplest remedy, and one that is as old a seafaring itself, is the self-locking drawer. It has no hooks or bolts and only needs someone to remember to push it closed. Since drawers are not usually left open, even when the boat is not at sea, there is every chance that it will be closed, and then without any further requirement, it will remain closed no matter what sort of convulsions the boat goes through when she encounters a big sea.

The secret lies in a small recess at the bottom of the drawer, immediately behind the front panel and a slightly raised sill on the front of the drawer recess. When the drawer is pushed closed, the recess in the drawer drops

Self-locking drawer.

down over the raised sill and locks it firmly into position. To open the drawer merely requires it to be lifted to clear the sill and the drawer slides out quite normally.

LAID DECKS

Nothing adds more to the appearance of a yacht or motor boat than laid decks. Fiberglass, steel and aluminum decks may be much more practical and are undoubtedly less prone to wear and tear than wood, but by the same token, the synthetic or metal materials do little to enhance the aesthetic appeal of a boat and as a rule wood fittings are used to give more visual attractiveness. Wood is often used for rails around the outside of the hulls and sometimes for the rubbing strake. Wood trim gives a softer appearance to the cockpit and polished wood gives a touch of class to interior furniture. But nothing gives any vessel quite the appeal of laid decks; once a major feature of all craft, now used mostly for cosmetic purposes.

Originally, the problem with laid decks was that they required constant maintenance or they leaked. Hot sun dries out the wood and shrinks it, causing the seams between the planks to open and allow water in which can be more than inconvenient, even if they close up again after being wetted by rain or seawater. For this reason, boat owners welcomed the arrival of fiberglass or metal decks which were generally totally watertight and required little maintenance, regardless of sun, wind and weather. But the cold, clinical feel of the plastic and the harsh, sterile feel of the steel or aluminum reduced the aesthetic appeal and gave the boat a practical, utilitarian feel instead of the warm, fuzzy feeling most boat owners enjoy in their boats.

The solution was simple: combine the practical utility of the fiberglass or metal deck with the warmth and classical appearance of the wood laid deck, thus avoiding the problems of leakage and at the same time enhancing the appearance of the boat. To achieve this, the wood decking is laid on top of the plastic or metal deck and the boat

The pitch or synthetic compound is poured into the seam to secure the caulking, then sanded off.

achieves the desired metamorphosis, as well as, of course, increasing her value. Although a small amount of maintenance is still required—as it is with any wood, to counter the effect of wear and tear—the opening and closing of deck seams are no longer a problem, since beneath the laid deck is a totally waterproof second deck.

There are a number of ways of fitting a laid deck over the fiberglass or metal, but it is a fairly complex job since cutting and fastening the planks in place needs professional experience and a shipwright should be called in, otherwise the end result may lack the appearance and effectiveness aimed for and thus negate the purpose of the laid deck. Apart from the main deck, many other parts of a boat can be enhanced with a laid deck, notably the cockpit and fly bridge. The appearance of the laid planks, plus the warm, soft colors that can be brought out in the wood make the world of difference to what would otherwise be clinical white plastic or harsh, cold metal.

Depending on the planking used, the laid deck may be left untreated. Teak is perhaps the best wood for this as it requires virtually no maintenance. However, it is very expensive and takes on a rather grey, unattractive appearance without treatment, although a coat of varnish will take care of that, bringing out the warm wood colors and adding even more to its appearance. Sikkens oil is a good treatment for wood decks and has good weathering properties which help reduce the effect of the elements. Take care when using any form of oil or varnish on a deck since it can become slippery when wet.

If necessary, non-skid strips or pumice dust in the surface coating will reduce this problem, which is one that must be kept in mind, for an accident can easily occur on slippery decks.

Maintenance of a laid deck covering a glass or metal deck consists of simply renewing the impregnated surface as it wears. Stained or marked decks can be sanded back to bare wood to regain their original appearance but this should not be necessary if the deck is recoated periodically. Paint can be used but this rather defeats the purpose of the laid deck, since the pleasant appearance of the wood and planking is covered by the paint.

LAMINATING WOOD

Laminating consists of combining a series of thin layers of wood to create a special shape that is extremely strong and in sections can provide a most attractive appearance. Plywood is a form of laminated sheet wood and is used widely as a construction material in wood boat building as well as for furniture and fittings in all types of boats. The thin layers of wood are laid cross grain and glued together with a strong glue; in the case of marine ply this is a strong marine or waterproof glue. It is important when buying laminated wood or plywood for use on boats to ensure that it is marine grade; the standard grade will just disintegrate when it gets wet.

From a maintenance point of view, the greatest use of laminated wood is when repairs need to be made that require sharply bent wood or when adding or renovating interior furnishings. The attractive appearance of the layered wood can add enormously to the appeal of a cabin interior and is at the same time very strong and practical. It can be used to create curved shapes for galleys, bunks and salon furniture where the use of normal wood would allow only straight lines and sharp corners. It need not be painted for the layered appearance, especially when built from different colored woods, is most appealing when finished with a clear varnish. Laminated tillers add a delightful touch to a cockpit.

Laminating does take a little more effort than using purchased wood, but the result in terms of appearance and strength make it worthwhile. A mold must be carefully constructed to the exact shape required and with accurate measurements since the completed laminations will not allow any bending or straightening once out of the mold although, of course, surface shaping with a plane or sander will always be possible. The strips of wood should be around 1/8" thick although they can be slightly thicker if

the bending is not too severe, and the grain should run along the length. The first strip is secured onto the mold and coated with a thin layer of marine glue. The second strip is laid onto it and clamped firmly into position. The procedure is repeated until the required thickness is achieved. Each layer of glue must be given time to cure before the next wood strip is applied and when the final layer is in position the whole lamination clamped securely and given time to cure properly.

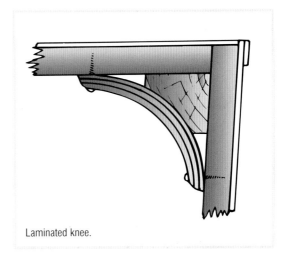

Laminated knee.

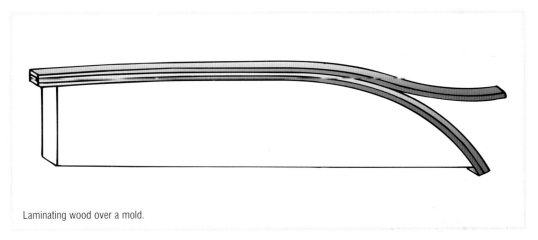

Laminating wood over a mold.

A shipwright's work frequently involves bending and shaping wood.

When removed from the mold, the laminated wood can be worked in the normal way to fair off edges and plane and sand down the surfaces until the desired result is achieved. Apart from its attractive appearance, laminated wood is very strong and ideal for repair jobs such as replacing curved structural sections like beam knees in a wood boat. Shipwrights consider it a sin to paint neatly laminated woods and many go out of their way to use the procedure for enhancing interior appearances while at the same time ensuring structural strength.

STEAMING WOOD

Since a boat is effectively curved in all directions, maintenance and repair of boats frequently calls for curved sections of wood to be used, either externally or internally. There are two methods that can be used to permanently bend the wood without breaking it and both are within the capability of the average handyman. Laminating, described above is ideal for great strength and an attractive appearance, but where the repair is not visible, or the appearance is not important, bending a straight piece of wood may provide a simpler and quicker way, and the easiest way to bend wood is by steaming it. This will not be possible with large sections but where relatively long, thin woods are required, steaming is simple and does not require professional skills.

A steamer can be made up from a section of metal pipe closed off at one end and angled over a heat source. Water in the pipe is heated to form steam and the wood to be bent is placed inside. Steaming will take some time, depending on the thickness of the wood to be bent, but while the steaming is in progress, the mold can be prepared to the shape in which the wood is to be bent. There are a number of ways a mold can be constructed, but a simple method for long pieces of wood is to nail sections of scrap wood to the floor of a garage so that when the steamed wood is placed around the template so formed it will fall into the required shape. Other methods can involve the use of clamps or brackets—much depends on the size of the wood to be bent and the shape it is to take.

Once it is sufficiently steamed to bend easily, the wood is placed in or around the mold and secured in position. As the wood dries it will take up the required shape, although thick sections or tight curves may require the process to be repeated a few times, starting with moderate

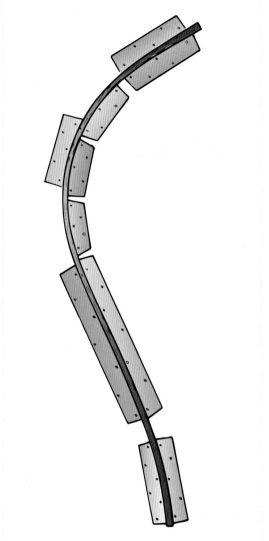

Plan view of mold nailed to floor in which steamed wood can be bent to shape.

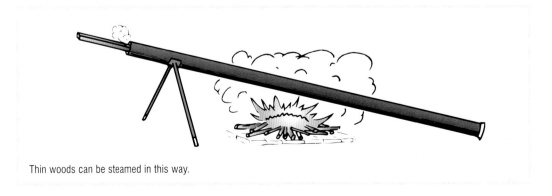

Thin woods can be steamed in this way.

A few fitting out ideas   261

Steaming or laminating are just two ways in which wood can be curved to shape.

bending and gradually building up to the required shape. Steaming wood in this way is ideal for interior work such as cabin furniture, bunks, and galley and cockpit fittings. It is best done with softwood because many hardwoods are brittle and will not bend easily. An attractive appearance can be achieved by ensuring that the grain of the wood follows the bend.

SHEATHING A WOOD DECK

As mentioned, laid decks are notorious for leaking. One way of curing this is the opposite of that described on page 256 where a fiberglass deck is covered with a laid deck. Now the laid deck is covered with fiberglass. This stops the leaking but retains the attractive appearance of the wood planks. The procedure is known as 'sheathing' and is very effective providing the original wood deck is in good shape.

The old woods of the deck will need to be sanded back hard to remove all traces of oil, dirt, grease and any patches of paint or rot since the sheathing will only take to clean, dry wood. This is often difficult, because after years of suffering wind, weather and sun, to say nothing of trampling feet and myriad objects dropped or manhandled across its surface, a wood deck can be expected to show serious signs of wear and tear. If it is not possible, then the sheathing can still be carried out but the attractive effect of the laid planks will be lost. This is because a new surface must be first laid— almost inevitably plywood—over the original deck and onto which the fiberglass sheathing can be placed.

So the decision will need to be made; keep the original laid deck and risk the possibility of the sheathing coming unstuck after a period of time, or lose the aesthetic appeal of the laid woods but gain a totally waterproof deck. The plywood must be of the best quality marine plywood, cut and shaped to fit the deck space to be sheathed, carrying it right out to the gunwale. A thick layer of quality marine glue is laid over the old deck and the plywood screwed into place. If the original decking is badly deteriorated and the screws will not hold, some fastenings may need to be secured right through to the deck beams beneath to prevent any chance of the new deck lifting.

While the new plywood deck or the old laid deck (whichever is being used) is still clean and dry, the fiberglass should be laid. The resin is made up in moderate quantities and painted across the deck and the previously-shaped glass cloth laid onto it overlapping the edges if possible, otherwise snugged up against it to create a good seal. Any form of glass cloth is suitable although some boat builders favor chopped strand for this job as the uneven finish gives good non-skid properties to the deck. The deck is glassed in sections with the resin thoroughly worked through the mat and combining with the first layer beneath. A stiff brush or metal roller can be used to work it in hard and get rid of any trapped bubbles of air or uneven patches.

Another layer of resin might be needed, depending on how thoroughly the first has covered the wood deck. Ensure that the resin is completely covering the cloth and there are no 'hairy' bits sticking up. Check also that whatever arrangement has been made that the gunwales are secure and unlikely to lift or allow water to get under the GRP. When the resin has hardened it can be sanded back to remove any bumps or lumps to ensure a smooth, even deck surface, after which it can be primed and painted if required, or left clear to show the wood through beneath. Correctly laid and finished, this type of decking will be totally waterproof and will outlast the life of the boat!

TIP: TO TRIM THE EDGES OF EPOXY SHEATHING AFTER IT HAS HARDENED, SOFTEN IT WITH A HEAT GUN FIRST.

FITTING FIBERGLASS FURNITURE AND TANKS

The convenience of GRP does not lie simply with its ease of maintenance, it is also a very easy material to use for fitting out. All kinds of extra furniture and features can be installed in a boat simply by molding and securing them with GRP or building them in position. In small fishing boats, for example, bench seats, bait tanks and other useful containers can either be molded in situ or molded ashore and later fitted into the boat.

With larger craft interior furniture, fuel and water tanks and canopies can all be molded from this versatile material. The procedure is much the same for any type of work, the only difference being the thickness of the laminate and the type of cloth used plus, of course, a mold into which or around which the GRP can be laid.

A typical example of the useful way in which GRP can be used would be to fit extra fuel or water tanks. The procedure described here for this task needs only slight modification to enable a handy person to construct any item that might be needed and fitted as part of the winter lay-up and maintenance program. This description deals with the fitting of GRP tanks in a GRP hull, but much the same procedure would be followed for fitting the same tanks in a wood hull providing, of course, that the wood surface is dry and clean. GRP does not bond too well on metal hulls, and tanks fitted to an aluminum or steel hull will need to be made first and fitted separately, securing them to the hull with pop rivets or some other suitable fastening and then sealing them all round.

Materials required for making a GRP tank will be as follows:
- Plywood for creating the mold or core.
- Masking tape for securing it into position.
- Woven glass mat (carbon or kevlar are rather expensive).
- Resin mix.
- Release agent (for female mold).
- Sandpaper and epoxy thinners for cleaning and preparation.

TIP: ALWAYS USE GLOVES, BREATHING APPARATUS AND OTHER SAFETY EQUIPMENT WHEN HANDLING GRP, ESPECIALLY IN CONFINED SPACES.

MALE MOLD

A male mold is one around which the GRP is laminated on the outside. The mold can then be removed or left in place, or particularly with a tank or furniture, it can be glassed all over and the mold retained as core material. This will leave the plywood showing through the finished product, but if that is not required it can easily be painted with primer and polyurethane paint to match surrounding surfaces. Any roughness on the finish of the laminate can be sanded back to reasonable smoothness, but if a really good quality finish is required, the use of a female mold is a better option.

FEMALE MOLD

This is a more satisfactory method for furniture or other items where a smooth, polished finish is necessary. The mold is made up in much the same way, using plywood or some other material, but in this case the laminate is laid up on the inside of the mold which must be carefully cleaned and prepared as the finish on the interior of the mold will determine the finish on the final product.

Typical of the useful fittings that can be easily made: a bait tank constructed of plywood core with GRP sheathing. The interior has been painted.

The following steps are a general guide to molding a tank or similar item in situ. The same procedure is followed if the tank is laid up separately and glassed into position later although there will usually be more working room if the molding is done ashore than in the tight confines of the hull. Obviously there will be considerable variations on this basic theme, depending on the required shape, size and the individual use of the finished product. However, the procedure given here can be adapted quite easily to meet any special requirements.

1. Shape and fit the plywood mold into position.
2. Ensure the surface to be used is clean and dry and has the required finish. If it is a female mold, apply a good coating of release agent to the inside. This should not contain silicones.
3. Cut the glass cloth to shape.
4. With a female mold, apply a layer of gel coat to the inside, allow it to dry then place the cut mat onto it to obtain an even coverage with overlapping or doubled mat where additional strength is needed. The gel coat is not required if the mold is to be left in situ.

5. Mix the resin and hardener to the manufacturer's instruction and work well into the glass cloth until it is thoroughly wetted out.
6. Apply further layers of laminate as required.
7. Allow to cure. Trim off edges with scissors before the resin has hardened completely ('toffee' stage).
8. Remove the female mold by gently prying it off the laminate. If the mold is incorporated in the job as a core, use sandpaper when the GRP has cured to remove unevenness and prepare the surface for painting.
9. Sand off the rim to a straight edge, then build the top to the exact measurements, using the same technique, and bond it into place to complete the tank. Pipes or other requirements can be put in place before the laminate is laid up or holes can be drilled in the finished product and the pipes glassed in.

MAKING A HATCH COVER

Hatch covers, unless they are hinged or battened down, can easily be lost overboard, but a replacement is simply made with GRP that has the same dimensions and even looks the same as the original hatch cover. If there is a tendency for a cover to be lost, it might pay to be prepared by taking a mold off the original cover and putting it away against future need. This mold can be simply made by coating the original cover with a release agent and laying up a laminate over the top of it. When the laminate has cured and

Small hatch covers are quite easy to make.

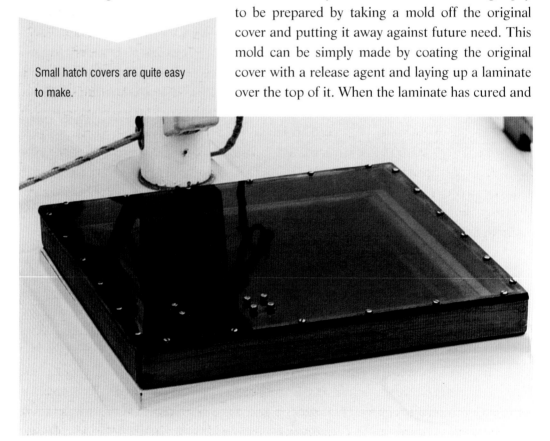

Molded fiberglass hatch covers are very durable and if well made should be watertight.

been removed, a perfect female mold duplicate of the original hatch cover will be left, with only a little trimming and tidying needed to get it into shape.

Some boat owners might find such prior preparation a little tedious, so if a hatch cover is lost and a new one has to be made without the original, the process described above for molding tanks or furniture will need to be followed. This will require a plywood or similar mold to be carefully constructed to fit the now open hatchway and then the new hatch cover laid up in it. The rounded edges and corners that smooth off the hatch cover will require careful shaping of the mold—a somewhat tedious and time-consuming task involving the use of epoxy filler, putty or some other malleable substance. It is so much easier to take a mold off the original before it is lost.

TIP: FOR THE SAKE OF SAFETY, FIT A LANYARD TO THE INSIDE OF THE COVER AND SECURE IT UNDER THE DECK ON ONE SIDE OF THE HATCH.

FITTING COCKPIT DRAINS

Self-draining cockpits are a boon in all craft, but especially in those that put out to sea. Heavy rain can soon turn a small cockpit into a bath, and a big boarding sea can create a very dangerous situation by filling the cockpit. Drains which run off any sort of water from the cockpit area ensure that it stays dry and comfortable at all times. There is only one condition required in order to fit self-drainers to any deck area, and that is the level of the cockpit floor, which must be well above the normal waterline. If it is below the waterline then the water will drain in and not out, which could lead to a disastrous situation. And even if the waterline is close to the level of the cockpit floor, problems can arise. A yacht heeled on one side, for example, will induct water through the lee drain unless it is closed off, and constantly closing off seacocks on the drains is a tedious operation.

So the level of the cockpit floor must be well above the boat's normal waterline, and since the hull will be pierced in the process, the fitting of the drains must be done out of the water. Winter maintenance time when the boat is on shore for some period of time provides a good opportunity for such work, or if the boat can be trailered, then she can be taken somewhere where the work can be done under more favorable conditions. Although some boat owners do not use seacocks on the drains, it is a wise procedure to fit them against the possibility of a broken or leaking drain pipe. Without a seacock there will be nothing to stop the water pouring directly into the hull and the vessel will sink. The diameter of the drain is not important although obviously the larger the pipe the faster the cockpit will drain; an important factor when a big sea comes aboard. The procedure for fitting standard self-drainers is as follows:

1. With the boat out of the water, cut two holes in the lower end of the cockpit floor and secure a skin fitting to each. These can be bonded into place with fiberglass, or fastened with screws or bolts. Bedding compound should be placed between the fitting and the cockpit floor on both fittings.
2. Cut two matching holes in the hull closely aligned to the cockpit holes and repeat the procedure with skin fittings securely bonded or fastened into place in the hull skin and mounted in bedding compound or suitable sealant.
3. Fit a seacock on the inside of each hull skin fitting.
4. Join the cockpit deck fitting to the seacock on either side with matching flexible pipe or hose. Use hose clamps to ensure a tight fitting at both ends of the pipe.

This system can also be fitted to small motor boats although the shallow draft of these craft usually means the waterline is above the deck level. However, if the deck is raised or a false deck fitted, there is nothing to stop self-drainers being used, and if, because of the low waterline, the water tends to come in through the cockpit fittings when at sea, plugs can be placed in the holes and removed as required.

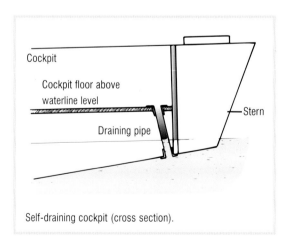

Self-draining cockpit (cross section).

Drains fitted in the lower (forward) end of the cockpit floor, drain off rainwater as well as the result of any boarding seas.

Self bailers are ideal for small craft and
are easily fitted in the hull skin.

SELF BAILER

Where this system is not practical, there are other ways of removing water from the inside of the boat. Sailing dinghies frequently fit small self bailers in the bottom of the hull which suck out the water as the boat moves along. A similar system can be employed with small motor boats; the self bailer can be purchased from any chandlers and secured in position about one quarter of the length of the boat from the transom. Although this will mean cutting a hole in the bottom of the boat, it should not be a problem and the self bailer pop riveted (aluminum) or bonded (GRP) into position with a watertight seal. The vortex action of the water moving past the outside of the hull sucks out any water inside. However, it is important to remember to close the self bailer when the boat slows down or stops, or the draining actions will be reversed and water will come into the boat instead of going out!

SELF-DRAINING DECK

Larger motor boats, usually have welldecks at the stern rather than the narrow cockpits of sailing vessels. Although self-draining systems such as that described for a cockpit previously can still be used, and indeed are frequently used, a draining system which is particularly popular with working boats such as trawlers may be more appropriate for this kind of deck. This is the self-draining deck which allows any water that comes aboard to freely run out over

Freeing ports must be large enough to cope with any water which is liable to board.

Self-draining decks are popular with fishing boats as they can be easily washed down.

the side. As a rule, such decks are fitted when the boat is built but some designers make no provision for removing water that comes aboard, particularly in small fishing and sailing boats.

The self-draining deck eliminates the need to open or close self bailers or seacocks; any water which comes on board simply runs across the deck and over the side through freeing ports or elongated holes cut in the bulwarks at the side of the boat at deck level. This is the system originally used by the big windjammer sailing vessels who were constantly inundated with seas that flooded the deck. Freeing ports along the side at deck level allowed water to run back into the sea while hinged port covers prevented the sea from coming back in the same way. Modern boats do not take sufficient water to warrant the use of hinged ports as a rule, so the water simply runs unhindered through the freeing ports and over the side.

Once again, the only requirements for fitting freeing ports to a self-draining deck is that the deck is well above the waterline and is totally watertight so no boarding water can get into the hull. It goes without saying that water getting into the hull can create a dangerous situation, and if the deck is not well above the waterline, water will slosh aboard far too frequently and make life uncomfortable for passengers and crew who will have their feet constantly in water. The freeing ports need not be very large unless the vessel is likely to be working in big seas, as they will drain rapidly. Depending on the size of the deck area, two freeing ports on each side, three at most, should take care of most vessels. An examination of commercial fishing vessels will give a good indication of the number and size most suited to the deck space.

SHEATHING AN OLD DINGHY

No matter what you do, sometimes it is impossible to stop leaks. This is particularly the case with old boats, and even more so with small wood boats such as tenders or dinghies. Structurally the boat may be quite sound and it would seem a pity to condemn it to the woodpile, yet it still leaks and nothing is more frustrating and embarrassing than taking guests out to a moored yacht or cruiser and having them arrive with wet feet or worse—wet bottoms! Or coming back after a day out and finding the dinghy full of water and needing to be bailed out before anyone can step in. Bailing out a waterlogged dinghy can be a very aggravating business, albeit perhaps amusing to onlookers, for a water-logged dinghy is the most unstable craft afloat and is very likely to tip out anyone who steps into it!

The answer to leaking dinghy problems is relatively easy and a good chore to undertake during the winter lay-up period. Sheathing with fiberglass or some GRP material such as Dynel, will ensure that the boat will not take a drop of water when it is re-launched, and can be left on the mooring for weeks when the only chance of water getting in is through a shower of rain. Large hulls can also be sheathed, but this can be a major task since there is a lot of preparatory work to be done if the sheathing is to be successful, and the place to do this work is on shore, preferably in a garage or somewhere warm and dry. Sheathing does not work well with metal hulls and fiberglass dinghies should be patched rather than sheathed overall.

First step in preparing a leaky wooden dinghy for sheathing is to get it out of the water and into shelter where it can stay for many weeks drying out. The success of the sheathing will be determined by how dry the hull woods are, for if even the remotest dampness remains in the planks or plywood, the sheathing will not take. The boat should be first totally hosed off with fresh water, for salt also impairs the bond between sheathing and the wood hull, then put away to dry. If heating is available so much the better, otherwise the dinghy will need to remain closed under cover for quite some weeks.

When the hull is bone dry, it is sanded off hard with a good sander, removing all traces of old paint, dirt, grime and anything which might affect the bond between the sheathing and the wood. Like the drying process, the cleaner the hull the better the bond will be and ideally the hull should be taken back to bare wood, which will provide a perfect surface for the sheathing. This is a similar procedure to that used when sheathing a deck, as described on page 262. A light sand to smooth off the surface will ensure a good finish and then the boat is ready for sheathing.

Almost any fiberglass materials will serve to make a good sheath, but there are special resin mixes such as International Epiglass HT9000 epoxy resin which is ideal for the job. A woven glass cloth around 6 oz/yd^2 should suit, although it might be a little heavy for very small craft so a lighter cloth can be used. Where more strength is required, the

Old dinghies can be given a new lease of life by sheathing with GRP.

layers of cloth can be doubled. The cloth is carefully cut to totally encase the hull, preferably in sections so that the job can be done in stages rather than having to handle large sections of resin-soaked cloth. Each section should overlap the one above.

With the cloth cut it is time to turn the boat over. This is the best way to work as it avoids overhangs and awkward angles, and most small craft offer easy access to the entire hull when turned over. Any fittings that cannot be removed should be masked. A thorough wipe down with thinners will remove any remaining dirt or dust and allow good penetration of the resin into the wood.

Mix a reasonably small quantity of resin and hardener so that it does not go off while the job is in progress and lay the first sheet of cloth along the hull against the keelson, running it up and over the keel bottom. Some glass workers prefer to place a layer of resin on the wood before laying the cloth in place, and this is quite a good practice, especially with heavy cloth. But light cloth can just be placed into position and then thoroughly saturated with resin, working out any bubbles and ensuring that plenty of resin soaks through to the wood. A small metal or rubber roller or brush can be used and the resin worked firmly into the weave of the cloth. When finished, the cloth should be transparent so that the finished job looks somewhat like a varnished wood surface.

Before the resin dries the next strip of mat is laid, overlapping the first slightly—which will help hold it in place—and smoothing out to cover the next section of the hull evenly.

The process is repeated with resin being soaked into and worked through the mat until the second stretch is done. When one side of the dinghy has been sheathed, it is time to do the other side, merging the cloth over the base of the keelson so that it is overlapping the initial layer. This not only ensures a good bond that will not come adrift when the dinghy is dragged down the beach, but also provides double thickness in an area which is liable to be hard used when the boat is back in business. An even better way is to remove the keelson before glassing and replace it afterwards, but that can create problems with older boats where the fastenings are often impossible to move.

From there it becomes a matter of completing the coverage around the stem and transom until the entire boat is sheathed up to and over the gunwale, after which it is left to dry. Depending on how smoothly the resin was applied, the finish might need only light sanding or perhaps no sanding at all. The gunwale can be finished by turning the boat over onto her keel and cutting off any overlap of the sheathing, preferably before it hardens completely, then either fitting wood trim around the circumference of the gunwale over the sheathing, or by laying a thick layer of tape over the gunwale and glassing it into position with resin as before. The wood trim gives the most attractive appearance, especially if it is made with new wood and given a clear coat of resin which gives it the permanence of GRP and the appearance of varnish.

TIP: IN COLD WEATHER STAND THE RESIN IN A BUCKET OF WARM WATER BEFORE MIXING WITH THE HARDENER.

GLOSSARY

Aerofoil: the cross-section shape of the sail which resembles the cross-section shape of an aircraft wing.

Anti-fouling: chemical composition used on underwater areas to prevent marine growth attaching to the hull.

Arc: a spark which jumps from welder to metal being welded and melts the welding rod.

Atomizers: units on a diesel motor which spray fuel into the cylinder, also sometimes called injectors.

Bead: strip of molten metal laid down by the welder.

Bleed: rust marks on a hull or structure.

Bulkheads: partitions that divide up the interior of the hull into sections.

Careening: landing a boat on the sea bed in order to carry out work on the underside of her hull.

Caulking: sealing the gap between hull planks with cotton packing or some similar material.

Chocks: blocks placed beneath the hull when out of water to keep it level.

Cleat: fitting used to secure the end of a rope.

Coaming: the raised lip around a hatch or cockpit.

Corrosion: disintegration of metal due to weathering or galvanic action.

DAR (Dressed All Round): wood planed on all sides.

Deviation: error on the compass caused by magnetism on the boat.

Dodger: canvas protection over or around the cockpit.

Dowel: small wooden plug used to conceal screw heads.

Dressed wood: wood that has been planed back to a smooth surface.

Electrolyte: liquid that will convey electrical currents.

EPIRB (Emergency Position Indicating Radio Beacon): a satellite-linked emergency and distress beacon.

Epoxy resin: chemical liquid used among other things to encase fiberglass material for hull construction.

Etch primer: special paint used as a primer for fiberglass and aluminum surfaces.

Ferrule: the fitting which secures an eye splice in wire rope.

Fiberglass: resin reinforced fiberglass.

Flux: grease-like material used to assist soldering.

Galley: the boat's kitchen.

Gel coat: outermost coat of a laminated fiberglass molding.

GRP (Glass Reinforced Plastic): better known as fiberglass or glass fiber.

Gunwale: the outer edge of the deck (or surrounding edge of dinghies).

Halyard: a rope used to hoist a sail.

Hogging: stress on a hull created when the middle is supported and the ends sag.

Hounds: the point at which the standing rigging is attached to the mast.

Hull stringers: longitudinal members of a hull structure.

Knee: angled support piece between hull sides and deck.

Lee side: side opposite the wind.

Leech: trailing edge of a sail.

Luff: leading edge of a sail.

Mast step: the base at the bottom of the mast.

Osmosis: blister in the fiberglass laminate caused by water impregnation.

Pintles: fittings on which a transom rudder is hung.

Polyurethane paint: resin-based paint, can be in one- or two-pot packages.

Pop rivets: rivets 'popped' into place by means of a special tool.

Potch: filler made up from resin to patch GRP.

Purchase: an arrangement of blocks and ropes.

Resin: chemical liquid which cures to a hard, impregnable solid when mixed with a catalyst.

Rift sawn: wood cut with the grain running vertically up and down the plank.

Rough sawn: wood that has not been planed to a smooth surface.

Rubbing strake: also called the sponson; the surrounding wood strake which protects the hull, usually at or near deck level.

Runabout: small outboard powered boat used mostly for leisure or water skiing.

Sacrificial anodes: zinc blocks used to prevent electrolytic corrosion eating away underwater fittings.

Sagging: stress on a hull created when the ends are supported and the middle sags.

Sandwich: construction material using two layers of GRP between which is placed a layer of a light but strong material.

Scarfing: butt join between two planks cut at an angle.

Sheathing: usually covering wood with fiberglass.

Sheave: wheel inside a block over which the rope runs.

Sheet: a rope used to control a sail.

Skin fitting: end of intake or discharge pipe where it pierces the hull skin.

Slag: crust on top of a newly welded seam.

Slash sawn: wood cut with the grain running across the plank.

Slipway: railway tracks with cradle for pulling boats out of the water.

Splining: sealing the gap between hull planks with wood strips.

Stern drive: inboard engine with outboard drive leg.

Tabernacle: the deck fitting into which a mast foot is placed.

Tackle: an arrangement of blocks and ropes.

Tinning: preparing the tip of a soldering iron for a soldering job.

Warp: sailcloth made with the main fibers running along the length of the cloth.

Woods: the boat's ribs (in hull construction).

Wracking: a twisting action resulting from a hull corkscrewing in a seaway.

INDEX

swaging tools, 66

tackles *see* blocks and tackles
teak, 32
teredo worms, 175
thinners
    fiberglass, on, 18
    hand and eye protection, 18
tiller steering, 238
tools, 51–66

underwater fittings, 185–188
underwater maintenance, 167–192
    painting, 177–182
    preparing to paint, 177
    removal of marine growth, 177–179

ventilators, 202, 204

warp, 236–237
weed
    marine fouling, 176–177
welding, 79–83
    electric arc welder, 79, 80
    striking the arc, 81–82
    technique, 82
wet rot, 199–203
    preventing condensation, 200
window seals, 212
wire and pulley steering system, 239
wire brushes, 66
wire cutters, 66
wire rope
    flexible, 136
    galvanized steel, 123–132
    splicing, 127–128
    stainless steel, 123–125
wood
    additional maintenance required, 31
    ash, 32

    beauty of, 30
    buying, 34–37
    cedar, 31
    characteristics, 35
    cleaning, 39–41
    clear finishes, 100–101
    direction of grain, 36
    dressed, 35
    elm, 32
    fastenings, 68–76
    grading, 35
    hard wood, 30
    knees, 37
    laminating, 258–260
    mahogany, 32
    maple, 32
    oak, 32
    Oregon pine, 31
    plywood, 33–34
    popularity of, 29
    rot in, 12, 30
    rough sawn, 35
    seasoned, 36
    selecting, 34
    soft wood, 30
    spotted gum, 32
    spruce, 31
    steaming, 260–262
    structural strength, 35
    teak, 32
wood fittings, 37–38
wood hulls
    cleaning, 39
    repairing damage, 42
'wracking,' 11

NOTES